Satan has met his match

with the words CHRIST has given us for
His power and purpose!

by

Michael I. Kaplan

Satan has met his match with the words Christ has given us for His power and purpose!
Copyright © 2023 by Phase2 Advantage

ISBN-13: 979-8218289058

All rights reserved.
Printed in the United States of America.

No part of this publication may be reproduced, stored, or transmitted in any form or by any means, except as permitted under 107 and 108 of the 1976 United States Copyright Act, or for brief quotations in articles and reviews, without the express written permission of the author. For information, please contact:

Phase2 Advantage
P.O. Box 14071
Savannah, GA 31416
(912) 335-2217

Table of Contents

Chapter 01
The Power and Promise of God's Written Word — 07
- 7 Reasons to Study the Bible — 12
- 7 Reasons to Trust and Defend the Bible — 19
- The 3 Critical Components of Bible Study — 27
  - A Caveat Prior to Examining the Bible — 28
- Component #1: EXAMINATION — 30
  - The Value of Terms over Words — 30
  - Emphasis of Theme — 31
  - Repetition of Words and Phrases — 31
  - Scriptural Relationships Between Themes — 32
  - Examining Cultural Context — 34
  - Examining Literary Genre — 35
- Component #2: INTERPRETATION — 36
  - 5 Guidelines for Correct Interpretation — 36
- 7 Common Interpretation Mistakes to Avoid — 39
- 12 Practical Tips for Studying the Bible — 46
- Applying God's Biblical Truth to Your Daily Life — 50

Chapter 02
The Mission to Advance Christ's Kingdom on Earth — 51
- The Biblical Path to Christian Discipleship — 53
- 7 Reasons Christians Do Not Share the Gospel — 54
  - Fear of Engaging People — 55
  - Unaware of Biblical Obligation — 56
  - Negative Perception of Evangelism — 57
  - Lack of Biblical Knowledge — 58
  - Lack of Practical Mentorship — 59
  - Sense of Personal Guilt — 60
  - Insufficient Level of Compassion — 61
- Jesus' Approach to Making Disciples — 62
  - Public, Personal, and Fundamental Conviction — 62
- The Making of Disciples vs. Congregants — 64
- The Cost of Christian Discipleship — 67
- How Jesus Perceived the Value of His Disciples — 70
- How Jesus Perceived the Value of Non-Disciples — 72
- Jesus' Expectations for His Disciples — 74
  - Jesus Expected Unconditional LOVE — 75

Jesus Expected Unconditional PURITY	78
Jesus Expected Unconditional SACRIFICE	81
Jesus Expected Unconditional OBEDIENCE	83
Jesus Protected His Disciples from Hell	85
7 Challenges of Modern Christian Discipleship	88
7 Ways to Practice Faithful Christian Discipleship	92
7 Tips for Sharing the Gospel with Confidence	95

Chapter 03

Planning for Victory with Lessons from History — 99

The Importance of History and Historical Theology	101
The 7 Periods of Christian Church History	103
The Apostolic Age	104
The Patristic Period	109
Council of Nicaea to the Fall of Rome	111
Medieval Church to the Renaissance	113
The Period of Reformation	115
The Period of Enlightenment	117
The Modern / Post-Modern Periods	119
12 Major Influencers in Christian Biblical History	121

Polycarp	(69 – 155 A.D.)	122
Tertullian	(160 – 220 A.D.)	123
Athanasius the Great	(298 – 373 A.D.)	124
Augustine of Hippo	(354 – 430 A.D.)	125
Gregory the Great	(540 – 604 A.D.)	126
Anselm of Aosta	(1033 – 1109 A.D.)	127
Thomas Aquinas	(1225 – 1274 A.D.)	128
Martin Luther	(1483 – 1546 A.D.)	129
John Calvin	(1509 – 1564 A.D.)	130
Jonathan Edwards	(1703 – 1758 A.D.)	131
John Wesley	(1703 – 1791 A.D.)	132
John Nelson Darby	(1800 – 1882 A.D.)	133

7 Benefits of Studying Historical Theology	134
The Importance of Studying Biblical Languages	138

Chapter 04

Defending Christ Against the Adversaries of God — 145

Championing the Christian Faith in Modern Society	147
Disturbing Facts and Trends: ADULTS	149
Disturbing Facts and Trends: YOUTH	150
Disturbing Facts and Trends: PASTORS	151
7 Benefits of Studying Christian Apologetics	152
Obeying God's Word Establishes the Standard	153
Develop a Strong and Mature Faith	155

  Confidence Fulfilling the Great Commission 160
  Reverse the Trend of Apostasy 167
  Combat the Teaching of False Doctrine 169
  Create Stronger Unity in Fellowship 173
  Replace Cultural Ignorance with Truth 177
 The Biblical Basis for a Well-Reasoned Faith 179
 7 Logical Fallacies used to Discredit Testimony 180
  Argumentum Ad Hominem 181
  Ad Hominem Tu Quoque 181
  Argumentum Ad Ignorantiam 181
  Argumentum Ad Populum 182
  Post Hoc, Ergo Propter Hoc 182
  Non-Sequitur 183
  Onus Probandi 183
 7 Common Arguments Against God 184
 Objecting to God: Atheists or Antichrists? 189

Chapter 05

The Priority of Prayer in the Christian Mission 191
 Learning to Pray: It is Always the Perfect Time 193
 7 Scriptural Truths that Reveal God's Nature 194
 The Power and Presence of a Holy God 195
 Honesty Does Not Create Reality – It Reveals It 198
 The Role of Prayer in Christian Life 199
 "Our Father": The Model for Christian Prayer? 201
 The Value of Christ's Teachings on Prayer 203
 The Right Way to Approach God in Prayer 208
 7 Components of Purposeful Prayer 209
  Focused Introspection 209
  Deserved Exaltation 210
  Repentant Confession 210
  Obedient Petition 210
  Thankful Recognition 211
  Empathetic Intercession 211
  Glorifying Praise 211
 The Wrong Way to Approach God in Prayer 212
 7 Reasons Why Christians Pray Every Day 215
 Biblical Fasting in Support of Purposeful Prayer 218
  Ezra 8:21-23 222
  Esther 4:16 222
  1 Kings 21:25-29 223
 7 Reasons Why Christians MUST Practice Fasting 223
 12 Tips for Successful Biblical Fasting 226

Chapter 06

Forging Spiritual Strength with Testing and Trials — 229

- Discerning the Sources of Testing and Trials — 231
- The Biblical Version of the Spiritual Realm — 235
- The Biblical Perspective of Spiritual Warfare — 238
  - Battles within the HEART — 238
  - Battles within the MIND — 238
  - Battles within the WORLD — 239
- The 4 Satanic Entities of Spiritual Warfare — 241
  - Principalities — 241
  - Powers — 243
  - Rulers of the Darkness of this Age — 243
  - Spiritual Hosts of Wickedness in Heavenly Places — 245
- The Seasons and Cycles of Spiritual Warfare — 247
- Satan: A Profile of the Christian's Adversary — 248
- Our Example: Satan's Temptation of Jesus — 252
- Satan's 3 Temptations and Jesus' 3 Victories — 253
- Does God Tempt Man to Sin? — 255
- Could Jesus have Yielded to Temptation and Sinned? — 256
- The Reality of Sin in Christian Life — 260
- Christ Came to Defeat the Works of Satan — 261
- Every Christian Experiences Temptation — 262
- The Nature of Habitual Sin is Idolatry — 265
- 12 Tips for Defeating Satan's Temptation — 267

Chapter 07

Advancing Christianity with Faith in Action — 271

- 7 Goals of Practicing "Experiential Christianity" — 273
- 5 Categories of Timeless Lessons in the Bible — 281
  - Lesson #1: DIRECT COMMANDS — 282
  - Lesson #2: UNIVERSAL TRUTHS — 283
  - Lesson #3: DIRECT EXAMPLES — 284
  - Lesson #4: INDIRECT EXAMPLES — 285
  - Lesson #5: REASONABLE ASSUMPTIONS — 286
- 7 Learning Styles: Choose the Best for YOU — 287
- 7 Components of a Successful Biblical Lifestyle — 288
- 7 Biblical Strategies to Overcome Adversity — 291
- 7 Benefits of Applying Biblical Truth to Life — 299
- 7 Daily Habits to Reinforce a Biblical Mindset — 303

Glossary

Glossary of Terms — 307

Chapter 01

The Power and Promise of God's Written Word

"So Philip ran to him, and heard him reading the prophet Isaiah, and said, 'Do you understand what you are reading?' And he said, 'How can I, unless someone guides me?' And he asked Philip to come up and sit with him."

~ Acts 8:30-31 ~

Chapter 01: *The Power and Promise of God's Written Word*

You might expect a chapter discussing Bible study methods and interpretation to launch directly into a variety of strategies, methodologies, and tactics for studying the Bible. It will, shortly, but the reality of our modern culture demands another topic be addressed first: *continual learning*.

The demands, responsibilities, and time constraints imposed on working adults have increased significantly in modern society. The difficulty many experiences while attempting to maintain a balance between their personal and professional life has given rise to a cottage industry of self-help books worth billions of dollars.

Concurrently, trends in technology, dissemination of information, and social pressure imposed on our youth have also increased significantly in modern culture. The difficulty many youths experience while attempting to maintain a balance between their ability to focus and data-driven sensory overload has given rise to a new industry of pharmacological products.

Texting + Facebook = Textbook

Yes, mom. I'm studying.

Considering these cultural trends, it seems reasonable to begin a chapter, dedicated to the topic of studying, by discussing first the need for learning. This need exists for everyone, regardless of their age.

Life is a process of continual learning. When we are young, learning presents itself as formal education, and as we advance in life it presents itself in the form of experience. Each of us has an innate desire to grow and expand – personally and spiritually – and it is learning that allows this to happen.

One of the primary factors that determines the success of spiritual growth is the degree of intentionality brought to the process of learning. Empowered Christians, who see the world as a series of endless opportunities, view learning as a process to be actively pursued. Given their defining characteristics this should come as no surprise. The ability to adapt to change, accept risk, seek opportunity in the face of adversity, and benefit from mistakes –

Chapter 01: *The Power and Promise of God's Written Word*

and doing so upon a strong foundation of unshakable faith – all require a genuine appreciation for learning.

This does not mean that to be spiritually mature you need a degree in Biblical Studies or enroll in seminary. If that is your goal it would be a wonderful accomplishment, but the commitment to learning I refer to is much more self-directed and informal. I realize for many the natural inclination is to associate learning with formal education, but for a variety of reasons – such as time, finances, and adult learning styles – this may not be the best option.

A piece of paper on the wall that tells the world you completed a formal degree or certificate program is not a true measure of what you know. As Albert Einstein once wisely stated, *"Education is what remains after one has forgotten what one has learned in school."* If you are committed to learning, you have other options.

I recall having a fiery debate with a teacher during my high school years. My confidence was greatly overextended, my ego was insatiable, and I felt the need to prove myself to my peers. After allowing me to finish what I thought was a brilliant argument, the teacher presented his rebuttal, proved his information to be factual and reduced my self-image to zero.

Upon observing my obvious embarrassment, he landed the "kill shot" with the following statement: *"Michael, do not be upset. It is not your fault you did not know that. The government hides information like that from people like you … in books."* The lesson had been learned, albeit painfully.

From that moment forward I dedicated myself to being a prolific reader and it has reaped huge rewards. I encourage everyone to keep a book on hand and read continuously. Before you say, *"I do not have time,"* be aware that if you read just five pages per day – and the average Bible is 1,281 pages – in one year you will have read the entire Bible one-and-a-half times.

Consider those 1,821 pages of divine inspiration as push-ups for your brain and your soul. Use it or lose it.

Regardless of what form it takes, incorporating continual learning into your daily Bible study regimen provides much more than just factual knowledge. Continual learning also creates:

Chapter 01: *The Power and Promise of God's Written Word*

1. **A Hungry Mind**. A mind committed to learning soon realizes just how little it knows, and that is a good thing. It inspires you to want to learn more, and the habitual practice of this mindset leads to a genuine love of learning. Once the mind develops an appetite for knowledge it must be fed constantly.

2. **A Strong Mind**. Your brain, like any other part of your body, needs exercise to remain strong. Analytical and problem-solving skills are perishable commodities that diminish in time when not used. The focus of the learning is not nearly as important as the action of learning. Regular mental exercise (learning) keeps the mind sharp and your brain operating at peak capacity.

3. **An Open Mind**. The mind, like a parachute, only works when it is open. Learning provides a continuous stream of knowledge that broadens perspectives, reveals unique solutions, and allows you to identify answers to problems that had not been known previously. Providence favors the well-informed and prepared mind, and those with the most information available usually make the best decisions.

4. **A Social Mind**. Most learning requires interaction with others, and in instances in which it does not, the *application* of that learning does. Knowledge has no intrinsic value until it is applied, and it is the application of that knowledge that conditions the mind for social interaction. In fact, it is the exchanging of ideas that forms the foundation of our social orientation and Christian fellowship.

These are just a few of the benefits you will experience because of your commitment to continual learning. It is not difficult to see how learning supports a strong and unshakable faith.

The rewards of learning promote faith in God, trust in God's Word, and confirm your continued determination to pursue a biblical lifestyle. With the general topic of *learning* addressed, let's talk about the reasons to *study*.

Chapter 01: *The Power and Promise of God's Written Word*

7 Reasons to Study the Bible

When considering statistics in printed literature, no publication can come close to matching the Bible. It is the most printed, most quoted, and the most recognized book in human existence. However, it is also one of the least read books in many Christian households. When one considers that the Bible is the centerpiece of the Christian faith – the divinely inspired, inerrant, infallible Word of God – that fact appears to run counter to logic. As counterintuitive as this may be, there are several reasons for this unfortunate fact.

Many Christians view reading the Bible as an intimidating endeavor; the sheer size of the text, written in a grammatical style that can be confusing at times, is enough to prevent them from making the attempt. This is typically rationalized with a question such as, *"why should I read the Bible myself, when my Pastor reads it to us every Sunday?"* This issue will be dealt with specifically later in the chapter.

For others, the Bible is an archaic text possessing little relevance to the moral and ethical issues confronting Christians in our modern culture. In a culture embracing varying degrees of moral relativism, the absolute standards imposed by God can appear to be "out of sync" and intolerant. Nothing could be farther from the truth, but that fact goes unnoticed when time is not taken to become acquainted with the text.

There are numerous reasons to study the Bible regularly, the most obvious of which is God: it is His message, His story, His commands, His promises, and His means by which Salvation becomes available to faithful Christians who believe in Him. The seven reasons listed below represent a starting point and serve to have the most significant impact in our daily lives.

1. **The Word of God leads to FAITH.**

> *So then faith comes by hearing, and hearing by the word of God.*
>
> ~ Romans 10:17 ~

Chapter 01: *The Power and Promise of God's Written Word*

Walk into any retail bookstore and you will find no shortage of self-help publications on any topic of interest. They typically follow the same general premise: to show **you** how **you** can change **yourself**, and how **you** can make improvements in **your** life. While a few of these publications may provide superficial value, the majority do not accomplish the task, as most readers cannot summon the power to create real and lasting change in their lives.

The Bible is not a self-help book. It is the divinely inspired and authoritative Word of God, containing an infinite amount of power, and written by the God with the power to create everything. The power of God contained within the pages of the Bible – tangible, palpable, and accessible – activates faith within any reader with the ears to hear His message. Whether meditating on God's Word when reading the Bible, or sharing His Gospel aloud to an unreached population, the power flowing through His word leads to the activation of faith.

2. **The Word of God STRENGTHENS our faith.**

> *But those who wait on the Lord shall renew their strength; They shall mount up with wings like eagles, they shall run and not be weary, they shall walk and not faint.*
>
> *~ Isaiah 40:31 ~*

Although our family and closest friends may let us down occasionally, God always keeps His promises. We may forget that at times and experience spiritual weakness in our thoughts. *Does God really forgive me? Does He really love me? Is He really in control? Why am I so worried about the future if God is here?* When you ask yourself those questions, be assured God's Word has the answers.

When friends offer mistaken advice, remember God's Word is perfect, truthful, and eternal. If God says it, you believe it. Reading the Bible reveals a God who loves us despite our sinful nature, promises Salvation even though we do not deserve it, and guarantees rewards when it is never possible for us to earn them.

3. **The Word of God reveals our PURPOSE.**

   > But indeed for this purpose I have raised you up, that I may show My power in you, and that My name may be declared in all the earth.
   >
   > ~ Exodus 9:16 ~

   Reading the Bible reveals God's purpose for us on two distinct levels. First, the Bible makes it abundantly clear that God created Man, in His image, to glorify Him. We are created in His likeness and image; therefore, we cannot do anything apart from Him. You will also discover God glorified us *first*, as evidenced by His special act of Creation and His adoration of us, His children.

   On an individual level, the Bible makes it clear that God imparted to each of us a unique set of skills, gifts, and talents to maximize our potential as His creation. Our special abilities allow us to excel and attract recognition that immediately gets redirected to glorify God instead. As we grow in our relationship with God and utilize the gifts He's given us, our glory to Him increases, which He then responds with His glory to us. One would expect nothing less from a Father who adores His children.

4. **The Word of God provides HOPE.**

   > Let us hold fast the confession of our hope without wavering, for He who promised is faithful.
   >
   > ~ Hebrews 10:23 ~

   Many people will conceive a plan, develop a series of contingency plans in the event things do not work out, and then hope for the best. In this sense, earthly hope is nothing more than making a wish, without the expectation that it is guaranteed to happen.

   The Bible reveals God's Hope to be much different: it is dynamic, active and it commands results. When we rely on His hope, we change our perspective, and alter the way we plan. Biblical hope is based on God's promises.

5. **The Word of God leads to FREEDOM.**

*It is for freedom that Christ has set us free.
Stand firm, then, and do not let yourselves
be burdened again by a yoke of slavery.*

~ Galatians 5:1 ~

In the secular world, no single concept has such a significant importance – from the individual to entire nation states – as that of *freedom*. It is a powerful word that shapes our entire society: the way we think, the way we act, and the way we express our thoughts. The United States was founded on the concepts of freedom and liberty, ideas so powerful that Colonists were willing to make extraordinary sacrifices and suffer extreme hardship in their revolution against the British Empire.

The concept of freedom is also deeply rooted in the Bible, and while many Christians know instinctively that "*the truth shall set you free*" (John 8:32), they have difficulty reconciling the concepts of Biblical freedom and cultural freedom in their daily lives. When one considers that cultural freedom requires rules, regulations, and laws – all sacrifices made to be "free" to pursue other goals – the concept of Biblical freedom becomes easier to understand.

God's Word tells us that *true* freedom is faith in God and trusting Him enough to be obedient to His word. In return, the Christian is free from the things that matter most. These include but are not limited to the bondage of sin, the slavery of addiction, false worship of temporal gods (money, pride, power, vanity, etc.), and the eternal judgment associated with breaking God's laws that Man does not have the ability to follow. In short, those things cultural freedom suggests make us free are the things that place us in bondage and move us away from God.

God's Word promises we have the freedom to be what God intended us to be: a people made in His image, created to share in His eternal glory. When one considers that the average lifespan is eighty years, and eternity looks more like ten billion years, trusting in God's Word, and having obedience to Him makes complete sense.

Chapter 01: *The Power and Promise of God's Written Word*

6. **The Word of God imparts WISDOM.**

   > *To the person who pleases Him, God gives wisdom, knowledge and happiness, but to the sinner He gives the task of gathering and storing up wealth to hand it over to the one who pleases God. This too is meaningless, a chasing after the wind.*
   >
   > ~ Ecclesiastes 2:26 ~

   In secular terms, *wisdom* can be described as the knowledge, experience, and good judgment that leads to sound decisions. We typically acquire our limited earthly wisdom in reverse order: a lack of knowledge leads to poor judgment, which causes us to experience the suffering associated with poor decisions. If and when we learn from our mistakes over time, we become wiser with age. Our fallen nature drives this process, but God never intended it to be this way.

   The Bible reveals numerous examples of believers who placed their faith and trust in God's Word and were rewarded with His wisdom and blessings. God does not impart wisdom through His Word in a linear and incremental fashion; when faith and obedience in Him inspires us to seek His wisdom through prayer, He imparts it to us exponentially in ways that defy understanding.

7. **The Word of God gives us ETERNAL LIFE.**

   > *Whoever believes in the Son has eternal life, but whoever rejects the Son will not see life, for God's wrath remains on them.*
   >
   > ~ John 3:36 ~

   Take a quick survey of Christian believers and ask them to define the term "Eternal Life," and the majority will offer familiar terms in their response: going to heaven, not going to hell, and spending the rest of eternity in the presence of God and His angels inside the Pearly Gates. On the surface, there is nothing wrong with this response – until you understand they are missing the bigger picture.

Chapter 01: *The Power and Promise of God's Written Word*

Yes, God the Father did send Jesus to the world as part of His redemptive mission.

> *For God so loved the world that He gave His only begotten Son, that whoever believes in Him should not perish but have everlasting life.*
>
> ~ John 3:16 ~

Yes, Jesus did die for the sins of mankind as part of His redemptive mission.

> *It shall be imputed to us who believe in Him who raised up Jesus our Lord from the dead, who was delivered up because of our offenses, and was raised because of our justification.*
>
> ~ Romans 4:24-25 ~

Yes, our professed faith in Christ guarantees we will be able to join our Father in heaven.

> *For our citizenship is in heaven, from which we also eagerly wait for the Savior, the Lord Jesus Christ.*
>
> ~ Philippians 3:20 ~

Yes, our professed faith in Christ guarantees we will not be removed from God's sight and be banished to hell.

> *But the cowardly, unbelieving, abominable, murderers, sexually immoral, sorcerers, idolaters, and all liars shall have their part in the lake which burns with fire and brimstone, which is the second death.*
>
> ~ Revelation 21:8 ~

Those are all very valid reasons to profess faith in Christ as Lord and Savior. However, if Christians are only drawn to faith to be taken out of the waiting line for hell, and given a ticket to heaven, they are missing the true meaning of Eternal Life. Heaven opens when we die but benefits of Eternal Life are available to Christians *now*.

Chapter 01: *The Power and Promise of God's Written Word*

Words are important; we use them to describe the world around us, and to create images in the minds of others. If the words used are not fully understood, an accurate image cannot be created to help visualize what is being described. This proves to be especially true when reading the Word of God.

> *And this is eternal life, that they may **know** You, the only true God, and Jesus Christ whom You have sent.*
>
> ~ John 17:3 ~

God's promise to Man of eternal life means to *know* Him. It does not mean to know *of* Him or *about* Him, but to truly *know* Him in the Biblical sense. Yes, you just read that correctly.

> *Then Mary said to the angel, "How can this be, since I do not **know** a man?"*
>
> ~ Luke 1:34 ~

When Mary asked this of the angel Gabriel, she knew she was a virgin who had never had intimate relations with a man. The word in the original Greek text **γινώσκω** ("ginóskó," to know) is the same in both Scriptures and implies the same idea: an intimate relationship. Obviously, this does not imply a physical relationship, but in matters of the heart and soul the message is clear.

The Word of God reveals the He wants us to have an intimate relationship with Him and, in so doing, He gives us the promise of an Eternal Life that starts now. Does a person change when they have an intimate relationship in the world? Everything changes: the way they feel, act, and speak. If that holds true for worldly relationships, how much more would that hold true for God the Father?

Going to church and hoping things get better when you get to heaven is not taking full advantage of the Eternal Life the Word of God promises you *now*.

Chapter 01: *The Power and Promise of God's Written Word*

7 Reasons to Trust and Defend the Bible

To become proficient in any task requires study and practice; becoming familiar with the Word of God is no different in this regard. You were presented with seven reasons to study the Bible, the last of which discussed an intimate relationship with God as the foundation of Eternal Life. The foundation of any intimate relationship, if it is to be successful, is the element of *trust*.

Prior to committing any amount of time to a relationship – in this case, a relationship with God through the studying of His Word – one must be confident that the information being presented is always truthful. If not, we begin to call everything into question. The Bible is the inerrant, infallible, and divinely inspired Word of God – perfect and truthful in every regard. That makes the Bible an "all or nothing" proposition: Christians cannot selectively decide to declare some parts of it to be true, and others to be false.

Imagine for a moment what life would be like without any trust in the earthly realm. It would be intolerable, miserable, and would cease to function. There could be no way to know if cars would stop for red lights or stop signs, and no way to guarantee a cashier at a register would give you change for a purchase. You would never experience friendship at any level, much less love.

Now imagine that scenario, not with finite humans, but with an infinite and eternal God. Resist the immediate temptation to say, "*never ... that is unimaginable.*" That is exactly the type of doubt and distrust your adversary, Satan, tries to deceive you with daily. The topic of Spiritual Warfare will be discussed at length in Chapter 06, but for now be aware that every time you study the Word of God, your adversary is present and attempting to undermine your trust in His Word.

In the following pages, seven practical reasons will be presented to trust the Bible you've committed yourself to study. Given the onslaught of hostility directed at the Christian faith, one can never have enough ammunition at their disposal.

Chapter 01: *The Power and Promise of God's Written Word*

Reason #1: The Bible Passes the BIBLIOGRAPHIC Test

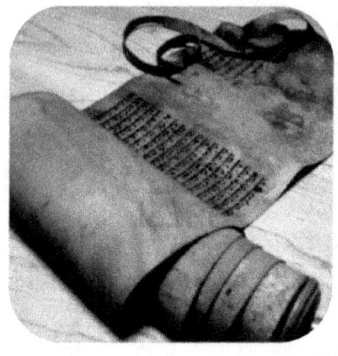

When historians study any form of ancient writing, they utilize several standardized methods to gauge the reliability of the document. The bibliographic test does this by comparing the number of extant manuscripts (earliest surviving copies) and the dates they were written the autograph (original text) and the date it was written. If no autograph exists – to date we do not possess an original for *any* ancient document, not just the Bible – comparisons are made between extant manuscripts in the areas of dating, consistency, and the number that exist.

As a rule, the ancient manuscripts historians have accepted as authentic – such as Homer's *Iliad*, Tacitus' *Annals*, or Caesar's *Gallic Wars* – the average amount of time between original writing and earliest known copy is approximately 400 to 800 years, with the number of extant copies ranging from 2 to 1,800. As archeologists and historians discover additional copies the numbers will change, but the averages and scientific standards of authenticity remain constant.

Compare those same standards of authenticity to the Word of God – both the Old and New Testaments – and the race to the finish line is not even close. The Bible wins every time.

We currently possess over 5,800 extant manuscripts of the New Testament written in Greek, the earliest of which can be dated to within 50 years of original authorship. When considering early translations of the Greek New Testament, the number of existing documents increases to over 18,000 copies. Add to this the Old Testament scrolls and codices discovered to date, and the number of extant manuscripts increases to more than 65,000 copies that have been determined by historians to be authentic.

No one questions the authenticity of ancient writers like Caesar, Homer, and Plato – their manuscripts are being taught in universities every day – and their writings do not approach the level of evidence the Bible must meet to pass the bibliographic test. What is the conclusion? The Bible can be trusted.

Chapter 01: *The Power and Promise of God's Written Word*

Reason #2: The Bible Passes the HISTORICAL Test

The historical test – also referred to as the external test – determines if the document being examined contradicts known historical facts. It compares the document to other authentic writings of the period. The larger the number of documents from a wide range of sources that support these historical facts, the more authentic that fact becomes. The most prevalent methods of conducting historical tests are by comparing the writings of authors, and discovery of physical evidence through archeology.

The historical test cannot prove the Bible to be true, but it can confirm the historical writings to be accurate. The authors of the divinely inspired Word of God put a significant amount of effort into cataloging details in their writing, demonstrating a commitment to accuracy. Reason dictates that the greater the number of details that can be confirmed, the greater the chance what the authors were writing was true.

Archeologists have made amazing discoveries that support the Bible, writings that had originally considered to be myth and superstition. The cities of Sodom and Gomorrah were thought to be myth until the 1970's, when the Elba Tablets, a collection of more than 1,800 clay tablets dated 2,500 BC, were discovered in Syria, and found to mention both cities by name. They also listed all the kings referenced in the Old Testament in chronological order. It is accurate to state that archeology has never discovered anything to contradict details provided in the Bible.

The authors of written history have also corroborated many details in the Bible. Josephus, a first-century historian and author of *Antiquities of the Jews*, mentions both the crucifixion and resurrection of Christ. He was not a follower of Jesus, and like many Jews of the time considered Him a "sorcerer," a fact that speaks to the miracles Christ performed. He wrote about James, the brother of Jesus, and the beheading of John the Baptist as well. In total, there are hundreds of supporting facts documented by historians writing at the time Jesus lived. What is the conclusion? The Bible can be trusted.

Chapter 01: *The Power and Promise of God's Written Word*

Reason #3: The Bible Passes the CORROBERATION Test

The corroboration test – also known as the eyewitness test – determines if anyone was a witness to the event, how many witnesses were there, were the witness statements documented, and do they all support each other? If so, the historian conducting the test has reliable primary source evidence that can be considered authoritative. The witnesses do not have supporters of the event, either; they can be hostile enemies. Friend or foe, the question focuses on the reliability of their testimony.

Given the early dating of extant texts, the authors of the New Testament were writing within the same period as the events being described. In numerous instances the authors are writing to an audience they presuppose are familiar with the facts (*as you yourselves also know* – Acts 2:22). In other instances, the writers are referencing witnesses in writing they know are still alive (*After that He was seen by over five hundred brethren at once, of whom the greater part remain to the present, but some have fallen asleep* – 1 Corinthians 15:6). If they had written false documents and circulated them to an audience that knew otherwise, their writing would have been dismissed as a lie immediately.

While the eyewitness accounts support each other, they are not rehearsed "parrot-speak." If four news channels report on the same story, the facts will remain constant even though the reporters choose to focus on different details – such as the authors of the Bible did in their writing. However, if a series of witnesses offer the same word-for-word accounts, it is obvious they've been coached. That is not the case with the witnesses to biblical events: they are close enough in the details to support each other, but different enough in style to show that they are unique and truthful.

As with the historical test, there are enough witnesses from a wide range of sources – both friend and foe – to state with confidence that the detail of their testimony is true. What is the conclusion? The Bible can be trusted.

Chapter 01: *The Power and Promise of God's Written Word*

Reason #4: The Bible Passes the PROPHETIC Test

The prophetic test determines if the predictions made happened, assess the accuracy of the occurrence, and then measures the probability associated with the prediction. The role of Bible prophecy is not just to predict future events, but to reinforce faith in a God that sees and controls the eternity of everything. Not all prophecy comes from the mouths of righteous men: the Word of God teaches us to discern between His prophecy and those false prophets speaking for the adversary. Consider the Scripture in Deuteronomy 18:22 –

"When a prophet speaks in the name of the Lord, if the thing does not happen or come to pass, that is the thing which the Lord has not spoken; the prophet has spoken it presumptuously; you shall not be afraid of him."

When a prophecy *is* from God – as were the more than 500 predicting the birth of Christ alone – it not only happens, but it is also 100% accurate in every detail. The prophecies listed below show the accuracy of His Word:

- **750 BC** / Micah 5:2 - The Savior born in Bethlehem: *But you, Bethlehem … out of you shall come forth to Me the One to be Ruler in Israel*
- **740 BC** / Isaiah 7:14 - The Savior conceived by virgin birth: *Therefore the Lord Himself will give you a sign. Behold, the virgin shall conceive and bear a son, and shall call His name Immanuel*
- **722 BC** / Hosea 11:1 - The Savior called out of Egypt: *When Israel was a child, I loved Him, and out of Egypt I called My son*
- **520 BC** / Zechariah 9:9 - The Savior enters Jerusalem by donkey: *Behold, your King is coming to you; He is just and having salvation, lowly and riding on a donkey, a colt, the foal of a donkey*

The Bible contains over 2,500 prophecies, 2,000 of which have been fulfilled with no error, and 500 remaining for the future. What is the conclusion? The Bible can be trusted.

Chapter 01: *The Power and Promise of God's Written Word*

Reason #5: The Bible Passes the CONSISTENCY Test

The consistency test determines if the component writings of the Word of God align and support each other. The three primary test categories are the manuscripts, the narrative (message) of the writing, and the theological focus. The consistency of manuscripts was addressed in Reason #2, so this section will address the narrative and theological focus. As you consider the historical development of the Bible, especially given the breakdowns in communication we experience in modern society, the consistency of God's Word is amazing.

Begin with a few facts:

1. The Bible contains 66 Books (39 Old Testament, 27 New Testament)
2. Written by 40 divinely inspired authors
3. Having very diverse backgrounds (Prime Minister, tax collector, fisherman, physician, Rabbi, etc.)
4. Living on three separate continents (Africa, Asia, and Europe)
5. In three different languages (Hebrew, Greek, and Aramaic)
6. Over a span of 1,500 years

Most of the authors did not know each other; thousands of miles separated them geographically, and hundreds of years separated them temporally. Each was written for a unique audience, and for a specific purpose. The one thing these authors did have in common was God, and the divine inspiration He provided to them to write His Word. It is for this reason – and only this reason – that the Bible remains such a consistent and harmonious Book.

Most "errors and contradictions" referenced in secular circles stem from mistakes in grammar and translation. The rest are resolved easily with detailed study and a deeper awareness of the cultural and historical context that existed at the time of the writing. The consistency of the Word of God is amazing. What is the conclusion? The Bible can be trusted.

Chapter 01: *The Power and Promise of God's Written Word*

Reason #6: The Bible Passes the ACCEPTANCE Test

The acceptance test determines how deeply a concept penetrates the society, how widely accepted it is to society and at what level within each society the concept is embraced. As you will read in Chapter 04, claiming an argument to be true just because many people believe it is a logical fallacy (Argumentum Ad Populum). However, if an item gets numerous excellent reviews from people we trust and respect, it makes sense to have a closer look at the item. In this case, the item in question – the divinely inspired Word of God called the Bible – has no competition in the acceptance category.

According to the Bible Society (and the Guinness Book of World Records), the Bible is the bestselling book of all time and continues to hold that title every year. Approximately 6 billion copies have been printed and distributed over time, in 636 different languages (full Bible).

Those numbers mean that 50 Bibles are sold every minute, every day. The Word of God penetrates every level of the society it touches – it is not an exclusive gift for the rich and famous – but those whose names you may know have inspiring words for God's Word.

> *"Of the many influences that have shaped the United States into a distinctive nation and people, none may be said to be more fundamental and enduring than the Bible."*
>
> ~ Ronald Reagan ~

> *"It is impossible to rightly govern the world without God and Bible."*
>
> ~ George Washington ~

> *"I believe the Bible is the best gift God has ever given to man. All the good of the Savior of the world is communicated to us through the Book."*
>
> ~ Abraham Lincoln ~

What is the conclusion? The Bible can be trusted.

Chapter 01: *The Power and Promise of God's Written Word*

Reason #7: The Bible Passes the EXPERIENTIAL Test

The experiential test determines the tangible, observable impact something has in the physical world. While God's nature is supernatural and beyond human measure, the impact His Word has on the lives of people around us can easily be seen. The experience of God's Word so impacted Christ's disciples they were willing to suffer in His name and be martyred. Thousands of people professed their faith, and with that profession their lives were changed forever, spiritually, and emotionally. In the words of the French novelist, Victor Hugo, *"nothing is more powerful than an idea whose time has come."*

What mechanism of human psychology can explain the radical transformation that one experiences – in mind, spirit, and soul – when the Word of God touches someone's heart? How can an uncompassionate, prideful human become an empathetic philanthropist overnight? How can a bitter and broken person leave the house cursing God in the morning, and return home that same evening praising Him? Modern social science does not know where to begin to explain these phenomena, but Christ revealed the answer to us over 2,000 years ago: *"With man this is impossible, but with God all things are possible"* (Matthew 19:26).

What mechanism of human social science can explain people professing their faith for God's Word in a country that profession carries a death sentence? Sharing the Gospel in a country that executes those in possession of Bibles? Walking away from prosperity and security to share God's Word in remote and dangerous locations? Once again, modern science falls short, but the Word of God reveals it perfectly.

> *"For I know the plans I have for you,"* declares the Lord, *"plans to prosper you and not to harm you, plans to give you hope and a future."*
>
> ~ Jeremiah 29:11 ~

What is the only possible conclusion? The Bible can be trusted.

Chapter 01: *The Power and Promise of God's Written Word*

The 3 Critical Components of Bible Study

You may recall "D-Day" from history classes in school; it was the military term assigned to the Allied invasion on the beaches of Normandy during World War II. You may have a family member alive today who served in that operation, or whose parents served and survived to pass along the details of the event to them. It was an epic event in world history that has shaped our civilization ever since. Imagine reading a written account of that event today, but with a few of the details missing.

1. You do not know the date, or the current state of the world affairs
2. You know nothing about world leaders: Roosevelt, Hitler, or Churchill
3. You know nothing about the commanders managing the war: Eisenhower, Montgomery, or Rommel
4. You do not know the geographical location of Normandy
5. The original account was written in a language other than the one you use today, so you do not know what the "D" in "D-Day" represents

The story would still be interesting to read – heroes, villains, battles, bravery, etc. – but the importance of the event and its consequences would be lacking in the absence of details. Details provide context, and the context provides meaning. That is what many people experience today when they read the Books of the Bible. In the following pages, three components will be discussed that will assist you in discerning the details of the text, interpreting the meaning of the text considering the contextual detail, and incorporating the meaning into a practical application that welcomes the Word of God into your life.

Remember the days of old; consider the generations long past. Ask your father and he will tell you, your elders, and they will explain to you.

~ Deuteronomy 32:7 ~

Chapter 01: *The Power and Promise of God's Written Word*

WARNING: A Caveat Prior to Examining the Bible

The first step to understanding the Will of God, as it applies to your life, is by examining (reading) the Word of God as it exists in the modern Bible. Prior to presenting the textual elements of examination – context, structure, emphasis, and correlation – a caveat must be put forward to avoid any chance of misunderstanding the point of this instruction.

In the original Greek New Testament, the concepts of "chapter and verse" did not exist. Individual Books were meant to be read in their entirety, as were groupings of specific Books written by the same author (such as the *Gospel of Luke* and *Acts*).

Stephen Langton, the Archbishop of Canterbury, was the first to divide the Bible into chapters in 1,227 AD. In 1,555 AD, the Bible was further divided into verses by Robert Stephens when he printed the Latin Vulgate.

Since this time, almost every Bible has been printed in the "chapter and verse" format. For the most part, it has been helpful; one can now directly navigate to a specific passage of Scripture. However, this format can lead to problems as well.

The first problem arises when readers discover "truths" in the Bible, based on the numbering of verses, that do not really exist. Consider the following Scripture:

> *From that time many of His disciples went back and walked with Him no more.*
>
> ~ John 6:66 ~

Is Satan a very real adversary, intent on turning believers away from Christ? Yes. Is there any correlation between the disciples turning their back on Christ, and the "6:66" numbering of this verse in the *Gospel of John*? No.

The second problem arises when numbered verses create independent messages that were never meant to be read

Chapter 01: *The Power and Promise of God's Written Word*

independently. Consider this Scripture from Colossians 2:21: *"Do not handle! Do not taste! Do not touch!"* It appears Paul is giving the reader a lesson in self-deprivation, but that would be the opposite of the intended meaning.

If the quotation marks do not give it away – authors do not quote themselves – a review of the text immediately preceding and following Colossians 2:21 gives us the truth:

> [20]*"Since you died with Christ to the elemental spiritual forces of this world, why, as though you still belonged to the world, do you submit to its rules:*
>
> [21]*"Do not handle! Do not taste! Do not touch!"?*
>
> [22]*These rules, which have to do with things that are all destined to perish with use, are based on merely human commands and teachings.*
>
> [23]*Such regulations indeed have an appearance of wisdom, with their self-imposed worship, their false humility and their harsh treatment of the body, but they lack any value in restraining sensual indulgence."*

This is not simply an issue of a thought being taken out of context; this is a problem with the numbering format itself. A quick review of the bolded superscript numbers reveals that Colossians 2:21 is not an independent sentence – it follows a colon – and obviously is meant to be a part of the verse preceding it.

When read as the author intended, Paul is not giving support for this concept, but a negative critique of it.

This caveat in no way suggests there are any errors in the Bible; this is a system of organization created by humans that in no way impacts the content of the Word of God. It is human nature to organize and categorize content, and at times our best intentions lead to unforeseen outcomes.

The sole purpose of offering this caveat is to advise you to pay close attention to the details when immersed in God's Word.

Chapter 01: *The Power and Promise of God's Written Word*

Component #1: EXAMINATION

To study the Word of God you first must read it. That said, reading quickly and superficially won't provide the insight God wants you to find. The Bible must be examined: approached inquisitively, read slowly, considered carefully, and studied daily. As you immerse yourself in God's Word, keep the suggestions listed below in the forefront of your mind. They will serve as useful guidelines for both New and Old Testament studies.

A. The Value of Terms over Words

As you approach the reading of any biblical text, keep in mind a rule that is applied consistently in daily life: words used to convey are terms, and terms are more complex than words. In short, words do not always mean what they say, and tend to vary in meaning based on culture and context. For example, read Christ's words in Luke 14:26 –

> *"If anyone comes to Me and does not hate his father and mother, wife and children, brothers and sisters, yes, and his own life also, he cannot be My disciple."*

Jesus was a proponent of the Old Testament Law and obviously believed God when He gave Moses the 5th Commandment: '*Honor your father and your mother*' (Deuteronomy 5:16). That indicates the word "hate" is to be read as a term, not just a word, and the term is being used to convey a more complex thought.

In the original language of the New Testament, the word used for "hate" is **μισέω** (miseó: detest, love less, esteem less). The word "hate" is a term used to convey the concept of assigning a lower priority to something. With that understanding in mind, the meaning of the Scripture becomes much less shocking: *love God (Christ) more than you love people*.

This is not creative wordplay to manipulate the "plain language" of the text. Those of us who speak a modern dialect in any language employ the use of terms in our speech every day and do not give a second thought to it. There is no language on earth – from the beginning of time until the present day – that hasn't incorporated idioms into their speech. With that in mind, can you imagine how your words would be interpreted in ancient Greece when they discovered you "loved" chocolate? YUCK!

Chapter 01: *The Power and Promise of God's Written Word*

B. Emphasis of Theme

In many instances a reader can discern an emphasis of a particular theme the author is conveying, even though it may be said in a few different ways. This type of emphasis can be observed within individual chapters, or throughout multiple chapters of the same Book. A good example of this can be seen in the *Gospel of Matthew*.

> *Therefore as the tares are gathered and burned in the fire, so it will be at the end of this age. The Son of Man will send out His angels, and they will gather out of His kingdom all things that offend, and those who practice lawlessness, and will cast them into the furnace of fire. There will be wailing and gnashing of teeth.*
>
> ~ Matthew 13:40-42 ~

The thematic emphasis of Chapter 13 is the *danger of disbelief* in Christ. In fact, the entire chapter is dedicated to the theme. Another emphasis is the use of parables; there are seven of them written in the chapter. Jesus often used parables to convey His most important messages – those with an open heart would understand, those with a hardened heart would miss the message.

C. Repetition of Words and Phrases

In certain instances, the Scripture will convey a theme through the repetition of a certain word or phrase. In the first example, the Apostle Paul is writing his epistle to the believers of the church in Rome:

> *Therefore we conclude that a man is justified by faith apart from the deeds of the law. Or is He the God of the Jews only? Is He not also the God of the Gentiles? Yes, of the Gentiles also, since there is one God who will justify the circumcised by faith and the uncircumcised through faith.*
>
> ~ Romans 3:28-30 ~

Paul uses the word "faith" 55 times to convey that it is belief in Christ, not external laws, that leads to Salvation.

Chapter 01: *The Power and Promise of God's Written Word*

In the second Scripture, we observe that a theme can be emphasized within the text by use of a repetitive phrase. A good example of this can be seen in the *Gospel of Luke*:

> *And Jesus said to him, "Today salvation has come to this house, because he also is a son of Abraham; for the Son of Man has come to seek and to save that which was lost."*
>
> ~ Luke 19:9-10 ~

Luke's Gospel focuses on the *humanity* of Jesus and provides the most detailed account of His earthly ministry. To reinforce that theme, the *Gospel of Luke* uses the phrase, *"Son of Man,"* 25 times – more than any other Gospel in the New Testament.

D. **Scriptural Relationships Between Themes**

A Scriptural relationship is a connection between two passages that creates a bridge between cause and effect. These correlations can appear in many ways.

A ***cause-and-effect*** correlation ties two separate themes together by saying, *"now that X exists, Y must happen."* A key indicator of this type of correlation is the word "therefore." An excellent example of this is found in the *Book of Romans*, a 16-chapter epistle written by the Apostle Paul to the believers in Rome. This epistle is easily divided into two distinct sections: chapters 1-11 focus on understanding Christian doctrine, while chapters 12-16 focus on a believers' duty to apply proper doctrine in their lives. The bridge between these two sections can be seen at the start of Chapter 12:

> *I beseech you therefore, brethren, by the mercies of God, that you present your bodies a living sacrifice, holy, acceptable to God, which is your reasonable service.*
>
> ~ Romans 12:1 ~

As you study the Word of God, pay attention for any occurrence of the word "therefore." Always read the message preceding it to better understand the Scripture's context.

Chapter 01: *The Power and Promise of God's Written Word*

A **comparison and contrast** relationship ties two separate themes together by saying, "*now that X exists, Y does not need to happen.*" A key indicator of this type of correlation is the phrase, "*...you've heard this said before.*" Jesus used this phrase many times in His teaching, followed immediately with the directive, "*...but I tell you, it is time to think differently.*" An excellent example of this is found in the *Gospel of Matthew*, and most predominantly appearing in Chapter 07.

> *You have heard that it was said, 'An eye for an eye and a tooth for a tooth. But I tell you not to resist an evil person. But whoever slaps you on your right cheek, turn the other to him also.*
>
> ~ Matthew 5:38-39 ~

A **conditional** relationship (if/then) ties two themes together by saying, "*if X happens, then Y is going happen*" – or vice versa. This is undoubtedly the most common relationship in the Word of God. God does not chasten or punish randomly; there is always a reason for His actions, and His actions are preceded with some type of warning (a conditional statement). When questions about God's wrath arise, try to trace it back to the original warning.

> *Now therefore, if you will indeed obey My voice and keep My covenant, then you shall be a special treasure to Me above all people; for all the earth is Mine.*
>
> ~ Exodus 19:5 ~

A **question-and-answer** relationship (why/because) ties two themes together by asking, "*if X is so, Y does exist*" – with the understanding that the question is typically rhetorical. While this occurs throughout the entire Bible, nowhere is it more noticeable than in the *Book of Job*. The final chapters of the Book (38 – 42) are entirely dedicated to this type of exchange.

> *Then the Lord answered Job out of the whirlwind, and said: Who is this who darkens counsel by words without knowledge? Now prepare yourself like a man; I will question you, and you shall answer Me.*
>
> ~ Job 38:1-3 ~

Chapter 01: *The Power and Promise of God's Written Word*

D. **Examining Cultural Context**

Considering a cultural context requires the reader to understand the society a person is residing within, and then consider how the culture may impact the person's actions or – in the case of the Word of God – their message. Take the culture of the period into account, and very often a back-story emerges that explains the nature and tone of the text. Listed below are two examples of how cultural context influences the style, tone, and content of a message to a specific audience.

1. **The *Gospel of Mark***: This Scripture was written by Mark, a disciple of Peter (1 Peter 5:13), and a teenager during Christ's earthy ministry. He was present in Mary's house during Pentecost (Acts 12:12) and was an eyewitness to the presence of the Holy Spirit. The Gospel was written around 65 AD, one year after Peter had been martyred, and one year after a major fire engulfed Rome that Nero blamed on a new sect called "Christ-followers." The emperor's persecution of Christians was brutal; Nero would tie them to tall poles, dowse them in kerosene, and use them as human torches for his palace garden while his guests dined.

   After Peter was martyred, Mark was driven to share God's Word with the gentile community in Rome – so there wasn't much need to include teachings on Jewish tradition or Old Testament messianic prophecies. Mark's message was tailored specifically to the culture of a Roman audience that valued power, action, and elevated teachers to a position of high esteem. Its words focus on action and immediacy in Christ's teachings, and portrayed Christ as a revered and divinely inspired teacher of God's Word. The *Gospel of Mark* was the right message, at the right time, for the right audience.

2. **The *Gospel of Luke***: This Scripture was written by Luke, a first-century physician who traded a comfortable life to accompany the Apostle Paul over 30 years during his three missionary journeys (Luke also wrote the *Book of Acts*). He was a man of science, and a detailed observer of people and events. Luke used the meticulous attention to detail required for medical practice and applied it to his very well-researched writing.

Chapter 01: *The Power and Promise of God's Written Word*

Luke is the Bible's only Gentile author, and his writings were meant to reach the wider non-Jewish audience. Luke's Gospel casts Samaritans in a positive light – Jews considered Samaritans to be "dogs" (Matthew 15:26) – by sharing two of Christ's "Samaritan Parables." In the first parable, Jesus heals 10 men with leprosy, but it is only the Samaritan leper that returns to give thanks for being healed (Matthew 17:11-19). In the second parable, a man who had been robbed, beaten, and left for dead in the road was helped by a Samaritan (Luke 10:30-37) after being ignored by a Jewish Sadducee and a Jewish Pharisee. The *Gospel of Luke* was the right message, at the right time, for the right audience.

E. **Examining Literary Genre**

A literary genre is a category of writing that is determined by the style, tone, technique, length, and content. The Bible can be divided into nine primary genres; the categories are listed below, followed by examples from both the Old and New Testament.

1. History   (Exodus, Acts)
2. Law   (Leviticus, Deuteronomy)
3. Wisdom   (Proverbs, Ecclesiastes)
4. Poetry   (Psalms, Lamentations)
5. Prophecy   (Isaiah, Ezekiel)
6. Apocalyptic   (Daniel, Revelation)
7. Parable   (The Gospels)
8. Epistle   (Romans, Ephesians)
9. Romance   (Song of Solomon, Ruth)

As with modern languages, different meanings can be applied to words depending upon the genre. During any given day one may read a novel, a menu, a business report, and a love letter, all written in the same language. However, the way these different categories of writing will be approached and interpreted will be very different.

In many instances, it is the tone and style, not the content, that changes the meaning of words. Imagine reading a business report with the tone of a love letter to your CEO, or a love letter with the tone of a legal document to that special person in your life. As you are examining the Word of God, pay attention to genre (for tone) even when the language is clear.

Chapter 01: *The Power and Promise of God's Written Word*

Component #2: INTERPRETATION

The purposes for studying the Word of God (listed previously) presuppose the intended meaning of the Scriptures is understood by those who read them. Given the tendency of cults and hate groups – such as white supremacists and apocalyptic doomsday cults – to justify their evil actions on the Bible, it is obvious that the inspiration in God's Word can be distorted to support perverse goals.

A less dramatic but equally egregious misinterpretation of God's Word can be found in the mouths of modern "prosperity preachers," who deceive millions of unknowing "believers" that the Word of God promises wealth beyond all imagination – providing those hearing the words "sow their blessed seeds" in the form of large checks and cash contributions.

Hermeneutics, a formal name for the study of methods for interpretation, is a theological discipline that attempts to discover and explain the meaning of Scriptural texts using an exegetical approach. *Exegesis* derives from Greek (to guide out of); one is supposed to draw the meaning out of biblical text.

The opposite of this approach, *eisegesis* (to guide in to), is to be avoided at all costs: one is reading meaning into God's Word based on their own perspectives and opinions.

> *All Scripture is given by inspiration of God, and is profitable for doctrine, for reproof, for correction, for instruction in righteousness;*
>
> ~ 2 Timothy 3:16 ~

5 Guidelines for Correct Interpretation

Listed below are five general guidelines to use when studying the Bible. Their importance will be made apparent when the common errors of interpretation are discussed in the next section.

Chapter 01: *The Power and Promise of God's Written Word*

1. **Respect the Obvious Context**

    The plain language of God's Word reveals the meaning in most cases. When ambiguity exists, a review of the near context (verses immediately before and after the text) typically resolves the matter. If questions remain, a review of the distant context (paragraphs and/or chapters immediately before and after the text) will illuminate the meaning of the text in most cases.

2. **Cross-Reference Related Scripture**

    An established truism of hermeneutics states, "*we study a Scripture by studying all Scripture.*" If the meaning of a word or phrase is not immediately known, reviewing related Scripture can reveal the meaning. For example, while reading *Romans* in the New Testament, you discover that the meaning of the word "justified" (God's act of declaring sinners to be innocent of their sins) is not clear. Reviewing the other letters written by Paul to churches (the Pauline Epistles) would reveal he used the word in various forms 29 times in his writing. A high degree of probability exists that its usage in a related Scripture would clarify the meaning.

3. **Respect the History of Culture**

    Although the eternal Word of God remains unchanged, the language used by Man evolves over time. If the meaning of a word or phrase is not immediately known by reviewing the context, a consideration of the history and culture may be of assistance. Begin the process with the "Five W" questions used by investigative reporters:

    a. **W**ho wrote it, and to whom was it written?
    b. **W**hat is the primary theme and message?
    c. **W**hen was it written?
    d. **W**here is the writer and the recipients?
    e. **W**hy did the author write the text?

4. **Respect the Authors' Conclusions**

    When the meaning of a passage of Scripture is not clear, notate the chapter and verse, and revisit it when the reading has been concluded. In many instances, Scriptural passages will end with a summarization of key points, and the stated conclusion of the author. Once the author's conclusion is known – and with it, the author's intent for the writing – revisit the verse in question. If the meaning originally assigned does not support the author's intended conclusion, the meaning was misinterpreted. Always give respect and deference to the author's intent over opinion.

5. **Consult the Commentaries**

    Bible commentaries are a collection of systemized series of works written to provide explanations of Scripture. There are many reputable commentaries to assist with biblical study, most which fall within four categories:

    a. **Expository**: teaches verse by verse, and tends to include notes, maps, illustrations, teaching outlines, and practical application

    b. **Exegetical**: written by theologians and Bible scholars, tends to be academic and technical, with a focus on biblical languages

    c. **Devotional**: written for personal reflection and inspiration, tends to focus on daily Bible verses with sections for notation and journaling

    d. **Cultural**: written by historians and Bible scholars, focuses on cultural and geographical details meant to enhance the understanding of the biblical text

In addition to commentaries, a variety of supporting texts are available to assist in biblical studies. These include:

   e. **Bible Dictionaries**
   f. **Biblical Encyclopedias**
   g. **Study Bibles**
   h. **Biblical Concordances**

These resources are readily available and have been created to minimize the chance for making the types of mistakes listed below when studying the Word of God and its meaning.

Chapter 01: *The Power and Promise of God's Written Word*

7 Common Interpretation Mistakes to Avoid

The Bible is the Word of God: it is inerrant, infallible, and inspired. How man interprets God's Word, however, is far from perfect at times.

It is inevitable that imperfect Man will arrive at competing interpretations for the perfected message of the Bible. But when competing interpretations of His message contradict His Word, the consequences are no longer harmless; they rise to the level of hazardous and have the potential to become heretical. This holds especially true for those who twist God's Word intentionally to propagate a non-biblical agenda.

The common mistakes listed below presuppose the desire to understand (and apply) the truth of the Bible, with no ulterior motive or agenda. Avoiding these mistakes will provide a fertile field in your heart for the Holy Spirit to guide your studies, and a spirit of truth in your heart that will draw you into an intimate relationship with Christ through His Word.

1. Choosing Information over Inspiration

From a secular perspective, the Bible is a fascinating literary composition to study for numerous reasons: history of ancient societies and cultures, the study of biblical languages, and the origin of Judeo-Christian ethics are a few that come to mind immediately. This fact is not restricted to secularists; any believer will find the Bible fascinating for the same reasons.

For Christians, however, the Bible is much more than a fascinating literary composition: it is the divinely inspired, inerrant and infallible Word of God. It is how God communicates with us through the Holy Spirit and instructs us to pursue a path of righteousness that leads us closer to Him.

> *All Scripture is God-breathed and is useful for teaching, rebuking, correcting and training in righteousness, so that the servant of God may be thoroughly equipped for every good work.*
>
> ~ 2 Timothy 3:16 ~

Chapter 01: *The Power and Promise of God's Written Word*

There is nothing inherently wrong with Christians studying the Bible for knowledge; God commands us to do just that. The danger arises when we subjugate inspiration to information, intellectualizing a religion instead of inspiring our faith.

The second danger arises when we pursue knowledge for its own sake. The often-quoted maxim, "*Knowledge is Power,*" is patently false. Knowledge has no intrinsic power or value; the application of it *does*. The revised maxim, "*Applied Knowledge is Power,*" is true. Confirmation of this truth is clearly stated in God's Word:

> *But be doers of the word, and not hearers only, deceiving yourselves. For if anyone is a hearer of the word and not a doer, he is like a man observing his natural face in a mirror; for he observes himself, goes away, and immediately forgets what kind of man he was.*
>
> ~ James 1:22-24 ~

Study God's Word constantly for knowledge. That said, subjugate knowledge to the wisdom that can only come from God's inspiration, and apply what you learn daily in a world that needs to observe Christians as positive examples of His Word.

2. Redefining the Intent of the Author

Even though the Bible was written to a specific audience with a specific need, the inspired Scripture remains as relevant to Christians today as it did when it was written. Even so, the application of the Scripture has limits and restrictions that are often violated because of misinterpretation. The mistake is obvious in the sermons of "prosperity preachers," pastors that have deceived their church by twisting the Word of God into a form that is unrecognizable. Did you know God wants you to have a mansion, a private jet, and a yacht? It says so in the Bible; all you need to do is ask God for it and claim your prize.

> *So I say to you, ask, and it will be given to you; seek, and you will find; knock, and it will be opened to you. For everyone who asks receives, and he who seeks finds, and to him who knocks it will be opened.*
>
> ~ Luke 11:9-10 ~

Chapter 01: *The Power and Promise of God's Written Word*

Is that what the Scripture really says? This verse is used constantly by "prosperity preachers" promising wealth to their members in exchange for substantial donations. When Jesus spoke these words, was He referring to material wealth? A quick review of the last sentence of the paragraph reveals the true intent of His message:

> *If you then, being evil, know how to give good gifts to your children, how much more will your heavenly Father give the Holy Spirit to those who ask Him!*
>
> ~ Luke 11:13 ~

The "it" referred to in the Scripture "prosperity preachers" quote to the deceived masses does not refer to wealth or material possessions; the "it" is the Holy Spirit, and the intended message of Jesus' words are clear. The deception occurs when 1) believers do not study the Bible themselves, and 2) they prefer to hear a message of material wealth than one that guides them to an intimate relationship with Christ.

3. **Creating False Combinations (Collapsing Contexts)**

The Words of God written in the Bible are true – provided they remain in the correct verse, paragraph, chapter, and Book. When words with a specific meaning are combined with unrelated Scriptures – then blended and synthesized to create a message to support an agenda – the words are no longer true, even though they were taken from God's Word. For example, did you know that God will bless you if you quit your job, never work again, and party all the time? It says so in the Bible:

> *It is vain for you to rise up early; There is nothing better for a person than that he should eat and drink and find enjoyment. Rest a while, Keep your life free - Then you will win favor and a good name in the sight of God.*
>
> ~ ? ? ? ~

Does the Bible really say that? Yes, it does – those are accurate quotes from God's Word – the problem is that they were taken from five different Books and combined out of context to create a short paragraph. The verses, in order, are: Psalm 127:2, Ecclesiastes 2:24, Mark 6:31, Hebrews 13:5, and Proverbs 3:4.

Chapter 01: *The Power and Promise of God's Written Word*

4. Rationalizing the Morality of Difficult Scripture

The Word of God is true, perfect, and authoritative in all situations. Uplifting verses are available for inspiration and offer us God's strength when it is most needed. However, there are times when Scripture is not pleasant to read – especially when it speaks to God's plan for righteous living and runs counter to our earthly desires. As a Christian pursuing an intimate relationship with Christ, how would you counsel a young Christian couple, engaged to be married, who want to live together beforehand?

> *Marriage should be honored by all, and the marriage bed kept pure, for God will judge the adulterer and all the sexually immoral.*
>
> ~ Hebrews 13:4 ~

Does living together first to see if "things work out" make sense? It might. Would it be better to fail in a dating relationship than in marriage? It might. If God knows we plan to get married anyway, would it really be a problem? Yes, it will. God's Word is not always what we want, but it is always what we need to hear and live in our lives.

As a Christian pursuing an intimate relationship with Christ, how would you counsel a best friend having marital problems, who wants to divorce their spouse for the sole reason of habitual arguing over reckless spending?

> *But I say to you that whoever divorces his wife for any reason except sexual immorality causes her to commit adultery; and whoever marries a woman who is divorced commits adultery.*
>
> ~ Matthew 5:32 ~

You may offer sincere advice with the best of intentions, but would it be consistent with what the Word of God teaches us in plain language? You may offer supportive comments: "*If **my** spouse did that to me, I would not hesitate to walk away.*"

The true test for any Christian when it comes to the Bible is this: when you encounter Scripture that runs counter to your desires, which one wins? Do **you** want to be the one who says, "*I know God says this, but I know better?*"

Chapter 01: *The Power and Promise of God's Written Word*

5. Developing Doctrine in Isolation

Developing doctrine in isolation refers to the act of interpreting Scripture and assigning meaning to passages that is so far outside the mainstream it makes it absurd and heretical. This is precisely how cults and Christian fringe groups justify their radical positions and rationalize their teachings to members. The Word of God provides instruction on this topic with perfect clarity:

> *Above all, you must understand that no prophecy of Scripture came about by the prophet's own interpretation of things. For prophecy never had its origin in the human will, but prophets, though human, spoke from God as they were carried along by the Holy Spirit.*
>
> ~ 2 Peter 1:20-21 ~

If you find yourself making the statement, "*I know everyone else believes the Scripture means this, but I believe it means that,*" there is a chance you may be incorrect. In instances such as these, step back and consider other alternatives. When it comes to the Word of God, the ego of Man takes lowest priority.

6. Applying Modern Meaning to Biblical Words

Language is a living thing; it grows, evolves, and changes over time. If this occurs within the same language over a short span of time – English, for example, over the last 100 years – imagine the potential for misinterpretation between different languages over a period of thousands of years. Understanding this fact is critical when interpreting biblical text.

This mistake can be found in arguments for same-sex relationships that appeal to Scripture for support. In the example below, not only is the meaning of the original language ignored, but the Scriptural reference is also taken entirely out of context.

> *A new command I give you: Love one another. As I have loved you, so you must love one another.*
>
> ~ John 13:34 ~

Chapter 01: *The Power and Promise of God's Written Word*

The argument goes as follows: *"Jesus never addressed homosexual relationships in the Bible. He did say we should love one another – Bill and Bob love one another – so Jesus would be OK with our relationship."* The purpose of the information that follows is not to engage in political debate, but to demonstrate how easily (and how frequently) this mistake is made when interpreting Scripture.

First, there were many topics Jesus did not address directly; He did not feel the need as they had already been established in the Old Testament Law:

> *You shall not lie with a male as with a woman.*
> *It is an abomination.*
>
> ~ Leviticus 18:22 ~

Second, it is obvious from a reading of Scripture that Christ fully supported the Old Testament Law:

> *For assuredly, I say to you, till heaven and earth pass away, one jot or one tittle will by no means pass from the law till all is fulfilled. Whoever therefore breaks one of the least of these commandments, and teaches men so, shall be called least in the kingdom of heaven; but whoever does and teaches them, he shall be called great in the kingdom of heaven.*
>
> ~ Matthew 5:18-19 ~

Finally, the original language used in John 13:34 did not speak to physical relationships. In the English language, there is one word for *love*: "love." In Greek, the original language of the New Testament, there are four words that are commonly used to express the concept of "love" – two of which were used by the authors of the Bible.

Storgē	Familial Love	Στοργή
Phileo	Brotherly Love	φιλία
Agape	Godly Love	ἀγαπάω

The word Christ used – and John used for this verse – is "agape." This is godly love that moves the heart to charity, good works and spiritual deeds that bring Man closer to God. A modern meaning has turned this biblical truth into its opposite: a lie.

Chapter 01: *The Power and Promise of God's Written Word*

7. Studying to Prove, not Learn

The last of the "7 Deadly Interpretation Mistakes" is studying the Word of God to prove a point, instead of attempting to learn a truth. Immersing oneself in the Bible, after a quiet time of prayer and being guided by the Holy Spirit, is an amazing experience. The key to achieving the full potential of this time is an open mindset and a desire to discern God's truth.

When the Bible is approached with an eisegetical mindset – reading into the text to support an agenda, instead of drawing truth out of it – a misinterpretation of the text often occurs. The Word of God warns us about making this avoidable mistake:

> *Now the Berean Jews were of more noble character than those in Thessalonica, for they received the message with great eagerness and examined the Scriptures every day to see if what Paul said was true.*
>
> ~ Acts 17:11 ~

As stated in the Scripture above, examining the Bible with eagerness to discover and corroborate truth, not using the text to prove an existing thought, confers a noble character upon those who study the Word of God. Engaging biblical study with a proper mindset and methodology – Examination, Interpretation, and a heart for Application – will be a critical step in developing the type of intimate relationship with God that He desires with you. The alternative path leads to an unwanted ending:

> *... of whom we have much to say, and hard to explain, since you have become dull of hearing. For though by this time you ought to be teachers, you need someone to teach you again the first principles of the oracles of God; and you have come to need milk and not solid food. For everyone who partakes only of milk is unskilled in the word of righteousness, for he is a babe. But solid food belongs to those who are of full age, that is, those who by reason of use have their senses exercised to discern both good and evil.*
>
> ~ Hebrews 5:11-14 ~

Studying is the first step; interpreting His Word correctly and using it daily is when life-changing events start to happen.

Chapter 01: *The Power and Promise of God's Written Word*

12 Practical Tips for Studying the Bible

It is the duty, responsibility, and goal of Christians to know and understand the Word of God. A proper approach is crucial. A well-reasoned methodology that genuinely addresses examination, interpretation and application is crucial. To take advantage of this approach to studying the Bible, a few basic tips are recommended. With proper structure and planning, immersion in His Word becomes an enriching experience, not an activity done begrudgingly from a sense of guilt.

> *Be diligent to present yourself approved to God,*
> *a worker who does not need to be ashamed,*
> *rightly dividing the word of truth.*
>
> ~ 2 Timothy 2:15 ~

1. **Engage in Prayer**: Pray before, during and after your biblical study. Prayer is your way of communicating with God, and His Word is His way to communicate His message to you. Ask that the Holy Spirit be present to guide you in discerning the truth of His Word, and to provide inspiration and insight into the practical application of God's truth in your life. The same quiet space you choose for prayer is the same type of environment you should use for your studies.

2. **Discipline and Regimen**: Establish a schedule for your studies and discipline yourself to stick with the regimen. There are many excuses for allowing distractions to disrupt your study time; all you need is one reason not to allow that to happen. As you progress in your studies, you will not only ensure no distractions interfere with your regimen, but you will also look forward with joyful anticipation to your private time with God's Word.

3. **Manage Expectations and Goals**: Building an intimate relationship with God, like earthly intimate relationships, is a process that is refined over time. Manage your goals and make them sensible; if you expect to memorize everything

Chapter 01: *The Power and Promise of God's Written Word*

you read the first time, you will soon find yourself disappointed and frustrated. Allow your reading goals to be attainable, based on your own abilities and schedule.

4. **Plan to Study Systematically**: Reading a few pages from different Books each day does not work well. You probably wouldn't buy 66 novels, and then plan to read them on a rotating schedule. By the time you return to a previous novel you'd most likely have forgotten the few pages you read weeks before. Your plan does not have to be "start at the beginning and read to the end," but it does need to be a plan.

5. **Choose the Right Bible**: With so many versions of God's Word available today, what is the right Bible for you? It is the one you will read and enjoy. If you are not reading the Old Testament in Hebrew, or the New Testament in Greek – and most of us do not – the English language version does not make a significant difference. Eventually, you will have read many translations and have them on-hand to cross-check Scripture. This logic applies to audio and digital Bibles as well. Each of these formats are based on mainstream translations – KJV, NKJV, NIV, ESV and NASB – so the experience won't be diminished. The best version is the one that keeps you in God's Word.

6. **Read Whole Books**: Regardless of what system you plan for your studies – thematic, linear, etc. – reading the entire Book before moving to the next will provide you with a better understanding of the author's intent and meaning. From there, move to groupings of related Books to get the broader picture. Books that are related by theme (Daniel, Ezekiel, and Isaiah) or written by the same author (Gospel of Luke, and Acts) can make more sense when read sequentially.

7. **Take Detailed Notes**: The Bible has a significant amount of content and detail – all of it is important – and it is very difficult to recall all the material studied. Keeping a note pad handy ensures that questions are written down, and details from the previous study period are not lost. If you study on a computer, it is easy to keep a word processing program open to type notes. You can also make notes in the body of an email and send it to yourself when you finish

Chapter 01: *The Power and Promise of God's Written Word*

to be printed or filed. Taking notes, regardless of method, assists in keeping the details of God's Word fresh in your mind.

8. **Beginnings, Bridges, and Endings**: Pay close attention to the beginning of texts, as the introduction tends to lay out the framework and intent for the Book. Bridges, such as "therefore," provide signals to the reader that a relationship between two themes is about to be revealed. The end of a text may end with a summary or the author's stated intent, both of which assist in determining the meaning of the Book. All the content in between is important, of course, but these three portions of any text deserve special attention.

9. **Research Bible Characters**: There are main characters in the Bible with whom we are familiar, but like any story, the supporting characters have a significant amount to contribute to the message. There is no person mentioned in the Word of God that is not important; if that were the case, we'd never read their names. In many instances, characters that seem "minor" at first glance have roles that contribute meaning to the back-story of the text. Set some time aside to research the names of people you encounter in your studies. You will not only learn more about the text, but you will often discover details that add significant meaning and insight to the message.

10. **Research Unknown Words**: Take the time to notate any words or terms that are unfamiliar and set aside time to find out what they mean. Look at this example from the *Gospel of Mark* (3:17): *"James the son of Zebedee and John the brother of James, to whom He gave the name Boanerges, that is, "Sons of Thunder."* Boanerges? Sons of Thunder? It turns the Apostle John (and his brother James) both had anger management issues to the degree Jesus was compelled to give them a nickname. These are the same two disciples mentioned in the *Gospel of Luke* (9:54): *"And when His disciples James and John saw this, they said, "Lord, do You want us to command fire to come down from heaven and consume them, just as Elijah did?"* It appears their tempers were well-known, and their nickname well-deserved.

Chapter 01: *The Power and Promise of God's Written Word*

11. **Use Historical Maps**: Many study Bibles contain a variety of historical maps to accompany the text; if not, these maps can be researched online. They provide a visual reference based on modern geography that can assist in visualizing the events detailed in the text. Many of the cities mentioned in the Bible are no longer in existence (Antioch, Ephesus, and Babylonia), but the locations where they stood remain. For example, when the Apostle Paul was traveling on his four missionary journeys and stopped in Philippi, the theme of his epistle (*Philippians*) makes more sense when it is known that Philippi was in Macedonia (northern Greece), as was a military stronghold for the Greco-Roman Empire. Although the city no longer stands, it is history – and importance to the culture that influenced the Pauline Epistles – will always remain in God's Word.

12. **Apply Equal Time to Both Testaments**: The study of God's Word is incomplete without the Old Testament for numerous reasons. They are part of one story – God's redemptive plan for fallen Man – and serve as the root of the Gospel we share today. The Old Testament lays the historical foundation for Christ's earthly ministry; He believed God's Word as did His disciples. Without the Old Testament, the New Testament writers would have never been able to reveal Jesus' role as the foreseen Messiah: *But those things which God foretold by the mouth of all His prophets, that the Christ would suffer, He has thus fulfilled* (Acts 3:18). It provides invaluable truths about the nature of God, God's promises to humanity, and the nature of humanity. The Old Testament also provides the foundation for biblical prophecies yet to be fulfilled, prophecies that Jesus Himself taught: "*For the Son of Man will come in the glory of His Father with His angels, and then He will reward each according to his works*" (Matthew 16:27). For the reasons listed above – and many more that go beyond the scope of this brief section – make time in your schedule to give equal time to studying both the Old and New Testaments.

These 12 tips are meant to serve as guidelines, not rules written in stone, to assist in you in establishing the practices, mindset, and environment needed to develop an intimate relationship with God through the study of His inspired Word.

Chapter 01: *The Power and Promise of God's Written Word*

Applying God's Biblical Truth to Your Daily Life

How does one live a biblical lifestyle? The study of God's Word is ongoing, the interpretation is based on sound doctrine, so – how does the process of application begin? Jesus gave us the answer in the Gospel of Luke (10:37): *"Go and do likewise."* In basic terms, it is hearing the call of God's Word internally, and answering the call externally with the decision to *"go and do likewise."*

The challenge for many Christians is that while they embrace biblical truth in concept, the thought of putting it into practice – changing the way they must think and act – does not make them comfortable. Many who profess their faith claim a desire for a changed life, when all they want is a change in circumstances.

> *The things which you learned and received*
> *and heard and saw in me, these do, and*
> *the God of peace will be with you.*
>
> ~ Philippians 4:9 ~

Begin by asking yourself the questions, *"How does this biblical truth affect my …*

> … *relationship with God?"*
> … *relationship with those around me?"*
> … *my perception of biblical truth?"*
> … *my perception of myself as a Christian?"*

Once those questions have been answered – the internal call of God's Word being heard and acknowledged – your plan to *"go and do likewise"* can be created and implemented.

1. Identify the applicable situations in your daily life
2. Create a plan to apply God's Word in those situations
3. Identify potential obstacles and set up contingency plans
4. Make the decision to act – "Go and do likewise"

Successfully living God's Word is a long-term process, not a short-term event.

Chapter 02

The Mission to Advance Christ's Kingdom on Earth

"And to Him was given dominion, Glory and a kingdom, that all the peoples, nations and men of every language might serve Him."

~ Daniel 7:14 ~

Chapter 02: *The Mission to Advance Christ's Kingdom on Earth*

The Biblical Path to Christian Discipleship

What is your primary responsibility as a person professing faith in Christ? There are a variety of answers that seem obvious, but which answer gets top priority? Whether you grew up in a Christian church or recently gave your life to the Lord, the correct answer may surprise you. Just prior to Jesus' Ascension, He gathered His disciples and gave them a tasking order that would serve as the mission statement for the early Church. Their mission was clear: MAKE DISCIPLES.

> *And Jesus came and spoke to them, saying, "All authority has been given to Me in heaven and on earth. Go therefore and make disciples of all the nations, baptizing them in the name of the Father and of the Son and of the Holy Spirit, teaching them to observe all things that I have commanded you; and lo, I am with you always, even to the end of the age."*
>
> ~ Matthew 28:18-20 ~

Modern Christianity looks much different than the early Church, even though God's Word remains unchanged over time. Adherence to the faith is declining, apostasy in churches is increasing, and statistical data shows there is little difference between the lifestyles of believers and non-believers. Most Christians will admit there is a problem; that is a critical first-step for finding a solution. We need to know where we are before we decide where we need to go. The difference between those two points is the solution.

Before identifying the problems and presenting possible solutions, Christians need to address the "800-pound gorilla" in the room: *evangelism*. Christ's "mission statement" to the disciples, "*Go therefore and make disciples of all the nations*," propelled the early Church forward, and established Christianity as a global faith. The disciples had to share the Gospel of Christ with non-believers, create disciples, and teach them how to replicate their efforts. Unfortunately, modern Christians are very uncomfortable sharing the Gospel, and that is a problem.

Chapter 02: *The Mission to Advance Christ's Kingdom on Earth*

7 Reasons Christians Do Not Share the Gospel

It does not take much to realize how significant this problem is to the health of Christianity. When Christ issued His command (*The Great Commission*) to the disciples, He knew what needed to be done to save a fallen world before His Second Coming. Jesus taught a select group of believers – disciples – how to continue His work with His faith, words, and actions. Jesus committed to them, the disciples committed to Him and, after 3-1/2 years of experience in Jesus' earthly ministry, His disciples transformed the world. Something appears to have changed.

Many Christians attribute that change to culture and period, and reference Acts 2:44-45 as proof: "*Now all who believed were together, and had all things in common, and sold their possessions and goods, and divided them among all, as anyone had need.*" They suggest nothing similar could happen in modern society due to cultural differences. They would be incorrect. The fact that passage made it into Scripture means it was noteworthy: things like that "did not happen" in their culture of the period. However, it *did* happen, which suggests there is another reason for the change.

The short answer – discussed in detail following this section – is that Christ made *disciples*, not congregants. His disciples were not admirers, they were followers. They were not impressed with Jesus, they were *devoted* to Him. They did not applaud Him for His miracles, they *surrendered* to Him. They did not approve His divine authority, they *obeyed* it. They did not view Christ as a "ticket to Heaven," they viewed Him as a *way of Life*.

His disciples knew the cost of following Him and were willing to pay it, while multitudes turned away. The disciples did not view themselves as members of a religious culture, burdened with minimal entrance requirements. Perhaps that explains why the word "disciple" appears 270 times in the Bible (NKJV), and the word "Christian" only twice. The issue for the moment, however, is why Christians are hesitant to evangelize.

Chapter 02: *The Mission to Advance Christ's Kingdom on Earth*

Fear of Engaging People

The thought of public speaking is enough to cause many people to have panic attacks; surveys reveal most people would rather face death or a terrorist attack than speak to large audiences. While sharing the Gospel does not always involve speaking to groups, the same rules apply: what causes a person to be fearful of speaking to groups is the same thing causing them to fear speaking to an individual. The reason for this fear has nothing to do with the size of the audience, but resides within the person themselves.

Consider the reasons given for fear of public speaking: "*I might make a mistake;*" "*They may not like what I say;*" "*I do not know what they'll think of me, or my message.*" All stem from the speaker's focus on themselves, not on the message or the people to whom they are speaking. Once the concern shifts from the "self" to the recipient of the message, none of the arguments above apply.

Another contributing factor to a fear of speaking publicly is a lack of subject matter expertise. Those who possess a good working knowledge of the material being presented are much less likely to be fearful than those speaking on a topic of which they know little about. The ability to anticipate questions and objections – and formulate answers and rebuttals in advance – reduces the fear of speaking to others. The thought of telling someone "*just be confident*" is as absurd as telling a drug addict to "*just say NO;*" it does not work. However, telling a person to "*just be competent*" is well within reason, and works rather well.

Christians that share the Gospel have a benefit secular speakers lack: *Christ*. He promised when the Gospel was shared, "*I am with you always*" (Matthew 28:20). Believe His promise.

> *There is no fear in love; but perfect love casts out fear, because fear involves punishment, and the one who fears is not perfected in love.*
>
> ~ 1 John 4:18 ~

Chapter 02: *The Mission to Advance Christ's Kingdom on Earth*

Unaware of Biblical Obligation

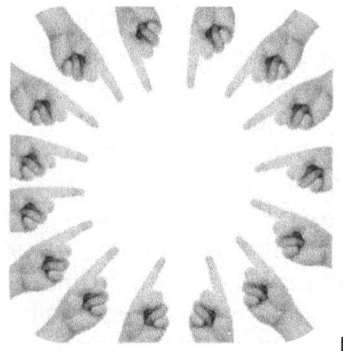

Who has the responsibility to share the Gospel? Many pastors will say it is their ministry or outreach team. Ask the congregants, and many will say it is their pastor or outreach team.

While Christians delegate the evangelical mission to anyone but themselves, the Gospel is not shared, and no one is making disciples. When believers realize that evangelism is every Christian's responsibility, they tend to respond in two ways: they accept the mission given to them by Christ, or they choose to invoke the list of *Spiritual Gifts* and absolve themselves from the responsibility altogether.

> *Preach the word; be ready in season and out of season; reprove, rebuke, exhort, with great patience and instruction.*
>
> ~ 2 Timothy 4:2 ~

The Holy Spirit endows Christians with spiritual gifts, the divinely-inspired abilities and talents Christians need to fulfill the mission of their faith. The New Testament gives multiple lists of these gifts (*Romans*, *1 Corinthians*, *Ephesians* and *1 Peter*), of which evangelism is but one. When Christians avoid sharing the Gospel by claiming "it is not my gift," several issues arise.

Jesus tells us evangelism is the mission statement for the Church; to invoke categories of gifts in defense is the type of legalism He preached against. Having other gifts does not negate the responsibility, even if the believer lacks ability. Offer to preach a sermon with the message, "*If giving* (a spiritual gift) *is not your gift, do not give to the church.*" The pastors' response will confirm multiple gifts are not just possible, they are a reality.

> *And He said to them, "Go into all the world and preach the gospel to all creation. He who has believed and has been baptized shall be saved; but he who has disbelieved shall be condemned."*
>
> ~ Mark 16:15-16 ~

Chapter 02: *The Mission to Advance Christ's Kingdom on Earth*

Negative Perception of Evangelism

Almost everyone in Western culture has experienced a case of evangelism run amok. It is the fire-and-brimstone street pastor, blocking the way of pedestrians, while screaming in their faces, *"Repent, or go to hell!"* It is the angry church pastor, caught on video, abusing and insulting his congregants. Regardless of what form it takes, it gives Christians a bad reputation and does not reflect the true spirit of sharing the Gospel. Unfortunately, for every one bad example people see, there are thousands of great examples they never experience.

Not only is this type of evangelism counterproductive, it is unbiblical as well. The apostle Paul gave clear instructions to the Body of Christ about judging non-believers:

> *For what have I to do with judging outsiders? Do*
> *you not judge those who are within the church?*
> *But those who are outside, God judges.*
>
> ~ 1 Corinthians 5:12-13 ~

Those misguided believers that take this approach to evangelism portray Christians as self-righteous, intolerant and preachy. No rational person would find that image appealing.

Similarly, many evangelists use a scripted greeting when engaging people in public places. Although they mean well and are typically well-mannered, talking to people as if reading from a PowerPoint slide is disingenuous, and the impersonal nature of this kind of exchange does not leave a good impression. Once again, for every one bad example people see, there are many great examples they never experience. Leave the bad examples behind, and focus on creating good experiences – and disciples.

> *Brethren, I do not regard myself as having laid hold*
> *of it yet; but one thing I do: forgetting what lies*
> *behind and reaching forward to what lies ahead;*
>
> ~ Philippians 3:13 ~

Chapter 02: *The Mission to Advance Christ's Kingdom on Earth*

Lack of Biblical Knowledge

Of all the reasons to avoid sharing the Gospel, this obstacle is the easiest to overcome. Many Christians believe they lack the biblical knowledge to evangelize, not realizing that sharing the Gospel is not an intellectual event. If one does believe they lack knowledge of God's Word, the solution is obvious: read the Bible. If you are a believer who can name ever member of a sports team – but you believe Joan of Arc was Noah's wife – you may need to reassess your priorities. However, sharing the Gospel is not a demonstration of biblical knowledge.

Evangelism is personal, heartfelt, and sincere. It is simply a conversation in which a Christian explains to a non-believer what type of person they were, how they came to Christ, and how the Holy Spirit has changed them into the person they are now. It is an opportunity to convey the power and impact of the Salvation experience.

Although sharing your testimony is personal, it does not have to be revealing. Everyone has sinned, including those with whom you share the Gospel. The fact that we've all sinned, and remembering God's promise to stand with you, is enough to get the conversation started: *"Do not fear, for I am with you; Do not anxiously look about you, for I am your God. I will strengthen you, surely I will help you, surely I will uphold you with My righteous right hand"* (Isaiah 41:10).

Satan does not want Christians to make disciples; that infuriates him. He wants to steal their voices, to make them believe their testimony is irrelevant, and the souls of the people they may approach are unimportant. However, Satan is not trying to conceal the voices themselves; he is trying to conceal Christ from the hearts of non-believers. The grace of God overshadows your message, and your faith in Christ strengthens it.

> *The mind of the prudent acquires knowledge,*
> *and the ear of the wise seeks knowledge.*
>
> ~ Proverbs 18:15 ~

Chapter 02: *The Mission to Advance Christ's Kingdom on Earth*

Lack of Practical Mentorship

Would you feel comfortable piloting a plane with passengers onboard if you have never taken a flying lesson? That would be absurd; lives are at stake and the risk is too great. Would you feel comfortable sending believers out into the world to share the Gospel of Christ if they have never taken a lesson in evangelism? That would be absurd; souls are at stake, and this time the risk is eternal. It makes sense that people are not comfortable performing tasks with little or no instruction.

True leaders lead from the front; Jesus knew this when He trained His disciples during His earthly ministry. He led from the front and taught His disciples by example: *"And He said to them, "Follow Me, and I will make you fishers of men." Immediately they left their nets and followed Him"* (Matthew 4:19-20).

This does not apply to sharing the Gospel with others in an informal environment – that is a personal conversation between a few people – but that type of exchange benefits from leadership as well. In the words of Benjamin Franklin, *"Tell me and I forget, teach me and I may remember, involve me and I learn."* The foundation for this style of teaching is well-established by leaders around the world.

However, the benefit of leading by example extends well beyond learning; it also creates the crucial element of trust. The disciples did not follow Him – and later die for Him – because they admired His teaching. They did so because they trusted Him, based on His example: *"When he puts forth all his own, he goes ahead of them, and the sheep follow him because they know his voice"* (John 10:4). If corporations are willing to train their staff for networking and sales, churches must be willing to invest in training for making disciples and the Salvation of lost souls.

Train up a child in the way he should go, even when he is old he will not depart from it.

~ Proverbs 22:6 ~

Chapter 02: *The Mission to Advance Christ's Kingdom on Earth*

Sense of Personal Guilt

Some Christians are hesitant to share their faith, and the Gospel of Christ, due to a sense of personal guilt that makes them "unworthy" to offer testimony. They ask themselves the question, "Who am I to tell someone about sin and Salvation after all that I have done?"

Although a good example leads to a credible testimony – one should never preach against the sin of alcoholism if they are drunk, holding a bottle of vodka – this sense of personal guilt shows a lack of understanding of the reason Christ died for our sins.

> *How much more will the blood of Christ, who through the eternal Spirit offered Himself without blemish to God, cleanse your conscience from dead works to serve the living God?*
>
> *~ Hebrews 9:14 ~*

Those believers who allow guilt to interfere with their responsibility to make disciples must understand that God's forgiveness includes a clean conscience. Through a profession of faith in Christ as Lord and Savior, the slate is wiped clean, and the stain of sin is removed forever. There is no residual stain; it is like it never happened at all. The indwelling of the Holy Spirit guides us through a process of Sanctification, and eventually we are empowered to walk away from sin altogether.

What happens when a believer sins again, and the guilt returns? Christians confess their sins before God, repent, and ask God for forgiveness. Then we pray for the strength that allows us to be victorious the next time we are tempted. With all that God does for our conscience, we must never be silent about Him.

> *I acknowledged my sin to You, and my iniquity I did not hide; I said, "I will confess my transgressions to the Lord"; And You forgave the guilt of my sin.*
>
> *~ Psalm 32:5 ~*

Chapter 02: *The Mission to Advance Christ's Kingdom on Earth*

Insufficient Level of Compassion

Imagine walking by a lake and hearing shouting in the distance. You see a person in the water, 25-feet out, panicked, and screaming for help: they are drowning. You see them, then look at the 50-foot rope coiled around your shoulder, then watch them as they start to go underwater. You turn your eyes away from them and go about your business. *"Someone else will save them,"* you tell yourself, *"or they'll find a way to save themselves."*

If your first reaction to that hypothetical scenario is disgust – *"I would **never** do anything like that"* – that is exactly what happens every time we intentionally forego an opportunity to share the Gospel of Christ with a non-believer.

The keyword is *intentionally*: there will always be missed opportunities beyond the control of believers, and it is terrible when it happens. This intentional silence tends to come from those who view Christ as nothing more than a "ticket to Heaven." They are willing to trust Christ with their eternal souls, but not the day-to-day actions of their lives. They are saved and that is all that matters.

Thankfully, they represent only a very small portion of believers, but they *do* exist. They must realize in a world of non-believers (drowning victims), they have the rope (the Gospel) that could pull the victim to safety (Salvation through faith in Christ). To have the means of saving a person's soul from an eternity in Hell, only to walk away hoping someone else will save them, is no different from the hypothetical scenario above.

In the event Christians throw the rope and the victim turns their back on them, refusing the rescue, there is nothing they can do but try again and pray. They are in God's hands now.

*Let us not lose heart in doing good, for in due
time we will reap if we do not grow weary.*

~ Galatians 6:9 ~

Chapter 02: *The Mission to Advance Christ's Kingdom on Earth*

Jesus' Approach to Making Disciples

It is a challenge that plagues modern Christianity: how can two people that claim to believe the same things act so differently? Two believers, of similar age and background, attend the same church. They both believe in Christ, and they both profess to adhere to the same doctrine. Yet for some reason, they are very different. One is filled with joy, is prayerful, and looks for ways to help other members of the church. The other is bitter, resentful, and tends to divide the church. The issue is their respective levels of conviction, something Jesus taught about continually during His earthly ministry.

Jesus often spoke against the Pharisees and Sadducees of His day, chastening them for the hypocrisy of their legalistic system. In short, the words they spoke regarding their beliefs did not match their actions in the world. He taught His disciples to recognize this behavior in themselves and, through the example set by Him, alter their exterior behavior by changing their level of conviction. Jesus understood those who followed Him – even His disciples – would not be equally convicted. Through His teaching and example, Scripture reveals that Jesus dealt with this issue preemptively.

There are three basic levels of conviction appearing in Scripture: *public*, *personal*, and *fundamental*. Jesus' mission during His ministry was to change the disciples' convictions at a fundamental level.

1. **Public Conviction**: This is the level of conviction claimed by someone in public. It may be true (as in the case of Jesus), or it may be a lie to further a personal agenda. A good example would be Judas Iscariot, the disciple who betrayed Jesus to the authorities (Matthew 26:14-16). Judas concealed his traitorous nature so well, the remaining 11 disciples had no idea of his true intentions, even after 3-1/2 years. Jesus knew this would happen – and allowed it to happen – so that Old Testament prophecy could be fulfilled: *"Did I Myself not*

choose you, the twelve, and yet one of you is a devil?" (John 6:70).

2. **Personal Conviction**: This is a level of conviction a person claims to hold, and really believes it to be true. It may be true (as in the case of Jesus), or it may be found to be false, failing under the pressure of certain conditions. A good example of this would be Peter, His primary disciple, who promised Jesus he would stand by Him under any condition: *"Peter said to Him, 'Even if I have to die with You, I will not deny You"* (Matthew 26:35). After Jesus was arrested, the disciples fled the Garden of Gethsemane, and Peter denied knowing Jesus three times (Luke 22:54-62). Jesus knew this was going to happen – and allowed it to happen – to teach Peter a lesson and strengthen his conviction.

3. **Fundamental Conviction**: This level of conviction is the most powerful; whether it is claimed or not, the person never violates it. People demonstrate their fundamental convictions through actions that come as naturally as breathing. For example, most rational people hold the laws of physics to be true, and will not walk in front of a car traveling at 75 MPH. They do not have to *think* about it; they simply *know* it to be true, the same way Jesus *knew* God the Father. A good example of this is Stephen, the first martyr in the New Testament, based on his words and *actions* as he was being stoned to death: *"But being full of the Holy Spirit, he gazed intently into heaven and saw the glory of God, and Jesus standing at the right hand of God"* (Acts 7:55).

All three levels of conviction were congruent in Jesus. He knew the level of faith leading to Salvation is fundamental, and worked to cause that transformation in His disciples. Jesus wanted them to have faith in Him, but also wanted for them to have His level of faith in God the Father. At the end of His earthly ministry, and from that time forward, the disciples viewed the world through the same lens as Jesus. That is the hallmark of good discipleship.

Holy Father, keep through Your name those whom You have given Me, that they may be one as We are.

~ John 17:11 ~

Chapter 02: *The Mission to Advance Christ's Kingdom on Earth*

The Making of Disciples vs. Congregants

In modern Christianity, the success of a pastor is often based on the size of the church. Popular opinion holds that a church with 20,000 members is more successful than one with twenty members. Is that the vision Jesus had in mind for His followers? The Bible tells us accounts of multitudes, in the thousands, following Jesus to hear His teaching. He fed them, healed them, and preached to them. After Jesus' Resurrection and Ascension, the number of adherents to the new faith of Christianity increased exponentially.

Many Christians believe Jesus wanted the multitudes to follow Him. They also believe He wanted to convert as many people as possible during His earthly ministry – the mission of most modern churches in society today. However, Scripture reveals that to be a myth, and nothing could be farther from the truth.

During His earthly ministry, Jesus divided the people He interacted with into two categories: *disciples*, and *everyone else*. The Bible refers to those who fall into the second category as "crowds" or "multitudes." In Jesus' mind, they are very different categories.

> *And He summoned the crowd with His disciples, and said to them, "If anyone wishes to come after Me, he must deny himself, and take up his cross and follow Me.*
>
> ~ Mark 8:34 ~

> *When he had left the crowd and entered the house, His disciples questioned Him about the parable.*
>
> ~ Mark 7:17 ~

In both examples above, the Scripture clearly defines the two groups as individual categories. Why is this important? His disciples viewed the world through the same lens Jesus did; the multitudes did not. This fact eludes many modern Christians.

Chapter 02: *The Mission to Advance Christ's Kingdom on Earth*

To illustrate this point, consider the following passages from Chapter 8 in the *Gospel of Luke*, the *Parable of the Sower*.

> "When a large crowd was coming together, and those from the various cities were journeying to Him, He spoke by way of a parable: "The sower went out to sow his seed; and as he sowed, some fell beside the road, and it was trampled under foot and the birds of the air ate it up. Other seed fell on rocky soil, and as soon as it grew up, it withered away, because it had no moisture. Other seed fell among the thorns; and the thorns grew up with it and choked it out. Other seed fell into the good soil, and grew up, and produced a crop a hundred times as great." As He said these things, He would call out, "He who has ears to hear, let him hear" (Luke 8:4-8).

In this parable, Jesus explains there are four types of people that hear His Gospel (the seeds sown). The first is the one who hears, ignores the Word, and belongs to Satan. The second hears the word, and has a shallow faith that disappears under pressure. The third hears the Word, but makes worldly concerns a priority, thereby negating the faith. The fourth type hears the Word, believes it, and follows it. Those seeds of faith multiply in the fertile soil of a disciples' heart.

Based on the Scripture, Jesus finds only one of the four categories valuable: those who hear the Word, believe it, and *follow* it. That is the only type that survives and multiplies. What about the second and third types? Where do they fit into the equation? For the answer, consider the next two sentences in the same passage of Scripture.

> "His disciples began questioning Him as to what this parable meant. And He said, "To you it has been granted to know the mysteries of the kingdom of God, but to the rest it is in parables, **so that** seeing they may not see, and hearing they may not understand" (Luke 8:9-10).

Does the Scripture mean Jesus was using parables to conceal His message from the crowds? Yes. *Why would He do that?* Jesus only wanted His disciples to understand His message. *Who were His disciples?* Those who took the time to question Him, asking Him what the parables meant. *What about everyone else?* Jesus did not worry about crowds of admirers, only disciples.

Chapter 02: *The Mission to Advance Christ's Kingdom on Earth*

The time of Jesus' earthly ministry was only 3-1/2 years. He had much to do in little time, and He knew that. He did not care about drawing large crowds or measuring the success of His movement on the number of "registered congregants." Jesus dedicated His attention to His disciples, and *only* His disciples.

Jesus had compassion for the multitudes; He fed them, healed them, and He preached to them. Those who listened to His message received His compassion. However, God sent His only begotten Son as part of the redemptive plan for all of humanity, and only those who **followed** – the disciples – got His attention.

Those who heard the Word, believed it, but were shallow in their faith – they liked the message, but would not fully commit – did not get His attention. Scripture makes that perfectly clear. Those who heard the Word, believed it, but were more concerned with wealth and possessions – they liked the message, but would not fully commit – did not get His attention. Scripture makes that perfectly clear.

A combination of modern culture, false teaching and biblical illiteracy have combined to portray Jesus' earthly ministry as a "come one, come all" event. Scripture makes it clear Jesus was not going to waste any time fertilizing rocky soil and thorns. Many Christians at this point may ask, "*If Jesus was not concerned about crowds, were did His thousands of disciples come from?*" That is a great question; Scripture reveals the answer:

> *And in those days Peter stood up in the midst of the disciples (altogether the number of names was about a hundred and twenty);*
>
> ~ Acts 1:15 ~

After 3-1/2 years, Jesus had about 120 disciples at the time of His Ascension: 11 primary, and the rest in supporting roles. That is all He needed to launch His divine mission.

> *Enter by the narrow gate; for wide is the gate and broad is the way that leads to destruction, and there are many who go in by it. Because narrow is the gate and difficult is the way which leads to life, and there are few who find it.*
>
> ~ Matthew 7:14 ~

Chapter 02: *The Mission to Advance Christ's Kingdom on Earth*

The Cost of Christian Discipleship

In modern Christianity, the phrase "carry your own cross" has come to mean shouldering a heavy burden in life. It is used when people are dealing with guilt or adverse circumstances. With a mournful look they exclaim, *"Woe is me. That is the cross that I must bear."* When Jesus said, *"take up your cross and follow Me,"* that is not what he meant. Over the course of nearly 2,000 years, the meaning of Jesus' teaching has changed drastically.

In Jesus' time, to "carry your own cross" meant only one thing: *death*. The practice of crucifixion was brutal, painful and humiliating. Criminals had to carry a heavy crossbeam to the site of their own death, humiliated and mocked by crowds along the way. Once crucified, the death was painful and slow. It was such a disgrace to die in this manner, crucifixions were not allowed to be conducted within the gates of a city.

The Jewish people had a similar custom, although it did not involve an actual crucifixion. The bodies of disgraced and reviled criminals would be hung on a tree after death to give citizens the chance to curse and mock them. In Jewish culture, God cursed anyone hung from a tree after death.

> *His body shall not remain overnight on the tree, but you shall surely bury him that day, so that you do not defile the land which the Lord your God is giving you as an inheritance; for he who is hanged is accursed of God.*
>
> ~ Deuteronomy 21:23 ~

In modern society, wearing a cross is a sign of reverence, piety, and respect; it is easy to forget the brutality associated with that image. However, in Jesus' day, wearing a cross would be equivalent to wearing a guillotine necklace during the French Revolution.

During His earthly ministry, Jesus did not mince words or withhold the truth when He preached his message. He told the

Chapter 02: *The Mission to Advance Christ's Kingdom on Earth*

multitudes, in advance, the cost of becoming His disciple. There were no surprises and nothing left unexplained. Jesus did not want uniformed disciples that would quit under pressure.

> *"Then Jesus said to His disciples, "If anyone wishes to come after Me, he **must** deny himself, and take up his cross and follow Me. For whoever wishes to save his life will lose it; but whoever loses his life for My sake will find it"* (Matthew 16:24-25).

The word "life" (**ψυχή** / sooh-CHAY) also means "soul" in Greek, the original language of the New Testament. The meaning of Jesus' teaching is clear: *if you are My disciple, be willing to die to save your soul*. That is not the typical evangelical message one hears in church on Sunday.

Jesus wanted His disciples to know their future in the world was uncertain; following Him meant they would face risk and possible death. In a world that rejected them, there would be no place they could call "home," except Heaven.

> *Now it happened as they journeyed on the road, that someone said to Him, "Lord, I will follow You wherever You go." And Jesus said to him, "Foxes have holes and birds of the air have nests, but the Son of Man has nowhere to lay His head."*
>
> ~ Luke 9:57-58 ~

Jesus wanted His disciples to know they would be rejecting everything in the world to follow Him: possessions, wealth, and even family members.

> *Then He said to another, "Follow Me." But he said, "Lord, let me first go and bury my father." Jesus said to him, "Let the dead bury their own dead, but you go and preach the kingdom of God."*
>
> ~ Luke 9:59-60 ~

Jesus wanted His disciples to know there was no turning back once they joined Him; those who turned away would not inherit the kingdom of God. In clear language, disciples that did not follow and obey Him would not go to Heaven.

Chapter 02: *The Mission to Advance Christ's Kingdom on Earth*

> *And another also said, "Lord, I will follow You, but let me first go and bid them farewell who are at my house." But Jesus said to him, "No one, having put his hand to the plow, and looking back, is fit for the kingdom of God."*
>
> *~ Luke 9:61-62 ~*

None of the individuals in the three cases above were willing to accept the cost of following Jesus. While that pained Him, He accepted that. He did not want lukewarm disciples. Every time Jesus taught, He instructed those wishing to become His disciple to carefully count the cost.

> *"For which of you, intending to build a tower, does not sit down first and count the cost, whether he has enough to finish it - lest, after he has laid the foundation, and is not able to finish, all who see it begin to mock him, saying, 'This man began to build and was not able to finish'?*
>
> *Or what king, going to make war against another king, does not sit down first and consider whether he is able with ten thousand to meet him who comes against him with twenty thousand? Or else, while the other is still a great way off, he sends a delegation and asks conditions of peace.*
>
> *So likewise, whoever of you does not forsake all that he has* ***cannot*** *be My disciple"* (Luke 14:28-33).

Jesus warned those wishing to join Him to consider the cost carefully. Staring an important task, only to quit halfway through, would be futile. He also warned listeners they would be fighting a war: accept the risk and go to Heaven, or make peace with the world and enjoy life's fleeting benefits.

However, Jesus also taught the cost of discipleship with Him – the price His disciples must pay – earns a reward much greater than any other the world can offer: Heaven, as a co-heir of Christ, and an eternity with God the Father.

> *Again, the kingdom of heaven is like treasure hidden in a field, which a man found and hid; and for joy over it he goes and sells all that he has and buys that field.*
>
> *~ Matthew 13:44 ~*

Chapter 02: *The Mission to Advance Christ's Kingdom on Earth*

How Jesus Perceived the Value of His Disciples

Jesus preached a difficult message to the multitudes, and taught lessons to His disciples that sounded severe at times. Scripture reveals three primary reasons that explain the motivation for His requirements.

First, Jesus knew their value in the world would be immeasurable. They would become the spiritual leaders responsible for guiding a lost world to God. Second, Jesus knew the expectations for His disciples would be very high; the level of standards He set for disciples needed a foundation that could support them. Third, the reward for the disciples who followed Him – and the penalty for those who did not – would be so great, they needed to understand the importance (and eternal consequences) of their decisions.

> *You are the light of the world. A city that is set on a hill cannot be hidden. Nor do they light a lamp and put it under a basket, but on a lampstand, and it gives light to all who are in the house. Let your light so shine before men, that they may see your good works and glorify your Father in heaven.*
>
> ~ Matthew 5:14-16 ~

Consider the power of Jesus' words when He told His disciples they would be "*the light of the world;*" it meant they would be the source of righteousness for a world that was utterly dark. Jesus placed extraordinary value on those who followed Him and obeyed His teaching. The value of true discipleship – and the importance Christ assigns to those choosing to follow Him per the example of the original disciples – has not lessened over time.

Jesus knew the importance of the disciples' mission would require a foundation of enormous strength, that could only be created through extraordinary faith in Him. The reason for this foundation is twofold. The first reason – and the most obvious at the time – was the building of the early Church. Jesus knew the disciples would be persecuted, hated by non-believers for their

Chapter 02: *The Mission to Advance Christ's Kingdom on Earth*

faith in Him, and targeted by an adversary (Satan) seeking to destroy the early Church.

> *I also say to you that you are Peter, and upon this rock I will build My church; and the gates of Hades will not overpower it. I will give you the keys of the kingdom of heaven; and whatever you bind on earth shall have been bound in heaven, and whatever you loose on earth shall have been loosed in heaven.*
>
> ~ Matthew 16:18-19 ~

Jesus also knew in latter times – our modern society today – the Christian faith would face a severe threat from within its churches. Many believers do not realize when Paul wrote his second epistle to Timothy, warning him about the 18 behaviors which would signal an approach to the End Times, he was not referring to a world of non-believers. Paul was describing the behaviors of Christians in modern churches. Jesus knew it would take a revival of true discipleship – with the same standards and requirements He imposed 2,000 years ago – to have a foundation strong enough to combat this level of threat.

> *"But realize this, that in the last days difficult times will come. For men will be lovers of self, lovers of money, boastful, arrogant, revilers, disobedient to parents, ungrateful, unholy, unloving, irreconcilable, malicious gossips, without self-control, brutal, haters of good, treacherous, reckless, conceited, lovers of pleasure rather than lovers of God, holding to a **form of godliness**, although they have **denied its power**"* (2 Timothy 3:1-5).

Jesus knew a diluted message of faith and an increase in biblical illiteracy would create the necessary conditions for the apostate church. Jesus also knew He'd call for a revival in biblical discipleship, with the same rewards for those who follow Him.

> *And He said to them, "Truly I say to you, there is no one who has left house or wife or brothers or parents or children, for the sake of the kingdom of God, who will not receive many times as much at this time **and** in the age to come, eternal life."*
>
> ~ Luke 18:29-30 ~

Chapter 02: *The Mission to Advance Christ's Kingdom on Earth*

How Jesus Perceived the Value of Non-Disciples

During Jesus' earthly ministry, He discussed two categories of people that followed Him: disciples, and everyone else (non-disciples). Non-disciples included those who opposed Him, rejected Him, or *would not commit to Him fully*.

As you read the Bible – especially Paul's letters to various churches – do not forget he is writing these words to, and for, Christians. When he wrote to Timothy and warned him about difficult times in the last days (2 Timothy 3:1-5), many believers view the world around them and at once agree with the text, not realizing Paul is describing members of the church itself. If you profess faith in Christ, Paul wrote his letters *to* you and *for* you – not those who are outside the faith. Just as Jesus discussed different categories of people, Paul makes a clear distinction between Christians and non-believers.

> *Conduct yourselves with wisdom toward outsiders, making the most of the opportunity. Let your speech always be with grace, as though seasoned with salt, so that you will know how you should respond to each person.*
>
> ~ Colossians 4:5-6 ~

The fate of non-believers is not an issue; Scripture makes it clear those who reject Christ as Lord and Savior are judged and condemned to eternal death (Hell). At issue are the varying levels of conviction, held by many individual Christians, who are told the "fully committed" requirement no longer applies. As the diluted Christian faith moves away from the plain language of the Bible, believers are not aware problems even exist. Consider what Christ told the church in Laodicea in the *Book of Revelation*:

> *I know your works, that you are neither cold nor hot. I could wish you were cold or hot. So then, because you are lukewarm, and neither cold nor hot, I will vomit you out of My mouth.*
>
> ~ Revelation 3:15-16 ~

Chapter 02: *The Mission to Advance Christ's Kingdom on Earth*

Christ tells the Church of Laodicea they are "lukewarm," and warns them of the consequences if they do not repent and fully commit to their faith again: He will *vomit them out of His mouth*. The word "vomit" in Greek (ἐμέω / em-MAY-oh) means "to reject with utter disgust." The message Christ sent the church was clear: If you are not fully committed, you are **not** a mediocre Christian – *you are rejected by God and doomed to eternal death*.

Those that may have a problem with the concept of Christ rejecting "professing believers" need look no further than the Bible for confirmation. While God is infinitely merciful and willing to forgive a repentant heart, those who continue in intentional disobedience – despite their public professions of faith – risk the rejection of God.

"My people are destroyed for lack of knowledge. Because you have rejected knowledge, I also will reject you from being My priest. Since you have forgotten the law of your God, I also will forget your children" (Hosea 4:6).

Throughout the New Testament, Jesus and His apostles continually warn believers of this reality. The apostle John could not have made the message clearer:

"Whoever transgresses and does not abide in the doctrine of Christ does not have God. He who abides in the doctrine of Christ has both the Father and the Son" (2 John 1:9-11).

Jesus discussed this issue as well, in plain language, with a very clear message:

*"Not everyone who says to Me, 'Lord, Lord,' shall enter the kingdom of heaven, but he who **does the will** of My Father in heaven. Many will say to Me in that day, 'Lord, Lord, have we not prophesied in Your name, cast out demons in Your name, and done many wonders in Your name?' And then I will declare to them, 'I never knew you; depart from Me, you who practice lawlessness!"* (Matthew 7:21-23).

An unshakable Christian faith is 100% committed, takes God seriously, and obeys His doctrine. This type of faith is the hallmark of a true disciple and follower of Christ.

Chapter 02: *The Mission to Advance Christ's Kingdom on Earth*

Jesus' Expectations for His Disciples

Jesus' expectations for His disciples were very high, which makes perfect sense given the stakes: eternal souls. His message was tough, His demands were radical, and the disciples faced extreme risk. Jesus accepted that in His obedience to God the Father, and expected the same from others who followed His example. Jesus never lowered His expectations to increase membership in His movement. Given the choice between Jesus' expectations, and the diluted faith we see today in modern churches, what type of disciple does God really want? Scripture reveals that to us:

> *"For My hand made all these things, thus all these things came into being," declares the Lord. "But to **this** one I will look, to **him** who is humble and contrite of spirit, and who trembles at My word"* (Isaiah 66:2).

Those who "tremble at God's Word" are those that hear it, do it, and fear the consequences if they do not. In modern times, many believers hear God's Word and do some of it begrudgingly, but very few live by it and tremble at the thought of disobeying God. This message was also difficult for some of His disciples:

> *"But there are some of you who do not believe. For Jesus knew from the beginning who they were who did not believe, and who it was that would betray Him. And He was saying, 'For this reason I have said to you, that no one can come to Me unless it has been granted him from the Father.' As a result of this many of His disciples withdrew and were not walking with Him anymore"* (John 6:64-66).

Despite the difficulties, Jesus' promise of Salvation made up for the hardship. The human lifespan is approximately 80 years; the average time a person spends dead after that is eternity. Trading present gain for future benefit is something we do often. We suffer today – long hours at work, school, etc. – for the hope of increased benefit tomorrow. If we do that for the world, how much more so for Christ and eternal Salvation?

Chapter 02: *The Mission to Advance Christ's Kingdom on Earth*

Jesus Expected His Disciples to Practice LOVE

If a believer was standing before the Almighty in Heaven, which of these attributes do you believe God would want you to have most: *faith*, *hope* or *love*?

The answer is *love*. You do not need hope; you are in Heaven. You do not need faith; God is real, and in front of you. However, you would still need love, the spiritual glue that binds us to a holy God. God takes love seriously, and He is passionate when it comes to protecting His children. Jesus knew this, and He trained His disciples according to God's Will.

We see this theme throughout the Bible. God tells Abram (later called *Abraham*), "*I will bless those who bless you, and I will curse him who curses you*" (Genesis 12:3). We see God's protective nature in Psalms: "*Do not touch My anointed ones, and do My prophets no harm*" (Psalm 105:15). This is important for Christians to know for several reasons.

Christians tend to view God as "somewhere out there," while view other believers as "here and now." Within the context of eternal life, that is a dangerous mistake to make. When you are a true disciple of Christ, you are one with Jesus and God the Father; dead to sin, the new creation, and indwelt by the Holy Spirit. The apostle Paul explains this clearly:

> *I have been crucified with Christ; it is no longer I*
> *who live, but Christ lives in me; and the life which*
> *I now live in the flesh I live by faith in the Son*
> *of God, who loved me and gave Himself for me.*
>
> ~ Galatians 2:20 ~

Jesus taught His disciples to love one another during His earthly ministry, and it was not to get them motivated about group hugs. Christ lives within every believer. Whatever you do to a fellow believer you also do to Christ and, as such, you do to God the father as well: "*Whoever receives one of these little children in My name receives Me; and whoever receives Me, receives not Me*

Chapter 02: *The Mission to Advance Christ's Kingdom on Earth*

but Him who sent Me" (Mark 9:37). The disciple John affirms this, *"Most assuredly, I say to you, he who receives whomever I send receives Me; and he who receives Me receives Him who sent Me"* (John 13:20), and the disciple Matthew reaffirms it: *"Assuredly, I say to you, inasmuch as you did it to one of the least of these My brethren, you did it to Me"* (Matthew 25:40).

When Saul of Tarsus was persecuting the new sect of Christ-followers – dragging them out of homes, throwing them in prison, and approving their deaths – he experienced the Lord on the road to Damascus. What did Christ ask him?

> *'Saul, Saul, why are you persecuting Me?' And he said, 'Who are You, Lord?' Then the Lord said, 'I am Jesus, **whom you are persecuting**.'*
>
> ~ Acts 9:4-5 ~

Christ viewed Saul's persecution of Christians as the persecution of Him. He still does, and it does not only apply only to persecution. Jesus teaches us it applies to sin as well: *"Whoever causes one of these little ones who believe to stumble, it would be better for him if, with a heavy millstone hung around his neck, he had been cast into the sea"* (Mark 9:42).

The word "stumble" (σκανδαλίζω / skan-dah-LEE-zoh) means "cause to sin" in the original Greek language. Causing a believer in the Body of Christ to sin is serious, and happens in four different ways:

1. **Direct Invitation**: Intentionally bringing a believer into sin in direct violation of God's Word.

2. **Indirect Temptation**: Intentionally sinning in front of a believer and causing them to stumble.

3. **Bad Example**: Blatantly sinning in sight of everyone, causing a believer to think "it is OK."

4. **Tacit Approval**: Having knowledge a believer is sinning and doing nothing to discourage it.

Causing a believer to sin – regardless of the way it is done – is equally offensive in the sight of God.

Chapter 02: *The Mission to Advance Christ's Kingdom on Earth*

Jesus taught His disciples clearly and outlined the penalty for participation.

> *"If your hand causes you to stumble, cut it off; it is better for you to enter life crippled, than, having your two hands, to go into hell, into the unquenchable fire. If your foot causes you to stumble, cut it off; it is better for you to enter life lame, than, having your two feet, to be cast into hell; If your eye causes you to stumble, throw it out; it is better for you to enter the kingdom of God with one eye, than, having two eyes, to be cast into hell"* (Mark 9:43,45,47).

Jesus was not suggesting self-mutilation was the answer to the problem; He said clearly to the Pharisees it was not the appearance that mattered, but what stemmed from the heart that was important (Matthew 23:27-28). A believer could have no arms or legs, be blind, and still be a sinner in the sight of God.

The message of His teaching was a mindset of pure righteousness before God, regardless of what a believer thought (eyes), did (hands), or went (feet). Jesus' message was it is better for the physical body to be dead than leading a brother or sister in Christ to sin. True love (*agape*) uplifts and encourages; it never leads to sin and the downfall of others.

You read in the previous chapter repetition of a theme was a rhetorical device that emphasized importance and urgency of a thought. The word "Hell" (**γέεννα** / GEH-eh-nah) means "Lake of Fire" in the original Greek language, and it is used three times in this one paragraph of Scripture. It clearly defines the penalty for leading another Christian to act in a contrary fashion to God's Will.

Once again, the message Christ sent the church was clear. If you cause another brother or sister in the Body of Christ to sin, you are **not** going to be a mediocre Christian – *you are rejected by God, and the penalty is Hell, the "Lake of Fire."*

Although this may sound severe by modern Christian standards, it spoke to a deeper issue than merely sin. Jesus knew this type of behavior was the fruit of an unrighteous heart and showed the lack of love (*agape*) needed to fully commit to Him.

Chapter 02: *The Mission to Advance Christ's Kingdom on Earth*

Jesus Expected His Disciples to Practice PURITY

During His earthly ministry, Jesus made the concepts of righteousness and purity a priority for His disciples. While He knew that Man's fallen nature predisposed him to sin - *"for all have sinned and fall short of the glory of God"* (Romans 3:23) – Jesus also knew escaping the punishment of eternal Hell was so important, radical purity was necessary. If professing faith in our Savior who died for our sins is all it takes to guarantee our "ticket to Heaven," why would Jesus spend so much time teaching His disciples about purity and righteousness? Scripture reveals a saving faith, with a level of conviction that seeks pure righteousness, was the key to inheriting the Kingdom of Heaven.

> *The Lord is not slack concerning His promise, as some count slackness, but is longsuffering toward us, not willing that any should perish but that all should come to repentance.*
>
> ~ 2 Peter 3:9 ~

After Satan tempted Jesus in the wilderness, He began His ministry with one mission in mind: *repentance*. *"From that time Jesus began to preach and say, "Repent, for the kingdom of heaven is at hand"* (Matthew 4:17). Many believers do not know the role repentance plays in their faith, nor its importance in true discipleship.

The act of repentance has a primary action, followed by a secondary action. In the original language of the New Testament, the word "Repentance" (μετάνοια / (meh-TAH-noy-ah) means "a change of mind, a change in the inner man." In plain language, it means "turning to God." The secondary action is "turning away from evil," a naturally-occurring byproduct of turning to God.

What does it mean to "turn to God"? It means to seek God, worship Him, obey Him, and live in the way He commanded to give Him glory through our faith, words, and deeds. The apostle Luke summed it up nicely in the *Book of Acts*:

Chapter 02: *The Mission to Advance Christ's Kingdom on Earth*

> *To open their eyes so that they may turn from darkness to light and from the dominion of Satan to God, that they may receive forgiveness of sins and an inheritance among those who have been sanctified by faith in Me.*
>
> ~ Acts 26:18 ~

What it does **not** mean is "never sin;" the fallen nature of Man dictates sin is inevitable. Even if believers could avoid every sin from this day forward, it would not erase the sins of our past. Only Christ's sacrifice on the Cross can do that – the necessity of Jesus is always present in our lives. When we sin (and we will), Scripture commands us to acknowledge the sin and confess it before God: *"If we confess our sins, He is faithful and righteous to forgive us our sins and to cleanse us from all unrighteousness"* (1 John 1:9). Then we repent – turn to God – and seek His strength and wisdom to prevent sin in the future. This is an ongoing process called *Sanctification* that does not end until we stand before God's Throne of Judgment.

However, we must never assume freedom to sin exists, resulting from God's gift of Salvation. Scripture clearly reveals Jesus never taught His disciples to believe that myth:

> *"If we say that we have fellowship with Him and yet walk in the darkness, we lie and do not practice the truth; but if we walk in the Light as He Himself is in the Light, we have fellowship with one another, and the blood of Jesus His Son cleanses us from all sin"* (1 John 1:6-7).

This presents an interesting question for true disciples of Christ. If knowing God's Word and rejecting it is apostasy, what is knowing God's Word, accepting it, while **not** rejecting evil? Is it possible for the two to exist concurrently? Jesus teaches His disciples the answer to that question is "NO."

> *"Grapes are not gathered from thorn bushes nor figs from thistles, are they? So every good tree bears good fruit, but the bad tree bears bad fruit. A good tree cannot produce bad fruit, nor can a bad tree produce good fruit. Every tree that does not bear good fruit is cut down and thrown into the fire. So then, you will know them by their fruits"* (Matthew 7:16-20).

Chapter 02: *The Mission to Advance Christ's Kingdom on Earth*

Jesus taught through His demonstration of leadership; His disciples learned the lesson of righteousness through His example and words. In teaching His disciples about divine love (agape), Jesus also taught that love can only come from the incorruptible righteousness of God.

> *"Since you have purified your souls in obeying the truth through the Spirit in sincere love of the brethren, love one another fervently with a pure heart, having been born again, not of corruptible seed but incorruptible, through the word of God which lives and abides forever"* (1 Peter 1:22-23).

Jesus also taught His disciples only a repentant heart – turned to God's Word and Will – would ever seek righteousness. Although outward actions considered to be "good" might fool people, they would never fool God on the Day of Judgment.

> *"The heart is deceitful above all things, and desperately wicked; Who can know it? I, the Lord, search the heart, I test the mind, even to give every man according to his ways, according to the fruit of his doings"* (Jeremiah 17:9-10).

Jesus did not want His disciples falling into the trap of meeting the outward expectations of righteousness – as the Pharisees and Sadducees did – without having a repentant heart that embraced God's Word and Will. Jesus knew that given a choice between the three levels of conviction – public, personal, and fundamental – only a fundamental conviction that led to a real change of the inner-Man would lead to Salvation. Anything less would fail to reject Evil entirely and, in so doing, would prevent them from truly turning to God (repentance).

> *"For if we sin willfully after we have received the knowledge of the truth, there no longer remains a sacrifice for sins, but a certain fearful expectation of judgment, and fiery indignation which will devour the adversaries. For we know Him who said, "Vengeance is Mine, I will repay," says the Lord. And again, "The Lord will judge His people." It is a fearful thing to fall into the hands of the living God"* (Hebrews 10:26-27, 30-31).

The fate of souls hung in the balance between Heaven and Hell; Jesus did not risk teaching a diluted message to His disciples.

Chapter 02: *The Mission to Advance Christ's Kingdom on Earth*

Jesus Expected His Disciples to Practice SACRIFICE

The concept of sacrifice is not foreign to most Christians; God gave His only begotten Son as a sacrifice for our sins. Scripture teaches the virtue of personal sacrifice as a reoccurring theme: *"And do not neglect doing good and sharing, for with such sacrifices God is pleased"* (Hebrews 13:16). However, when Jesus taught His disciples about sacrifice, He was giving it a much deeper meaning. When Jesus told His disciples, *"For everyone will be salted with fire"* (Mark 9:49), He meant His disciples must be ready to sacrifice their lives for Him, both figuratively *and* literally.

Many believers know Jesus referred to His disciples as *"the salt of the earth"* frequently throughout Scripture, and "fire" is typically associated with death and periods of trial. However, where do salt and fire come together in the Bible, and how does it apply to His disciples?

There are five types of sacrifices listed in the Bible: Burnt, Grain, Peace, Sin and Guilt. The grain sacrifice was a devotion to God, practiced to proclaim His glory. Except for one notable Gentile (Luke), all of Jesus' disciples – and authors of the Old and New Testaments – were Jewish. They were well-versed in Jewish tradition, Scripture and Law. Jesus, of course, knew this as well.

> *"Every grain offering of yours, moreover, you shall season with salt, so that the salt of the covenant of your God shall not be lacking from your grain offering; with all your offerings you shall offer salt"* (Leviticus 2:13).

Salt represents God's Covenant with His people, and the use of salt during sacrifices honored the continuance of it.

> *"When you have finished cleansing it, you shall present a young bull without blemish and a ram without blemish from the flock. You shall present them before the Lord, and the priests shall throw salt on them, and they shall offer them up as a burnt offering to the Lord"* (Ezekiel 23-24).

Chapter 02: *The Mission to Advance Christ's Kingdom on Earth*

When Ezra was leading thousands of exiles out of their captivity in Persia (formerly Babylon) to rebuild Jerusalem, the king made special provisions to include items needed for the sacrifices. To the Jewish people of the era, this was a critical and non-negotiable practice. The act of performing sacrifices confirmed God's Covenant, and salting the sacrifice confirmed its permanence, while consecrating it at the same time.

> *"Whatever is needed, both young bulls, rams, and lambs for a burnt offering to the God of heaven, and wheat, salt, wine and anointing oil, as the priests in Jerusalem request, it is to be given to them daily without fail, that they may offer acceptable sacrifices to the God of heaven and pray for the life of the king and his sons"* (Ezra 6:9-10).

In the language of sacrifice – requirements, importance, and outcomes – Jesus was teaching His disciples that following Him required a very real sacrifice. It was a sacrifice of devotion, consecrating a "new covenant" between Jesus and His disciples. Adding salt to the fire gave it a permanent status; His disciples were giving themselves over to Christ totally, as a consecrated offering before God the Father. The disciples knew their sacrifice in Jesus' name would extend well beyond the symbolism of Jewish culture:

> *My brethren, take the prophets, who spoke in the name of the Lord, as an example of suffering and patience. Indeed we count them blessed who endure.*
>
> *~ James 5:10-11 ~*

When we use the term "discipleship" in modern Christian culture, we must realize the importance that Jesus assigned to the word. He taught His disciples it required total commitment, surrender and sacrifice. If they had the faith and heart to persevere suffering, their reward would be the Kingdom of Heaven. That standard – God's Promise – has never changed.

> *"He who overcomes will inherit these things, and I will be his God and he will be My son. But for the cowardly and unbelieving and abominable and murderers and immoral persons and sorcerers and idolaters and all liars, their part will be in the lake that burns with fire and brimstone, which is the second death"* (Revelation 21:7-9).

Chapter 02: *The Mission to Advance Christ's Kingdom on Earth*

Jesus Expected His Disciples to Practice OBEDIENCE

Jesus expected His disciples to be the spiritual leaders of the word, the "salt and light" responsible for guiding a generation of lost souls to God and Heaven. As true followers of Christ, the disciples were entrusted with this task by virtue of their *love*, *purity*, *sacrifice* and *obedience*. When contemporary believers read the Bible and discover how Jesus defined obedience – and how He perceived those who were not – they are often surprised. Many Christians are not hearing messages that resemble Jesus' teachings.

The teaching His disciples considered fundamental, we view as fanatical. The values Jesus held to be intrinsic, we view as intensive. The core beliefs Jesus taught to His disciples as essential, modern Christianity considers to be extreme. Yet, Jesus taught and exemplified these lessons as an absolute requirement of true discipleship. Modern Christianity needs true disciples of Christ. However, it is not enough for modern disciples to hear the words; they need to understand the message behind them as well.

For example, most believers are aware Jesus told His disciples, "*You are the salt of the earth*" (Matthew 5:13), and know that salt is good. Most believers are also aware "salt that loses its flavor" is bad. Do they also know how bad it is, and why? Many Christians believe "tasteless salt" refers to those who are lukewarm in their faith. That is not what Jesus meant; He had something much worse in mind when He taught His disciples.

> *Therefore, salt is good; but if even salt has become tasteless, with what will it be seasoned? It is useless either for the soil or for the manure pile; it is thrown out. He who has ears to hear, let him hear.*
>
> ~ Luke 14:34-35 ~

We are told tasteless salt is so bad, people will not mix it with dirt or manure. Is that true, or is it a metaphor for another meaning? If that is true, how bad must something be to hear, "*Take that horrible stuff off my good manure NOW! Do not think about putting it on my valuable dirt, either!" It would have to be very bad and, as it turns out, it is not a metaphor. It is true.

Pure salt – sodium chloride – was very valuable in the first century as a seasoning and food preservative. However, there were varying grades of salt, and unscrupulous merchants would occasionally mix pure salt with gypsum to increase the volume. When gypsum combines with water it becomes plaster, the same substance the Roman Empire used to create sculptures. Manure and dirt have value – fertilizer and farming, respectively – but when corrupted with plaster they both become useless.

When Jesus taught His disciples to *be salt*, He meant pure salt (unmixed), with a high value. Salt that had been corrupted, or mixed, became useless. It also corrupted and destroyed other things with value: *"Draw near to God and He will draw near to you. Cleanse your hands, you sinners; and purify your hearts, you double-minded"* (James 4:8). Minds, faith, and obedience all become corrupted when "mixed" with impurities.

Jesus did not just teach His disciples about obedience and service, He set the standard in leading by example. *"If anyone serves Me, he must follow Me; and where I am, there My servant will be also; if anyone serves Me, the Father will honor him"* (John 12:26). In the original language of the New Testament, the word "serve" (**διάκονος** / Dee-AH-kah-nos) means "to serve," "to minister," or "to kick up dust" (run errands). Those that wanted to listen but not perform – the multitudes and crowds – never made it to the level of discipleship. Scripture reveals that hearing Jesus' message, but not obeying it, does not end well.

> *"Why do you call Me, 'Lord, Lord,' and do not do what I say? Everyone who comes to Me and hears My words and acts on them, I will show you whom he is like: he is like a man building a house, who dug deep and laid a foundation on the rock; and when a flood occurred, the torrent burst against that house and could not shake it, because it had been well built. But the one who has heard and has not acted accordingly, is like a man who built a house on the ground without any foundation; and the torrent burst against it and immediately it collapsed, and the ruin of that house was great"* (Luke 6:46-49).

A true disciple *always* obeys God's Word *and* His Will.

Chapter 02: *The Mission to Advance Christ's Kingdom on Earth*

Jesus Always Protects His Disciples from Hell

Jesus gave all who heard His voice a clear understanding of the risks, costs, and rewards of following Him. During His earthly ministry, Jesus fulfilled the mission given by God the Father: *"For God so loved the world, that He gave His only begotten Son, that whoever believes in Him shall not perish, but have eternal life"* (John 3:16). Many modern churches focus on Eternal Life without ever discussing the penalty for rejecting Christ. Many Christians joyfully discuss the Good News of the Gospel, without ever warning others of the bad news for making the wrong choice. Although the topic may be difficult to discuss, disciples of Christ *must* be willing to bring the truth to a world of non-believers.

> *If anyone does not abide in Me, he is thrown away as a branch and dries up; and they gather them, and cast them into the fire and they are burned.*
>
> ~ John 15:6 ~

From the *Gospel of Matthew* (5:22) to *Revelation* (20:14), Scripture reveals Hell as a physical place with real consequences. In the King James Bible (KJV), the word "hell" appears 31 times in the Old Testament, and 23 times in the New Testament. When Jesus taught about Hell – *a burning lake of unquenchable fire* – what were the images in His disciples' minds? The Old Testament gives a horrifying description of the image of Hell. In fact, Hell is much worse than the description.

In the original language of the New Testament, the word "Hell" (**γἐεννα** / GEH-eh-nah) means "lake of fire." The visual imagery originates from the Old Testament, in a valley found south and west of Jerusalem: The Valley of Ben-Hinnom.

> *"Then the border went up the valley of Ben-Hinnom to the slope of the Jebusite on the south (that is, Jerusalem); and the border went up to the top of the mountain which is before the valley of Hinnom to the west, which is at the end of the valley of Rephaim toward the north"* (Joshua 5:8).

Chapter 02: *The Mission to Advance Christ's Kingdom on Earth*

King Ahaz, a leader of the Jewish people, turned his back on God the Father, and worshiped the evil god, Molech. His occult practices included idol worship and sacrificing human children.

> *"Moreover, he burned incense in the valley of Ben-Hinnom and burned his sons in fire, according to the abominations of the nations whom the Lord had driven out before the sons of Israel"* (2 Chronicles 28:3).

King Ahaz died, and was eventually replaced by King Manasseh, whose evil rivaled that of Ahaz. His practices were equally horrific; the phrase "pass through fire" is a delicate way of saying "burning children alive."

> *"He made his sons pass through the fire in the valley of Ben-Hinnom; and he practiced witchcraft, used divination, practiced sorcery and dealt with mediums and spiritists. He did much evil in the sight of the Lord, provoking Him to anger"* (2 Chronicles 33:6).

King Manasseh's practices were so evil before God, the Lord told Jeremiah He was changing the name of the valley from Ben-Hinnom to the *Valley of Slaughter*.

> *"Therefore, behold, days are coming,"* declares the Lord, *"when this place will no longer be called Topheth or the valley of Ben-Hinnom, but rather the Valley of Slaughter"* (Jeremiah 19:6).

In the middle of this succession of evil leaders, one righteous man before God took charge: King Josiah. By the time Josiah began his rule of the Jewish people, the *Valley of Slaughter* became known as the *Valley of the Drum*. History records a time when so many infants and children were being sacrificed to the evil god Molech, drums were beaten 24-hours a day, 7-days a week, to drown out the sound of their screams.

The righteous King Josiah brought an end to this practice and restored religious order for the Jewish people.

> *"He also defiled Topheth, which is in the valley of the son of Hinnom, that no man might make his son or his daughter pass through the fire for Molech"* (2 Kings 23:10).

Chapter 02: *The Mission to Advance Christ's Kingdom on Earth*

King Josiah converted this deep valley into a refuse and sewage dump for human waste, spoiled food and dead bodies. The rotting flesh and food could not be buried; they had to be burned. The decomposing flesh produced methane gas that burned 24-hours a day, 7-days a week. The *Valley of Slaughter* became, quite literally, *a burning lake of unquenchable fire*.

Imagine the combined, documented history of these three kings, and the images it evoked in the minds of Jewish disciples that lived in the region and knew Jerusalem's history:

1. Worship of the evil deity, Molech
2. Witchcraft and sorcery
3. Divination and evil spirits
4. Human sacrifice
5. Babies and children burned alive, 24/7
6. Screaming and agony, 24/7
7. The smell of rotting flesh, 24/7
8. Thick, black clouds of putrid smoke, 24/7
9. Methane gas fires with flames hundreds of feet high, 24/7
10. An angry God punishing the Jewish people for turning their backs on Him, 24/7

That is a real scene from documented history; temporary and happening in the world. Most Christians would not want to live near that type of place.

Now imagine the same scene, albeit indescribably worse. This time, you are not living *near* it; you are living *in* it. This time, it is not *temporal* (your body), it is *spiritual* (your soul). This time, it is not *temporary* (a few hundred years), it is *eternal* (hundreds of billions of years ... and more).

However, this time there is one thing noticeably missing: *God*. There are no appeals, no petitions and no one to answer your prayers. The judgment is final and you are on your own.

This is the imagery Jesus and His disciples had in mind when they preached the kingdom of Heaven, and the message of Salvation. This is the reason Jesus died for our sins, and took our place in Judgment. This is the reason faithful disciples of Christ sleep well at night: *"For God so loved the world, that He gave His only begotten Son, that whoever believes in Him shall not perish, but have eternal life"* (John 3:16).

Chapter 02: *The Mission to Advance Christ's Kingdom on Earth*

7 Challenges of Modern Christian Discipleship

Whether you are an individual believer pursuing a deeper commitment to your faith, a pastor of a church, or a teacher in a Christian college, you probably sense Christianity is facing multiple challenges in our modern age. The most recent trend in addressing these problems is the creation of discipleship programs. Unfortunately, statistics show these programs have very little impact, if any at all. The good news is in many cases, deficiencies in these programs are internal, not external. Internal challenges – those within our control – are typically easier to fix.

Listed below are seven common challenges discipleship programs encounter at both the individual and corporate level. This list is not all-inclusive; it is meant to present those challenges most commonly experienced in modern Christianity.

1. **Lack of Absolute and Unshakable Faith**: Faith in God is the most fundamental principle of Christianity; a lack of faith is the most serious threat a believer will face. While most Christians stand firm on faith in their theology, many lack enough faith on a practical level to become disciples of Christ. Although these believers trust Jesus with their eternal souls, they will not trust Him enough to handle their daily lives. The source of this can be traced to a lack of biblical study, a shallow practice of their faith, and a misunderstanding of the promises of God. True faith is taking God at His Word, not treating Him like a "genie in a bottle," called upon when needed, with the hope He will respond to our every word. That is having faith in *faith*, not faith *God's Word*. Knowledge of His promises to us offers a level of strength that exceeds the "hope" seen today in many Christians, masquerading as faith in daily life.

   > *And without faith it is impossible to please God, because anyone who comes to him must believe that he exists and that he rewards those who earnestly seek him.*
   >
   > ~ Hebrews 11:6 ~

2. **Failure to Link Discipleship and Evangelism**: Jesus made disciples through His evangelism, and the successful early church did the same. Making disciples can only be done through sharing the Gospel, and only true disciples can share the Gospel in a way that makes disciples. Yet many believers in modern society see these as separate missions. When churches offer "discipleship programs" that do not include evangelism, they are not making true disciples of Christ. They are making educated students in a Bible study class, and the benefit of the knowledge tends to go no further than the students.

> *Tell of His glory among the nations, His wonderful deeds among all the peoples.*
>
> ~ Psalm 96:3 ~

3. **Lack of Willingness to Make Mistakes**: Human beings, regardless of their faith, do not mind making mistakes; they hate when they are punished and judged for making them. A person who's scared to make a mistake will never try anything new. The apostle Paul persecuted Christians and stood by approvingly when Stephen got martyred (Acts 7). The apostle Peter denied Jesus three times (Luke 22), and the apostles John and James were rebuked by Jesus for wanting to bring fire down onto a Samaritan village (Luke 9). Those all qualify as mistakes, and Jesus never held it against them. Based on Scripture, making mistakes was a hallmark of being a true disciple. Jesus may have rebuked and admonished them at times, but He always encouraged them to keep trying. The way Jesus taught is a lesson for churches and individuals alike.

> *We all stumble in many ways. Anyone who is never at fault in what they say is perfect, able to keep their whole body in check.*
>
> ~ James 3:2 ~

4. **Protectionism and Sectarianism**: Regardless of the movement within Protestant Christianity we belong, there is more that unites us within our faith than divides us. Scripture reveals Jesus wanted the Body of Christ to be united, but accepted separation when the goals of His

ministry were carried out. The apostle John took offense when he saw someone casting out demons in Jesus' name, and tried to stop him. Jesus' response to John was clear and to the point: *"But Jesus said to him, "Do not hinder him; for he who is not against you is for you"* (Luke 9:50). The apostle John had no problem with the actions of this believer; the issue was he was not part of their group. This type of divisiveness, especially with secondary issues (not core doctrine), undermine efforts in evangelism *and* discipleship.

> *I appeal to you, brothers and sisters, in the name of our Lord Jesus Christ, that all of you agree with one another in what you say and that there be no divisions among you, but that you be perfectly united in mind and thought.*
>
> ~ 1 Corinthians 1:10 ~

5. **Individualism vs. Relational Discipleship**: The core of true Christian discipleship is building relationships of trust, transparency, and example. This reality runs counter to Western culture's pursuit of individualism, liberty, and the right to privacy. Modern Christianity desires to make disciples, but the modern society adhering to the faith is not comfortable with "outsiders invading their private space." We are comfortable making disciples on our own terms, and in our own time – but woe betide those who would knock on the door of our home, at 3:00 am, in desperate need of help. Jesus often went to pray alone (Mark 1:35), but He was always available to disciples when they needed Him. Balancing the need for "private space" and selfless dedication is a critical need for true Christian discipleship.

> *They devoted themselves to the apostles' teaching and to fellowship, to the breaking of bread and to prayer.*
>
> ~ Acts 2:42 ~

6. **Focus on Being Disciples, not Making Disciples**: Jesus told us to "*make disciples of all the nations,*" not "*be disciples in all the nations.*" To be a disciple without making

disciples is to be a Bible study student. When a Christian proudly proclaims, "*I am a disciple of Christ,*" resist the urge to ask them, "*How many disciples have you made this year?*" Instead, ask them this: "*How many disciples have you made this year, that went on to make other disciples*? To lead a non-believer to faith is a great accomplishment; that is a precious soul saved from eternal death. However, to make a disciple means the person led to Christ went on to lead *others* to Christ, and never left their side in the process. True Christian discipleship is the act of multiplying, not adding, believers to the Body of Christ who are prepared, informed, and strong in their faith.

> *Do not merely listen to the word, and so deceive yourselves. Do what it says. Anyone who listens to the word but does not do what it says is like someone who looks at his face in a mirror and, after looking at himself, goes away and immediately forgets what he looks like.*
>
> ~ James 1:22-24 ~

7. **Blaming an Imperfect Church**: Individual believers and churches can come up with many reasons why discipleship programs will not work: there is never enough time, money, or training to make it happen. Despite all the reasons a thing *cannot* be done, a believer only needs one reason it *can* be done to make it a reality. Making disciples is a corporate responsibility within the Body of Christ, but it is an individual responsibility as well. We live in an age in which everything must be perfect for something to work: the perfect time, the perfect environment, the perfect speaker, or the perfect music for worship. That is an artificial limitation imposed on ourselves, by us. Such limits did not hinder Jesus and His disciples, and they are the example we are commanded to follow.

> *You, therefore, have no excuse, you who pass judgment on someone else, for at whatever point you judge another, you are condemning yourself, because you who pass judgment do the same things.*
>
> ~ Romans 2:1 ~

Chapter 02: *The Mission to Advance Christ's Kingdom on Earth*

7 Ways to Practice Faithful Christian Discipleship

The path of Christian discipleship is not an easy one; Jesus made that clear to the multitudes and His disciples. He did teach, however, that the reward of Eternal Life in the presence of God the Father made the cost worthwhile.

As you prepare to pursue your own path - as one who disciples, or one who is being discipled – there are steps you can take to overcome many common obstacles you will encounter during the journey. These seven practices apply to **all** Christian disciples, in any capacity they serve.

1. **Share the Gospel at every opportunity**: Sharing the Gospel of Christ is the hallmark of making disciples, being a disciple, and attracting potential disciples. It fulfills the command of Scripture, increase the faith of those sharing the message, and shows by example your willingness to be a leader in your faith.

   > *Preach the word; be ready in season and out of season; reprove, rebuke, exhort, with great patience and instruction.*
   >
   > ~ 2 Timothy 4:2 ~

2. **Practice radical obedience to Christ**: The Scripture is your instruction manual to a life centered around Christ; read it, use it, and follow it. A disciple is not a believer who shows up to church once a week and puts faith on like a sweater when it is needed. Radical obedience to Christ guides your actions from the time you wake up until the time you go to bed for the evening. It shows Gof you take Him as seriously as He takes Himself.

   > *Let your light shine before men in such a way that they may see your good works, and glorify your Father who is in heaven.*
   >
   > ~ Matthew 5:16 ~

Chapter 02: *The Mission to Advance Christ's Kingdom on Earth*

3. **Live like Christ in word and deed**: Jesus taught His disciples to follow Him meant to practice radical purity, love, sacrifice and obedience. That is not something a disciple can fake; it requires an inner change, a change of the heart. The indwelling of the Holy Spirit works in the believer as a progressive process of Sanctification, but actively imitating Christ – as did the apostle Paul – helps to guide and shape the transformation.

> *Imitate me, just as I also imitate Christ. Now I praise you, brethren, that you remember me in all things and keep the traditions just as I delivered them to you.*
>
> ~ 1 Corinthians 11:1-2 ~

4. **Practice spiritual disciplines daily**: Nothing in the human experience is accomplished without training and practice. The same holds true for spiritual disciplines. They help to develop the believers' new inner being, and support the transformation that accompanies Salvation in Christ. Each of these disciplines – such as Abstinence, Confession, Fasting, Fellowship, Prayer, Sacrifice, Service, Study, and Worship – are found in Scripture, and were practiced by Jesus and His disciples.

> *For the Spirit God gave us does not make us timid, but gives us power, love and self-discipline.*
>
> ~ 2 Timothy 1:7 ~

5. **Serve as the standard, model, and example**: Credible testimony happens when a believers words of faith match their deeds in the world. Excellent leaders and teachers like Jesus lead from the front; they set the standard, model the action, and serve as an example to those who follow. By the end of His earthly ministry, Jesus' disciples trusted that He was the Christ, and therefore believed in Him. That level of trust – the type of trust for which a person would give their life – does not come from words or doctrine. It comes from showing and doing. Rule #1: set the standard even when no one is watching. Rule #2: someone is always watching – see Rule #1.

Chapter 02: *The Mission to Advance Christ's Kingdom on Earth*

> *Remember your leaders, who spoke the word of God to you. Consider the outcome of their way of life and imitate their faith.*
>
> ~ Hebrews 13:7 ~

6. **Be a humble servant, prepared to serve**: Jesus made His mission clear to His disciples: *"For even the Son of Man did not come to be served, but to serve, and to give His life a ransom for many"* (Mark 10:45). In any field, the best leaders began as excellent followers; their leadership style reflects their commitment to serve. Jesus gave God the Father glory for everything, and kept no glory for Himself. A faithful disciple of Christ does the same.

> *Seek the Lord, all you humble of the land, you who do what he commands. Seek righteousness, seek humility; perhaps you will be sheltered on the day of the Lord's anger.*
>
> ~ Zephaniah 2:3 ~

7. **Practice full transparency and accountability**: During Jesus' earthly ministry, He had nothing to hide, nothing to hold back, from His disciples. A faithful disciple of Christ cannot be double-minded, engaged in sin in the darkness, while practicing faith in the light. That type of duality leads to fear, guilt and weakness. Every believer will sin; that is a certainty. Once those sins are confessed they are removed, the slate is wiped clean, and a clear conscious is left in its place. Habitual and intentional sin, however, cannot be hidden forever, nor should it be. Transparency and accountability builds the level of trust needed for others to believe in the Gospel of Christ, and to follow it as Jesus' disciples did: without questioning, waivering or quitting under pressure.

> *Everyone who does evil hates the light, and will not come into the light for fear that their deeds will be exposed. But whoever lives by the truth comes into the light, so that it may be seen plainly that what they have done has been done in the sight of God.*
>
> ~ John 3:20-21 ~

Chapter 02: *The Mission to Advance Christ's Kingdom on Earth*

7 Tips for Sharing the Gospel with Confidence

Christ's *Great Commission* – to make disciples of all the nations – was His command to all Christians to spread the Gospel. Jesus also gave us a plan to successfully execute His command.

This plan (Romans 10:13-15) has only one potential weak link: the believers' ability to make the message available to non-believers who need to hear it. *"How will they believe in Him whom they have not heard? And how will they hear without a preacher?"* (Romans 10:14).

If we do our part as the Body of Christ, He will do His part and bring the souls of non-believers to Salvation and Eternal Life. Listed below are seven tips to assist you in doing your part to share the Gospel.

1. **Do not be intimidated by other's testimony**: Some people have wild and exciting conversion stories, while others quietly came to faith in Christ. All testimony equally important in the eyes of God. The most important aspect of the experience is that it happened in the first place, and you gave God the glory for it. That is all that matters.

    > *I tell you that in the same way, there will be more joy in heaven over one sinner who repents than over ninety-nine righteous persons who need no repentance.*
    >
    > ~ Luke 15:7 ~

2. **Keep your testimony focused and relevant**: Every testimony has three parts: what you were, how you came to Christ, and what you are now because of your faith. There is no need for any embarrassing details or personal confessions of sin. Everyone has sinned; they "get it." There is no sliding scale for sin – it is all equally bad in the sight of God, and it all gets cleansed when a person makes their profession of faith in Christ.

> *For all of us have become like one who is unclean, and all our righteous deeds are like a filthy garment; And all of us wither like a leaf, and our iniquities, like the wind, take us away.*
>
> ~ Isaiah 64:6 ~

3. **Convey the impact of your Salvation experience**: The indwelling of the Holy Spirit is immediate and noticeable. The outward manifestation of the Holy Spirit is the fruit, and those results are powerful. Convey that sense of freedom and empowerment – available through the total surrender to Christ – and make sure the person knows that same reality is available to them through faith in Christ.

> *And suddenly there came from heaven a noise like a violent rushing wind, and it filled the whole house where they were sitting. And there appeared to them tongues as of fire distributing themselves, and they rested on each one of them.*
>
> ~ Acts 2:2-3 ~

4. **Do not let Satan steal your voice**: Satan hates when believers share the Gospel of Christ. He would rather see them burdened with religious activity – practicing with a band, building PowerPoint slides, et. – then out in the world, making disciples. Satan wants you to believe your testimony is unimportant, and your story of conversion is inconsequential. Satan does not care about you; he is trying to conceal Christ from the hearts of non-believers that may hear your testimony. Boldly proclaim and defend your Christian faith. You are not Satan's target, Christ is.

> *And through his shrewdness he will cause deceit to succeed by his influence; And he will magnify himself in his heart, and he will destroy many while they are at ease. He will even oppose the Prince of princes, but he will be broken without human agency.*
>
> ~ Daniel 8:25 ~

Chapter 02: *The Mission to Advance Christ's Kingdom on Earth*

5. **The grace of God overshadows your message**: Earlier in the chapter, the fear of engaging people – individually and in groups – was discussed. "*I may make a mistake;*" "*They may not like what I say,*" "*I do not know what they'll think of me, or my message.*" All stem from the speaker's focus on themselves, not on the message or the people to whom they are speaking. Once the concern shifts from the "self" to the recipient of the message, these arguments above do not apply. Evangelism is not about *you*; it is about sharing the Gospel of Christ. Keep that in mind, and remember God's promises to you as well.

   Do not fear, for I am with you; Do not anxiously look about you, for I am your God. I will strengthen you, surely I will help you, surely I will uphold you with My righteous right hand.

   ~ Isaiah 41:10 ~

6. **Your Salvation through Christ strengthens your message**: You professed your faith in Christ and accepted His message of Salvation. Once you have accepted God's forgiveness and Salvation, it is time to accept His strength as part of the agreement. With the Holy Spirit within you – and God's strength under you as a foundation – focusing on sharing the Gospel of Christ becomes invigorating. The jitters go away, and you are left with the exhilaration of leading a non-believer to God. He will make sure your message is perfected, established, strengthened, and settled when you share the Good News about Him.

   After you have suffered for a little while, the God of all grace, who called you to His eternal glory in Christ, will Himself perfect, confirm, strengthen and establish you.

   ~ 1 Peter 5:10 ~

7. **Sharing your faith increases your faith, and your understanding of it**. There will come a point in time while you are sharing the Gospel when a passage of Scripture you heard would be perfect to share with a non-believer ... but you cannot remember it. What will you do? You will look it

up, write it down, and remember it for the next occasion. There will also be people who challenge God's Word, and you know there is a perfect Scripture to show them the truth ... but you cannot remember it. What will you do? You will look it up, you will write it down, and you will remember it for the next time. The act of boldly proclaiming and defending our Christian faith is a biblical command: *"But sanctify Christ as Lord in your hearts, always being ready to make a defense to everyone who asks you to give an account for the hope that is in you, yet with gentleness and reverence"* (1 Peter 3:15). The act of forgetting the chapter, verse, and words of a perfect passage of Scripture is inevitable. You will have to learn how to deal with that fact – by constantly looking passages up, writing them down, and remembering them for the next time. It is a natural part of the learning cycle that comes with sharing the Gospel of Christ with others.

> *And I pray that the fellowship of your faith may become effective through the knowledge of every good thing which is in you for Christ's sake.*
>
> ~ Philemon 1:6 ~

The path of a faithful disciple of Christ is not an easy one to follow: there are hills, valleys, twists, and turns along the way. Jesus revealed this to the multitudes that travelled for miles – and sometimes days – to hear Him speak. He also taught this to His disciples who followed him daily throughout His earthly ministry. *"As a result of this many of His disciples withdrew and were not walking with Him anymore"* (John 6:66). That did not bother Jesus at all; He was looking for *quality* in His disciples, not *quantity*.

Although the path of a faithful disciple of Christ is not easy, it is worth every effort. The promise of an Eternal Life that begins now, not in the next life, changes the way believers view the world. The promise of Salvation changes the way believers act in the world, and the power of an indwelling Holy Spirit changes the way His believers impact the world. Disciples have everything to gain – an eternity in Heaven – and nothing to lose ... that they will not lose anyway when they leave this world. As Christians, we serve an awesome God, and it is worth every sacrifice we make.

Chapter 03

Planning for Victory with Lessons from History

"For inquire, please, of the former age, and consider the things discovered by their fathers; for we were born yesterday, and know nothing, because our days on earth are a shadow. Will they not teach you and tell you, and utter words from their heart?"

~ Job 8:8-10 ~

Chapter 03: *Planning for Victory with Lessons from History*

The Importance of History and Historical Theology

What is so important about studying the history of the Christian faith? The thought of spending hours learning about facts, dates, places that no longer exist and dead people does not sound appealing.

What is the value of spending time in the past, removed from a future that is difficult to manage, quoting historians of antiquity, when much of society either will net (or cannot) comfortably discuss their own theological doctrine? Those are valid questions, worthy of practical answers.

Before answering, let us begin with the definition of *Historical Theology*: it is the branch of theology that studies the social, historical, and cultural factors that influence theological ideas, doctrines, and structure. The discipline focuses on the relationship between theology and its contexts, as well as on the major theological, political, and philosophical influences upon the figures and topics studied.

Although the definition explains what Historical Theology *is*, and describes what it *does*, it is the Word of God that tells us why studying the history of the Christian faith is important. Although we focus in our study on the works of mankind, it is ultimately the study of God working through mankind:

> *And I also say to you that you are Peter, and on this rock I will build My church, and the gates of Hades shall not prevail against it.*
>
> ~ Matthew 16:18 ~

It is not Christians that have been creating, building, and spreading the church for the last 2,000 years – it has been Christ. The Christian faith revolves around His Word, accomplishing His Will, and trying to be more like Him. He's the Father to the Christian flock, the Body of Christ, and studying the history of the evolution of our faith – Historical Theology – is akin to learning about the genealogical branches that make up our Family tree. Brothers and sisters in Christ should know their family's history.

Chapter 03: *Planning for Victory with Lessons from History*

The Word of God, by its nature, is a living seed to be sown. Contingent upon the composition of the soil – stony, shallow, tare-ridden, or fertile – the seed of the Word grows, but the cycle has not been completed. If the seed produces fruit, it is harvested and distributed with a portion to be consumed, and a portion to be retained as seed for a new harvest.

The process of planting, harvesting, distributing, and consuming God's Word is a process that creates history and from that history, the study of historical theology follows.

> *So then neither he who plants is anything, nor he who waters, but God who gives the increase.*
>
> ~ 1 Corinthians 3:7 ~

It is inevitable that during this process, a few bad seeds – and occasionally tares – will be responsible for bad fruit and a poor harvest. Like most genealogies, the past is not always pleasant; the proverbial "skeleton in the closet" will always be a part of history. As our Christian doctrine has developed over time, it is had its share. For example:

1. The corrupt abuse of Indulgences
2. The persecution and eradication of the Knights Templar
3. The burning of Christian Theologians at the stake
4. Suppressing science and banning the Heliocentric Model
5. Refusing to allow access to Vernacular Bibles
6. The biblical justification of the Inquisitions
7. The millions killed globally in medieval Witch Hunts

> *Jesus answered and said to them, "Those who are well have no need of a physician, but those who are sick. I have not come to call the righteous, but sinners, to repentance."*
>
> ~ Luke 5:31 ~

Jesus knew what He was doing when He called disciples from the margins of society, when He set the stage for Paul and Peter to argue at the Jerusalem Council in 48 AD, and when the Church was losing its way prior to the Protestant Reformation. For those who yearn for the "Golden Apostolic Age," there was not one. Despite that, our Christian history has been amazing.

Chapter 03: *Planning for Victory with Lessons from History*

The 7 Periods of Christian Church History

The primary reason for studying any type of history is to establish a bridge, a connection, between the facts of the past and the ideas held to be truth in modern times. The reason for studying biblical history is the same, but the stakes are much higher. The questions asked to speak to the core of our faith, and the answers given shape the perceptions of divine truth that guide us in our relationship with God.

Imagine encountering an individual wandering aimlessly in the middle of the road, confused and concerned, suffering from amnesia. Not knowing who they are or where they came from would make it difficult (if not impossible) to guide them to where they needed to go. On an individual level, this would be alarming. On an institutional level, the consequences can be devastating. Yet, this type of institutional amnesia is present in many of our churches.

Those charged with leading churches are tasked with successfully guiding Christians, and a better understanding of the roots of our faith ensure a higher probability that the branches will grow to be healthy and strong. To study biblical history is to study God's Word, God's Will, and God's Work in the past, its application in the present, and its promise of hope for every Christian in the future to come. Throughout history, the people who served God in building His Church, suffering in His name, and fighting struggles – both external and internal – were human, like us. They must serve as examples to be **emulated**, not deified exceptions to be **venerated**.

> *Elijah was a man with a nature like ours,*
> *and he prayed earnestly ...*
>
> ~ James 5:17 ~

We are the same fallen sinners as were the Apostles, with the same capabilities and limitations. *Jesus Christ is the same yesterday, today, and forever* (Hebrews 13:8); the Holy Spirit still actively calls us today to *"go and do likewise"* (Luke 10:37).

Chapter 03: *Planning for Victory with Lessons from History*

The Apostolic Age: 30 A.D. – 100 A.D.

The next time you open your Bible or visit a church, ask yourself a question: how did Christianity – initially evangelized by 12 disciples of Christ with no modern methods of communication – become the worlds' largest religion with over 2.5 billion faithful believers?

Mainstream Christianity tends to hold a view portraying the Apostolic Age as cooperative and cohesive, being guided by believers with a common purpose and a unified message. There are movements such as Restorationism that call for a return to the "Golden Apostolic Age," envisioning a time when doctrine was pure, and sectarianism was nonexistent.

Unfortunately for those with this utopian yearning, nothing could be farther from the truth. The realities of the Apostolic Age have been documented by historians, validated by theologians, and documented in our Scripture.

As this back-story unfolds in the following pages, realize that it is not meant to disparage or minimize the contributions of those involved. In fact, it is meant to convey the exact opposite. When one considers that these factors and conditions existed – viewed against the backdrop of what we, as Christians, take for granted in our contemporary churches – the testament to their commitment is unquestionable, and the power of the Holy Spirit is undeniable.

Scripture informs us (and history confirms for us) that Jesus' brothers – Joseph, Jude, Simeon and especially James – played a prominent role in the Apostolic Age. Given the events detailed in the New Testament, that does not surprise anyone, until they discover that many of Jesus' family members did not believe Him or support His mission.

> *His brothers therefore said to Him, "Depart from here and go into Judea, that Your disciples also may see the works that You are doing. For no one does anything in secret while he himself seeks to be known openly. If You do these things, show Yourself to the world." For even His brothers did not believe in Him.*
>
> *~ John 7:3-5 ~*

Chapter 03: *Planning for Victory with Lessons from History*

It was not until after Christ's Resurrection that James and the rest of His brothers fully committed to the faith:

> After that He was seen by James,
> then by all the apostles.
>
> ~ 1 Corinthians 15:7 ~

With that in mind, the back-story of the Apostolic Age will begin with the Apostle Paul (formerly known as Saul of Tarsus).

The Apostle Paul: 4 Missionary Journeys
Acts 13:4 - 14:26   First Journey to Cyprus and Asia Minor
Acts 15:40 - 18:22 Second Journey to Macedonia and Greece
Acts 18:23 - 21:15 Third to Ephesus, Europe, and Asia Minor
Acts 27:1 - 28:16   Fourth Journey to Malta and Rome

Paul is one of the New Testament's most recognizable and active apostles. He authored 13 epistles (The Pauline Epistles) – some scholars believe the number to be 14 and include Hebrews – and evangelized Christianity as zealously as he persecuted it prior to his encounter with Christ and conversion on the road to Damascus (Acts 9:3).

Scripture reveals that Paul's life was one of constant suffering. He escaped assassination plots (Acts 9:29), was repeatedly stoned (Acts 14:19), repeatedly beaten with rods (Acts 16:22), repeatedly whipped (2 Corinthians 11:23), shipwrecked multiple times (Acts 27:42), and imprisoned twice (Acts 28:13). He would eventually be martyred in 64 A.D. – executed by beheading – per

Chapter 03: *Planning for Victory with Lessons from History*

the order of Emperor Nero. While the suffering he experienced personally was severe, the internal threats he encountered which were directed against Christianity were more significant.

Within the converted Jewish communities, *Judaizers* (those that believed Christianity to be "Judaism + Christ") were undermining Paul's teaching and acting as a divisive agent in newly planted churches. The severity of the issue lead to the Council of Jerusalem, a gathering of apostles and elders, in 48 A.D. The issue to be decided was the role Jewish law and tradition would play in the new faith. Peter and James took the pro-Jewish position, while Paul and Barnabas argued Mosaic Law was no longer needed. Paul's position prevailed, but the ripple effects of the confrontation remained, and the relationship between the apostles was severely strained.

> *Now when Peter had come to Antioch, I withstood him to his face, because he was to be blamed; for before certain men came from James, he would eat with the Gentiles; but when they came, he withdrew and separated himself, fearing those who were of the circumcision.*
>
> ~ Galatians 2:11-12 ~

At the time of Paul's final imprisonment, his relationship with the original Jewish apostles was virtually nonexistent. This is evident when Paul writes the final letter he will ever write, just prior to his beheading, ordered by Emperor Nero:

> *At my first defense no one stood with me, but all forsook me. May it not be charged against them.*
>
> ~ 2 Timothy 4:16 ~

Within the converted Gentile communities, *Gnostics* (those who believed philosophy and wisdom would bring 'oneness with God') were undermining Paul's authority, defaming his reputation, and profiting from teaching false doctrines that had infiltrated the church under the guise of "real Christianity." The Gnostics claimed Paul's teaching was insufficient to know God, his oratorical style was lacking, and he did not have the requisite intelligence to claim expertise and teach. Given the distance between churches and available modes of transportation, "rushing" to a location to defend oneself could take months.

Chapter 03: *Planning for Victory with Lessons from History*

Many of Paul's letters addressed this threat:

> *And I, brethren, when I came to you, did not come with excellence of speech or of wisdom declaring to you the testimony of God.*
>
> ~ 1 Corinthians 2:1 ~

The last threat to be discussed that Paul dealt with constantly did not involve religion or politics; it was a matter of economics. Paul's evangelism of Christ, and the subsequent conversion of Gentiles to the faith, was having a significantly negative impact on many industries within the Roman Empire.

For example, the silversmiths in Ephesus that created statues of the goddess Diana for the local pagan population were so enraged at Paul and his companions that they started a riot. The priestesses (prostitutes) at the Temple of Aphrodite in Corinth were losing income resulting from Paul's "new morality," a situation common to many of the major cities in the Roman Empire. In Philippi, Paul casted a demon of divination out of a slave girl – who generated large profits for her master – and ended up in jail with his companion, Silas. The next time you hear the phrase, "Voodoo Economics," consider the challenges faced by Paul in his journeys.

The widespread belief that Paul's trials and tribulations were solely caused by external threats, those opposed to the new sect of "Christ-followers," does not convey an accurate accounting of the challenges he faced in all directions. However, the apostles in Jerusalem were having their share of internal and external struggles as well. Scripture reveals that on Pentecost, all seemed cohesive and unified:

> *So continuing daily with one accord in the temple, and breaking bread from house to house, they ate their food with gladness and simplicity of heart.*
>
> ~ Acts 2:46 ~

However, as the numbers of believers grew – in a diverse, multicultural environment like the Roman Empire – challenges would arise. It is also reasonable to predict that when one erases cultural barriers with a common faith, problems will occur. It was

Chapter 03: *Planning for Victory with Lessons from History*

not long after Pentecost that cultural friction emerged between the Palestinian and Hellenistic widows, recent Jewish converts to faith in Christ.

> *Now in those days, when the number of the disciples was multiplying, there arose a complaint against the Hebrews by the Hellenists, because their widows were neglected in the daily distribution.*
>
> ~ Acts 6:1 ~

That problem was solved by the apostles by selecting seven elders of Hellenistic descent, to resolve the issue on their behalf. Persecution by leaders of the Jewish community continued, and despite Emperor Nero's dislike of the new sect of "Christ-followers," life for the Christian Apostles in Jerusalem remained relatively stable – until 64 A.D. It was then that the lives of Christians became intolerable and in many cases, short.

In July of that year, a fire swept through Rome – a city of more than 1 million people – that destroyed or severely damaged 10 of the city's' 14 provinces. Nero blamed the fire on Christians and began an organized persecution of the faith. The respected historians of the period, Josephus and Tacitus, reported the Emperor tied Christians to tall poles and used them as human torches to illuminate his palace garden during festive events. It was also in this year that the Apostles Paul and Peter were martyred.

Two years later, tensions between Jews and Hellenists erupted and led to *The Great Revolt* (66 A.D. – 73 A.D.), an armed conflict that led to a siege of Jerusalem, destruction of the Jewish Temple, and hundreds of thousands fleeing the region to escape the war. The dispersion of both the Jewish and Christian communities brought the faith into areas previously devoid of a Christian presence. God ensured adversity created opportunity.

By 100 A.D., all the apostles had been martyred except John, who died of old age exiled on the island of Patmos. During this adversity, early Christianity entered the Patristic Period.

Chapter 03: *Planning for Victory with Lessons from History*

The Patristic Period: 100 A.D. – 325 A.D.

One might expect the destruction of the Jewish Temple in Jerusalem, widespread persecution at the hand of a fanatical Roman emperor and the death of the original Apostles of Christ would be enough to thoroughly eradicate the fledgling Christian faith. By the Grace of God, the exact opposite occurred. Although persecution against Christians would soon reach its apex, several amazing tasks were accomplished: the official canon began to take shape, the Christian faith began to expand both influentially and geographically, and the writings of well-educated Christian converts had significant impact on the world.

The Roman Empire had tense relations with the Jewish population after destroying their temple, and from 132 A.D – 136 A.D., another Jewish-War consumed the region. The emperor during this period, Hadrian, was furious with the Jews and took steps to completely eradicate their faith. According to historians, Hadrian's troops killed more than a half-million residents, sold the ones that lived, and banned Judaism as a legal faith in 135 A.D. The emperor even changed the city's name from Jerusalem to *Aelia Capitolina*, an official name it retained until 638 A.D. While this war did not impact Christians directly, it did end Jewish leadership in the church. Prior to that date, the Bishops of Jerusalem had Hebrew names; after that date, only Hellenistic names appear.

The Roman Empire's persecution of Christians fluctuated, contingent upon the personality of the emperor at the time. However, in 303 A.D under the rule of the Diocletian, hostility towards the faith reached unprecedented levels.

Leaders of churches were tortured and executed, sacred texts were destroyed with the structures in which they were held, and entire communities were razed (and inhabitants slaughtered).

Instead of defeating Christianity, it strengthened it. Many chose martyrdom over submission, and their sacrifice inspired and attracted converts. Despite the individual suffering, the Body of Christ grew and expanded under the most extreme pressures. This level of persecution continued until 313 A.D., when the Roman

Chapter 03: *Planning for Victory with Lessons from History*

Emperor Constantine signed the *Edict of Milan*, a decree of religious tolerance for the citizens of the empire. Although written to include all religions, it afforded specific benefit to Christians that enabled the faith to grow and expand throughout the Roman Empire.

Contrary to popular belief, it did not become the official religion of Rome when Constantine converted in 312 A.D. – that occurred in 380 A.D. with the *Edict of Thessalonica*. He did, however, take major steps to lessen the burdens and suffering caused by hostility officially sanctioned by the Roman Empire.

The accomplishments of this period also included several significant steps to unify and codify the Christian faith. This had started at the end of the first century with the creation of the *Didache* – a brief codex addressing church ethics, rituals and organization – but a coordinated effort during this period set the framework for formalizing Christianity as a religion. Additionally, this period gave rise to the theological discipline of Apologetics.

> *But sanctify the Lord God in your hearts, and always be ready to give a defense to everyone who asks you a reason for the hope that is in you, with meekness and fear.*
>
> ~ 1 Peter 3:15 ~

The second and third centuries saw a significant increase in well-educated citizens converting to Christianity, and they put their formal education and skills to use for Christ's mission. The writings of the period tend to fall into one of two categories: Doctrine or Apologetics. Those in the first category considered the defining of the Church, its faith, and its unified practices. The second category focused on providing a reasoned defense for Christianity, and disarming the arguments being made against it. Writers in both categories were formally educated in rhetoric, philosophy, logic, and the classical theories of apologetics taught by Socrates. The advances in Christianity were so observable that Emperor Constantine convened the First Council of Nicaea, an event that ushered in the next age of the Christian faith.

Chapter 03: *Planning for Victory with Lessons from History*

Council of Nicaea to the Fall of Rome: 325 A.D. – 590 A.D.

Given the thousands of denominations of Christianity that exist in contemporary society, it is not unusual for believers to wish for "a unified faith like that which was practiced in the early Church." If you share that sentiment, be careful what you wish for; the unified doctrine you envision did not exist, and the process of creating it did not begin until 325 A.D. at the First Council of Nicaea.

Trinity

As Christianity spread throughout the Roman Empire, many competing doctrines began to emerge, creating division and tension within the Body of Christ. The Emperor Constantine was compelled to address the crisis and convened a meeting of Bishops in the city of Nicaea. The purpose of this ecumenical council was to secure a consensus within the Church regarding important doctrinal issues. This would be the first official meeting of Christian leaders since the Council of Jerusalem in 48 A.D. Constantine's goal was to resolve the disagreements dividing believers, and to establish a unified view for Christians in the Roman Empire. While the council did not solve many of the problems faced by believers, it proved to be a very important step in the process defining the Christian doctrine taken for granted in modern society.

> *But even if we, or an angel from heaven, preach any other gospel to you than what we have preached to you, let him be accursed.*
>
> ~ Galatians 1:8 ~

The primary issue was Christological: what was the nature of Christ as the Son of God, and what was His relationship to God the Father? The concept of the Trinity – the Father, the Son, and the Holy Spirit – proved difficult to define and highly divisive.

Another issue was the date of Easter, and the reliance on the Jewish lunar calendar to predict future dates. The issue did not get settled – it would take centuries for a day to be decided – but it was agreed that the day would be Sunday.

The council discussed organizational issues, such as dates for annual meetings, standards for clergy, the fate of sinners in the Church, and the role of secular philosophy in Christianity. The final accomplishment was the drafting of the first part of the Nicaean Creed, and an official statement of the Church's faith.

What may surprise many believers is what was not discussed at the council: the issue of an official biblical canon. It would not be until the Council of Carthage in 397 A.D. that the 27 Books of the New Testament – the Word of God we read today – became the official Bible for Christians. Additionally, there was no discussion about appointing one individual to lead and speak for the Church.

Christianity became the official religion of the Empire in 380 A.D., with the issuance of the Edict of Thessalonica, an initiative lead by Emperor Theodosius. Beginning in 381 A.D., the Church – tacitly supported by the Emperor – used its authority to suppress competing (non-Nicaean) versions of Christianity and began to aggressively persecute pagans within the Empire. Pagan worship was banned, temples were confiscated, and items that honored their gods (art, literature, statues, etc.) were destroyed.

Until Christianity became the official religion of the Empire, Popes had always claimed spiritual authority in Christendom; with a new sense of authority, they began to claim political authority as well. Beginning with Pope Leo the Great (440 – 461 A.D.), the Church exerted significant authority in political matters, taking advantage of the external pressures weakening the Western Roman Empire.

From 376 – 476 A.D., the Roman Empire suffered several defeats – losing property, power, and influence in the process – at the hands of the Visigoths, Vandals, and various Germanic tribes. From 476 – 590 A.D., the Western Roman Empire existed in name only. When Pope Gregory I assumed his position as the Bishop of Rome in 590 A.D., he became the *de facto* leader of Christendom from his office in Rome. However, with this power came difficulties: the next 1,000 years would prove to be a true test of faith for every professing Christian, all over the world.

Chapter 03: *Planning for Victory with Lessons from History*

Medieval Church to the Renaissance: 590 A.D. – 1517 A.D.

As the borders of the Roman Empire disintegrated, the Church went through a 1,000-year period that witnessed an unprecedented spread of the Christian faith, the expansion of the Church's influence, and division within the Church – driven by power and politics – that left it permanently fragmented.

This period also witnessed unparalleled acts of heroism, the rise of Christian intellectualism, and a movement to deliver the Word of God directly to believers that served as a foundation for the way Christians study the Bible in modern churches. If you've ever attended a university, read a Bible in English, and discussed the Word of God with others, you've experienced the benefit of this historic period.

In the words of Catholic historian Lord Action, *"Power tends to corrupt, and absolute power corrupts absolutely. Great men are almost always bad men."* No words could better describe the Church's ascension to a theocracy, and the internal battles for power between the five strongholds of the global Christian faith: Rome, Antioch, Alexandria, Constantinople, and Jerusalem.

The first major fragmentation, the Great Schism of 1054 A.D., occurred when Pope Leo IX in Rome, and the Patriarch of Constantinople, Michael Cerularius, excommunicated each other and declared the opposing church invalid. The next major divide, termed the Western Schism, occurred between 1378-1417 A.D. when three men, driven by politics, not theological doctrine, concurrently claimed the title of Pope. During this period, the impact on secular governments in Europe ranged from questions of allegiance to rampant violence in the affected regions.

In a parallel execution, nine major military campaigns between 1095-1291 A.D. that have come to be known as "The Crusades" pitted hundreds of thousands of European Christians – promised absolution (forgiveness of sins) if they fought – against the competing forces of Islam for control of Jerusalem and the Holy Lands. Crusades were conducted in Europe as well until 1492 A.D.,

Chapter 03: *Planning for Victory with Lessons from History*

directed against pagan tribes and Christians labeled "heretics" by the Church. The cost in lives, property, international relations, and reputation of the Church was monumental, and left a dark stain on the history of the Christian faith.

During the same period, advances made by Christian leaders in education and philosophical thought directly influence the way we study and interpret Scripture today. The first formal universities were created by the Medieval Church between 1088-1150 A.D. in Europe and began as cathedral schools before eventually evolving into secular institutions of higher learning.

Advances in the methodology of teaching and studying occurred in these universities as well, between 1100-1700 A.D. *Scholasticism*, which attempted to synthesize theology with classical philosophy, was developed to find answers to difficult questions, and resolve apparent contradictions found in written texts. Students would read a text, note points of disagreement and contradictions within the text, then research both sides of the argument thoroughly to bring the alleged contradictions into agreement.

This was done with *philological analysis* – examining words in original languages and context to determine if there could be alternative meanings – or logical analysis – proving that no valid contradictions existed except within the mind of the one reading the text. In his masterpiece, *Summa Theologica*, Thomas Aquinas uses scholasticism brilliantly to consider the natures of God, Christ, and Mankind. This method of studying, interpreting and reconciling God's Word in the Bible is used every day in the Christian faith.

Prominent Christian heroes laid the foundation for leaders of the Reformation, and the modern Christianity practiced today. John Wycliffe, a vocal opponent of the Pope, translated the Bible into English for the masses in 1382 A.D. This so infuriated the Church they exhumed his remains in 1417 A.D., burned them, and tossed his ashes in a river. John Hus, a follower of Wycliffe's, was condemned by the Church and burned at the stake. Events had aligned to usher in the period of the Protestant Reformation.

Chapter 03: *Planning for Victory with Lessons from History*

The Period of Reformation: 1517 A.D. – 1648 A.D.

The erosion of the Church's power and influence, amid a European Renaissance that questioned the authority of traditional thought, created an environment that allowed critical thinkers to challenge what they viewed as "corrupt practices" of the Church. The contributions this movement made in areas other than the Christian doctrine are equally significant: vernacular languages, messaging, mass media, and marketing.

In the opinion of Reformation leaders, the Church had strayed from God's Word and the teachings of Christ and had established several practices that appeared to elevate the Church over God. These practices included but were not limited to the selling of indulgences, the doctrine of transubstantiation, the elevation of Saints as mediators to God, confession of sin to priests, prayers for the dead, the concept of purgatory, and the unquestionable authority of the Pope.

The leaders of the Reformation were seeking reform within the Church, not separation from it, and established their doctrine on three fundamental principles: sole authority of Scripture, Justification by faith alone, and the concept of priesthood of the believer (every believer in the Body of Christ has the authority the Church assigned only to priests). Martin Luther, one of leaders of this movement, formally announced his grievances with the Church by nailing his *95 Theses* on a church door in Wittenberg, Germany, in 1517 A.D. Predictably, the response of the Church was not positive, and Luther was excommunicated.

> *For by grace you have been saved through faith,*
> *and that not of yourselves; it is the gift of God.*
>
> ~ Ephesians 2:8 ~

The core message of his doctrine was based on "*5 Solas*" that modern Christianity accepts as absolute truths. They are *Sola Scriptura* (by Scripture alone), *Sola Gratia* (by Grace alone), *Sola Fide* (by Faith alone), *Solus Christus* (through Christ alone), and

Soli Deo Gloria (glory to God alone). These "5 Only" beliefs were in direct opposition to the practices of the Catholic Church.

> **SOLA SCRIPTURA**
> **SOLA GRATIA**
> **SOLA FIDE**
> **SOLUS CHRISTUS**
> **SOLI DEO GLORIA**

Luther's doctrine spread rapidly in Germany and throughout Europe for several reasons, not the least of which was it was believed and needed by the Body of Christ. First, the invention of the Gutenberg Printing Press in 1440 – the same press that printed the Gutenberg Bible in 1455 – allowed for inexpensive, widespread distribution of Luther's message. Second, Luther's creation of a vernacular Bible (in German), allow non-clergy to read the Word of God that had previously only been printed in Latin and understood by the clergy. Finally, the support of nobility in various European countries who sought to exert authority over the Church allowed for a "top-down" acceptance of the Reformation doctrine.

The Reformation period, despite the spirit of Renaissance that engulfed Europe, was born in conflict, and tested by hostility. Educated adherents of Luther's doctrine used biblical prophecy to prove Rome was the new Babylon, and the Pope the antichrist who had replaced God, to cause mass defections from the Church. In response, the Church excommunicated hundreds of people, before labeling them as "heretics" and burning them at the stake. William Tyndale, credited with creating the first English language Bible translated directly from Hebrew and Greek, suffered this fate in England in 1536 A.D. It would be Tyndale's Bible that would serve as the model for the King James Bible in the next century.

The Church escalated its response to the Protestant Reformation move between 1618-1648 A.D. with a military campaign that's been labeled the "Thirty Year War." It is believed to have been one of Europe's most deadly and destructive wars; estimates put the total number of deaths from the campaign at over eight million. In 1648 A.D., peace was brokered through a series of treaties. The Church refused to acknowledge the treaty, Europe's nobility ignored the Church's opinion, and the power of the Church in Europe began a steady decline. The Protestant Reformation had secured independence from the authority of the Church, and the modern Christianity known today was born.

Chapter 03: *Planning for Victory with Lessons from History*

The Period of Enlightenment: 1648 A.D. – 1789 A.D.

The "Period of Enlightenment" spreading throughout Europe inspired a dramatic shift in social and political thought. Notable intellectual and philosophical leaders of the period gave primacy to reason as the driver for cultural progress, arguing that an unqualifiable force such as organized religion was irrational. The Arts flourished, a renewed interest in the Sciences emerged, and a cultural identity based on personal liberty and freedom was the foundation of prevailing political thought.

The conclusion of the Reformation period left the affected populations weary from religious wars, the Church's dominance in all facets of society, and resentful of the negative impact that Christian doctrine had imposed on intellectual progress. Leaders of the Enlightenment tended not to be "anti-God;" the majority embraced some variant of Deism or Theism. However, they were decidedly "anti-Church," and vehemently rejected and opposed the dogma of the Christian faith.

Intellectuals of the period took great measures to ensure that the Church would never again be able to impose a theocracy in Europe and advocated for a separation of "Church and State" in political writings.

This thought was embraced by leaders in the 13 North American Colonies as well and had a significant influence in the Declaration of Independence and the Constitution of the United States. The history of the Roman Catholic Church, and the European nobility that had mandated its practice on a national scale, demonstrated the need for the protection *from* religion as much as it did the freedom *of* religion. Although there was backlash against the Church, the Christian faith experienced a renewed sense of revival during this period.

The same Enlightenment that inspired the concepts of freedom, liberty and individual rights in European intellectuals influenced leaders in the Protestant Reformation as well. Access to Jesus Christ – formerly restricted and mediated by the Church – was now directly available to the Christian community.

Chapter 03: *Planning for Victory with Lessons from History*

> *Go therefore and make disciples of all the nations, baptizing them in the name of the Father and of the Son and of the Holy Spirit, teaching them to observe all things that I have commanded you.*
>
> ~ Matthew 28:19-20 ~

This period of Christian revival, known as *The Great Awakenings*, shifted emphasis from ritualistic practices and focused on making the faith a personal experience. These movements, which began in Europe and migrated to the American Colonies, radically changed the way Christianity was practiced, perceived and presented. Two movements were the primary drivers of this change: Methodism and Reformed Theology. Methodism – led by John Wesley, Charles Wesley and George Whitefield – began in Europe as part of the Church of England before becoming independent. Reformed Theology, led by Calvinist Jonathan Edwards, began in the New England Colonies in America.

Both movements contributed to the areas of doctrine, evangelism, and the practice of the faith. Sermons that were previously read to congregants and treated academically were being delivered emotionally, focusing on the listener's sense of guilt and need of Salvation through Christ. The need for personal morality and accountability replaced ceremonial rituals to remove sin. "Fire and Brimstone" had arrived.

John Wesley is credited with bringing music to church services that included instruments and audience participation. Charles Wesley is credited with writing almost 9,000 hymns, many of which are still used in contemporary Christian services. George Whitefield is credited with bringing the Christian faith out of buildings via "open air preaching," a radical concept at the time that had significant and positive impacts on evangelism. Jonathan Edwards, through his writing and pastoral style, is credited with making incredible advances in evangelical missions, especially those conducted abroad. As the French Revolution began in 1789, reformed evangelical Christianity in America was bringing Salvation to individual believers through Christ.

Chapter 03: *Planning for Victory with Lessons from History*

The Modern / Post-Modern Periods: 1789 – Present

Historians separate Christianity in recent history into two periods: Modern (1789 – 1970) and Post-Modern (1970 – Present). For this overview, events from both periods that have made a significant impact on contemporary Christian doctrine will be combined and presented. The Modern period in America saw the expansion of evangelism into the Western Frontier, the rise of a Christian Social Gospel to address critical social matters, and an increased acceptance of "Biblical Prophets" whose claims of "divine inspiration" reshaped many Christian denominations, or the creation of new denominations altogether.

As the Western Frontier expanded with settlers seeking new fortunes, evangelists from several movements expanded with them, seeking new converts to the Christian faith. The Methodists were extremely effective in this mission field. Having expanded initially with lay pastors for specific communities, they mobilized a new generation of itinerant lay pastors, known as "circuit riders," to reach the most remote locations. The Baptist movement was also effective in this mission. A key factor to their evangelical success was the use of rank-and-file citizens as lay pastors, a strategy that served to garner trust and support with the frontier communities.

This period produced several social challenges that forced the Body of Christ to apply biblical principles in support of social justice, human rights, and cultural morality. Christian converts were taught to *"be doers of the word, and not hearers only, deceiving yourselves"* (James 1:22), and many became leaders in a variety of activist causes. These social issues included abolition (slavery), temperance (alcohol), suffrage (women's rights) and poverty.

As the circuit riders were evangelizing the frontier, a new organization allowed God's Word to reach deep into the heart of inner cities: the YMCA. While its original purpose was to ensure rural youth did not stray from the Christian faith as they migrated to urban areas, they evolved into an arm of evangelical outreach for a mission field challenged by poverty and lack of education.

Chapter 03: *Planning for Victory with Lessons from History*

Individuals claiming to have experienced divine visions emerged between 1820 and 1930. Their impact on modern Christianity is undeniable and ever-present. Richard Brothers introduced Anglo-Israelism (1820), Joseph Smith introduced Mormonism (1830), Charles Russell founded Jehovah's Witnesses (1870), and Ellen White introduced 7th Day Adventist teachings. How God could have revealed His divine truth, to several people whose visions are contradictory, remains an issue of debate. Of all the new doctrines emerging during this period, Ralph Waldo Trine's "prosperity gospel" has arguably had the most profoundly negative impact on biblical Christianity.

Media personalities propagating the false doctrine of the prosperity gospel – such as Joel Osteen, Joyce Meyer, and Paula White – have amassed fortunes while leading millions of deceived "Christians" down the wide road to eternal death. A perfect storm of biblical illiteracy, societal pressures and desperation have combined to make this heretical movement (a satanic Ponzi scheme) successful. Followers believe *they* are the true source of divine creative power: know what you want, visualize receiving it, believe you'll receive it, and God provides it on demand. Jesus Christ becomes a "genie in a bottle" who exists to serve every whim and wish, and wealth replaces God as the object of worship.

The Post-Modern period has witnessed an exponential expansion of evangelism in foreign countries, with Salvation reaching millions that previously had never heard the Gospel. Advances in technology and communication have increased awareness, access and has allowed God's Word to reach the most repressive societies. Home churches in countries like China, Sudan, and Indonesia – highly repressive countries in which a professed faith in Christianity can result in imprisonment and/or death – have continued to be multiplied.

As the Christian community moves forward into the future, expanding and contracting, it will continue to face obstacles and challenges the Body of Christ will be required to overcome. Two things are certain.

Chapter 03: *Planning for Victory with Lessons from History*

First, the promises of God are eternal, His Grace is everlasting, and His Salvation is assured to all those who profess faith in Christ as our Lord and Savior. That ensures our ability to overcome suffering and challenges is certain.

Second, our biblical history reveals circumstances and events faced in the future have already been faced by believers in the past. The lessons learned from history and historical theology can assist in navigating events to come. If you doubt this second certainty, consider the following:

1. Believe Christ is Lord & Savior
   ➢ The Apostolic Age (30-100)

2. Stand ready to defend your faith with sound doctrine
   ➢ The Patristic Period (100-325)

3. Without fear of persecution for practicing an illegal religion
   ➢ Council of Nicaea – Fall of Rome (325-590)

4. Read the Word of God in your Bible
   ➢ Medieval Church – Renaissance (590-1517)

5. Believe in the Grace of Salvation through Faith alone
   ➢ Period of Reformation (1517-1648)

6. Enjoy the uplifting music at church service
   ➢ Period of Enlightenment (1648-1789)

7. Obey Christ's Great Commission with evangelism & missions
   ➢ Modern and Post-Modern Period (1789-Present)

Biblical history and God's Word have already proven it has been accomplished successfully. We, the Body of Christ, have only to continue that tradition of success for the generations that follow.

12 Major Influencers in Christian Biblical History

The following individuals have had a major influence on the evolution of Christian Doctrine listed in the preceding pages.

Chapter 03: *Planning for Victory with Lessons from History*

Polycarp (69 – 155 A.D.)

Polycarp, the Bishop of Smyrna (located in modern day Turkey), played a significant role in early Christianity. His importance is not due to influential writings, but because of who he knew and the example he set for Christians of the period.

Polycarp was a disciple of the Apostle John, and tradition holds that it was John that ordained him as the Bishop of Smyrna. The church of Smyrna was a large presence and an important role to play in Christianity. It was one of the seven churches John mentioned in the *Book of Revelation*:

> *And to the angel of the church in Smyrna write, these things says the First and the Last, who was dead, and came to life: I know your works, tribulation, and poverty (but you are rich); and I know the blasphemy of those who say they are Jews and are not, but are a synagogue of Satan.*
>
> ~ Revelation 2:8-9 ~

Polycarp's relationship with John made him a living bridge between the Apostolic and Patristic periods, affording him knowledge of the pure Gospel at a time when Christian Gnostic heretics were corrupting the teachings of Christ. It also gave him the authority to have his doctrinal position respected by other churches. Although Polycarp did not author many texts, his writings are some of the earliest historians that date to that period.

Polycarp was martyred in 155 A.D. for his faith, and his death served as an inspiration to persecuted Christians for hundreds of years. Brought before a Roman Proconsul and charged with being a Christian, he was given an opportunity to recant his faith and live. He refused, professing his faith and loyalty to Christ for his 86 years of life, and was burned alive at the stake. Tradition holds that as guards attempted to nail him to the stake, he told them not to bother; the same God who gave him Grace would give him the strength to endure the flames.

Chapter 03: *Planning for Victory with Lessons from History*

Tertullian (160 – 220 A.D.)

Tertullian, a Christian author, and orator in Carthage (modern day Tunisia), was an influential Apologist during the Patristic period. While not much is known about his early years, tradition holds that his father was a Roman Centurion, and his mother a pagan. He was formally educated – he spoke and wrote Greek and Latin – and some speculate training in law as well, prior to converting to Christianity in his 40's. Once he professed faith in Christ, he used his education, oratory skills and legal training to defend Christianity against the challenges of the period.

> *But sanctify the Lord God in your hearts, and always be ready to give a defense to everyone who asks you a reason for the hope that is in you, with meekness and fear.*
>
> ~ 1 Peter 3:15 ~

Tertullian is most well-known for writing *Apologeticus* (Apology), a defense of – and advocacy for – the Christian faith, written to the Roman Empire. In his writing, he labels the persecution of Christians unjust, hypocritical, and contrary to Roman law and practice. He then outlines the core tenets of the faith to dispel myths held by an uneducated pagan population and argues for Christianity to be accepted as a legitimate religion.

Tradition holds that he had great disdain for the revered Greek philosophers, believing them to be the source of Gnostic heretical thought that was corrupting the Christian faith. His writings against *Marcionism* – a doctrine created by Marcion of Sinope, a Church leader who blended Gnosticism with Christianity – would be used by Church leaders to eradicate heretics.

He composed many of his texts in Latin, allowing much of the population in the Western Roman Empire to read his doctrine. This unique act earned him the distinguished title of "Father of Latin Christianity," and led to widespread circulation of his work.

Chapter 03: *Planning for Victory with Lessons from History*

Athanasius the Great (298 – 373 A.D.)

Athanasius, the Bishop of Alexandria (modern day Egypt), was a formally educated leader in the Christian faith who is credited with many significant accomplishments. He spoke Coptic and Greek, had grown up as a disciple of the Church, and was uniquely qualified to help share early Christian Doctrine. He held his post for 45 years, 17 of which were spent in exile on the orders of several Roman Emperors. His exiles were not the result of his faith, but because his views on the Trinity (Father, Son, and Holy Spirit) ran against "mainstream orthodoxy" which was, at the time, *Arianism*.

> *For God so loved the world that*
> *He gave His only begotten Son.*
>
> ~ John 3:16 ~

Arianism rejects the concept of the Trinity, believing that anything that's "begotten" has a beginning. In this view, God (unbegotten) has authority over Christ (begotten) and the Holy Spirit (illuminating, but not God). Athanasius rejected this view as heresy, challenged the majority and was sentenced to exile for his views. Athanasius was vindicated at the Council of Nicaea in 325 – Arianism was labeled heretical and what we know today as Trinitarianism was made official – and the words "Father, Son and Holy Spirit" used in church services today can be linked to his efforts.

At the Council of Nicaea, Athanasius was a principal author of the Nicaean Creed, one of the most important doctrinal statements of faith in Christian history. He is also credited with creating the list of 27 Books that comprise the New Testament Cannon used in modern Bibles.

Athanasius' writings were not restricted to Christian doctrine; his biography of Anthony the Great was his most widely known work, translated into several languages, promoted the philosophy of asceticism throughout Christendom, and served as the inspiration for monastic movement (monasteries and monks).

Chapter 03: *Planning for Victory with Lessons from History*

Augustine of Hippo (354 – 430 A.D.)

Augustine, the Bishop of Hippo (modern day Algeria), was a prolific writer, innovative philosopher, and a Church leader whose theology would serve as a guiding doctrine for the proponents of the Protestant Reformation. His early life was spent outside of Christianity – his passions were women, sex, trouble and fun – but following his conversion he spent the balance of his life championing the Christian faith. His two most widely read writings, *City of God,* and *Confessions*, have impacted society far beyond religion.

City of God, a compilation of 22 books written over the course of 12 years, formulated, and formalized several of the doctrines subscribed to today in modern Christianity. His vigorous arguments for Creation *Ex Nihilio* ("from nothing") won support in the early Church and formed the core of Creation Theory Doctrine. His arguments align with the "Big Bang Theory" – the prevailing cosmological model explaining the origin of the universe – apart from God being removed as the Source of *ex nihilio*.

Augustine's writings addressed in detail the differences between "magic" and miraculous occurrences. The Church used these writings to establish official doctrines used in its battles with paganism. These doctrines were later used as a justification for "Witch Hunts" that continued throughout Europe and North America until the 18th-century.

He also discussed the use of force in the protection of life and faith, later coining the phrase "just war." He argued that while pacifism should be the standard practice, advocating pacifism when only violence can remove evil would be a sin. He believed this to be especially true when violence is sanctioned by legitimate authorities.

Finally, it was Augustine who formalized the doctrine of "Original Sin." Combined with his writing on Grace and Salvation, it became a principal doctrine for Protestant Reformation leaders such as Martin Luther and John Calvin. The Augustinian doctrine of Original Sin is currently used in contemporary Christianity.

Gregory the Great (540 – 604 A.D.)

Pope Gregory I, the Bishop of Rome (modern day Italy), was an innovative reformer of the Church, a masterful negotiator and administration, and the first Pope to oversee the evolution of the Church into theocratic rule.

His affluent family was active in the faith – Gregory was related to two Popes, and several of his aunts were nuns – and his formal training in law, politics, education, and religion provided the administrative skills needed to establish the Church's power and position within all of Christendom.

Despite his affluent upbringing, Gregory was an advocate of asceticism (extreme self-denial, abstinence, and austerity) and imposed his philosophy on Church leaders. He incorporated his experience as a monk to reform monastic training and practices, and his writings on education shaped views on apprenticeships and discipleship for centuries.

During the period in which Gregory was elected as Pope, Rome was experiencing natural disasters and barbarian invasions that left the region suffering from famine and plague. One of his first orders as Pope was to open the Church granaries to feed the starving population and establish a permanent system to help those in poverty. His administrative authority allowed him to fix failing aqueducts and raise the standards for public sanitation.

Gregory's experience as a formally educated administrator – and the absence of authority in the collapsing Roman Empire – allowed him to negotiate peace with barbarian invaders known as the *Lombards*. Where the Empire's policies had failed to bring a treaty, the Church's policies succeeded, and Gregory's influence and authority were widely accepted.

One of Gregory's achievements was the expansion of missionary work in Europe. During this period the inhabitants of Britain – Angles, Saxons, and Jutes – rejected paganism and converted to Christianity. A title he created for himself, "*the servant of the servants of God*," is still used by Popes today.

Chapter 03: *Planning for Victory with Lessons from History*

Anselm of Aosta (1033 – 1109 A.D.)

Anselm of Aosta, the Archbishop of Canterbury (modern day England), was a Christian theologian, philosopher, and accomplished author. Influenced by Augustine of Hippo, Anselm formalized the discipline of scholasticism, applied reason to understand and define faith, and considered theology to be "faith seeking understanding." After spending many years in France at a Benedictine monastery – during which time he wrote his two greatest philosophical works, *Monologion* and *Proslogion* – Anselm became the Archbishop of Canterbury in England. His theological and philosophical writings shaped the Christian doctrines of Christ as "God/Man" (Satisfaction Theory), and the existence of God (the Ontological Argument).

His reasoned explanation for Redemption (satisfaction) was based on the feudal system in which he lived; the price paid for transgression (sin) would increase proportionally to the rank of the offended. Since God's rank would never allow a sin to be paid in full by Man, Christ (God/Man) was needed to make the atonement (payment) for the trespass (sin) against the One offended (God). Anselm's *Satisfaction Theory of Atonement* replaced the earlier view of *Ransom Theory of Atonement* held by the Church and serves as the Redemptive model followed by modern Christianity.

Anselm is also credited for being the originator of the *Ontological Argument for the Existence of God*. The premise of his argument is as follows: Nothing greater than God can be imagined, therefore He must exist in reality; if He only existed in theory, a greater God could be imagined – a cycle that would continue forever. The reasonable conclusion to support the statement that "nothing greater than God can be imagined" is a God that exists conceptually (imagined) and materially (exists). His conclusion leads to three premises that state 1) God is the greatest conceivable thing, 2) God is not contingent; nothing contingent could be greatest, and 3) both premises make God necessary, and therefore a necessity, to existence. Philosophers have continually debated and challenged Anselm's position, the most notable being Christian philosopher Thomas Aquinas.

Chapter 03: *Planning for Victory with Lessons from History*

Thomas Aquinas (1225 – 1274 A.D.)

Thomas Aquinas, a Papal theologian, and University Regent (in modern day Italy), was a Christian philosopher, a Dominican Friar and a professor who advanced scholasticism in the Church's universities. Heavily influenced by the writings of Aristotle, he synthesized faith and reason, and founded the Thomistic school of philosophy. His teaching shifted Western focus from Plato to Aristotle and became the official doctrine of the Roman Catholic Church.

Aquinas' *Summa Theologica* (Theological Summary), a five-volume work consisting of more than 3,500 pages, written over the span of seven years, was created for students entering the clergy after university study. This comprehensive work, unfinished at the time of Aquinas' death, addresses a wide range of issues on the topics of God, ethics, and theology. Although it remained unfinished, enough content existed to form the foundation of the Church's doctrine.

One of the *Summa*'s most notable section, "*The Five Ways,*" presents five reasoned philosophical arguments for proving the existence of God. The five proofs – *unmoved mover, first cause, argument from contingency, argument from degree*, and the *teleological argument* – were written in opposition to Anselm's *Ontological Argument*. Aquinas believed Anselm's statement that "*nothing greater than God can be imagined*" was false, because the finite human mind couldn't perceive God's infinite nature directly. The fact that his doctrine became the official teaching of the Church speaks to its influence in the realm of philosophical thought.

The *Summa Theologica* also addressed many theological and philosophical issues that have become mainstream thought within modern Protestant Christianity. These issues include free will, teleology, moral objectivism, philosophical realism, and the immortality of the human soul. His arguments, based on reason and perception, won wide support over the *a priori* reasoning of his predecessors, which relied completely on theoretical (and therefore unprovable) deduction and conclusions.

Chapter 03: *Planning for Victory with Lessons from History*

Martin Luther (1483 – 1546 A.D.)

Martin Luther, a professor of biblical studies in Germany, was a reformer of the Church whose writings inspired the Protestant Reformation. He challenged the Church on its practice of selling indulgences – certificates absolving the purchaser from sin – and denounced the authority of the Pope's position. His experience as an Augustinian monk caused him to question the doctrine of the Church, and in 1517 he made his grievances publicly known by posting his *95 Theses* on the door of the Church in Wittenberg, Germany. Because of the invention of the printing press 40 years earlier, his document spread across the country within a few weeks. Luther was branded a "heretic" and excommunicated by the Church, and the Reformation began.

> *For in it the righteousness of God is revealed from faith to faith; as it is written, "The just shall live by faith."*
>
> ~ Romans 1:17 ~

Luther argued that justification was a gift of God's Grace resulting from faith alone; neither works nor the Church had the power to confer absolution from sin. He further argued that the practice of indulgences was not based in Scripture and interfered with true repentance by shifting focus from avoidance of sin to avoidance of punishment. Although the practice of indulgences fueled the debate with the Church, it was deviation from the truth of God's Word that inspired Luther to challenge the Church.

While Luther's actions are best known for inspiring the Reformation and creating the schism between Catholicism and Protestantism, their impact extend beyond theology and doctrine. His translation of the Bible from Latin to German brought God's Word to average citizens, advanced methods of translation, and assisted in standardizing the German language. His skill as a composer led to the writing of numerous hymns – currently sung in modern churches – and laid the foundation for music and singing to be incorporated into Christian worship services. Finally, the use of the printing press during this controversy ushered in a new era of media, messaging, and marketing for mankind.

Chapter 03: *Planning for Victory with Lessons from History*

John Calvin (1509 – 1564 A.D.)

John Calvin, a Christian theologian, and pastor in France, was a leader in the Protestant Reformation and the founder of Calvinism. He left the Church and became a Reformation leader in France, until persecution forced him to permanently relocate to Geneva, Switzerland. He was a prolific writer but is best known for *Institutes of the Christian Religion*, a 4-volume treatise addressing Christian doctrine and Reformed systematic theology. The final iteration has been translated into numerous languages and is still considered an authoritative text to be studied by theology students. Calvin supported the Reformation movement but rejected some of the doctrine embraced by Lutherans.

Calvin's Reformed Doctrine embraced the concepts of *predestination* and *election*: only some are chosen by God (election) to come to faith and receive the gift of Salvation. Man's "free will" was an illusion, removed because of Original Sin. The question of who is elected for Grace is unknowable, as the infinite nature of God and His purpose cannot be understood by Man. His doctrine also included the permanence of Grace – in response to the Church's teaching of meritorious works – to put at ease the minds of troubled citizens in France, which was predominantly Catholic, who broke from the Church to join the movement.

Calvin's Reformed Doctrine also shaped the structure of church government and discipline. He relied on Scripture to identify four elements of leadership – pastors, elders, deacons, and doctors – and built the governance of the movement around those positions. His model of church discipline reflected his support of the separation of Church and State, thereby limiting it to excommunication. It must be known that during the period in which Calvin was formulating his doctrine, the Church could extend its disciplinary measures to include civil and criminal penalties.

Although Calvin rejected greed and excess, he embraced the strong Protestant work ethic and capitalism, and preached that wealth was a just reward for those earning it legitimately.

Chapter 03: *Planning for Victory with Lessons from History*

Jonathan Edwards (1703 – 1758 A.D.)

Jonathan Edwards, a theologian, and revivalist pastor in Connecticut, has been credited by historians as being "America's greatest theologian." His education at Yale University and the influence of the Enlightenment inspired Edwards to synthesize faith and science in his philosophical writings. His leadership role in the First Great Awakening in the mid-1700's helped to fuel a spirit of Christian Revival that expanded beyond New England and into the remaining British colonies. Edwards is credited with writing eloquent sermons – the most notable titled *Sinners in the hands of an Angry God* – that fueled people's passions and sparked the first wave of revival.

Edwards played a significant role in bringing Calvinism to the Colonies, and his doctrine of "justification by faith alone," in combination with a "fire and brimstone" message, gained him both widespread acclaim and criticism. Tradition holds his message of predestination was so powerful that on more than one occasion, when attendees of revival meetings did not "feel moved by the Spirit," some would commit suicide afterwards believing they hadn't been elected for Salvation.

Edwards believed that faith in Christ was an intensely personalized experience, consistent with Enlightenment thoughts that placed primacy on individual liberty and freedom. He rejected the suggestion that reason could be used to make the nature of God known, and instead argued that the emotions and affections of the heart were the only way to know Christ. Even though Edwards was not a charismatic personality, his message began a trend of highly charged and emotionally driven worship services.

His writings on evangelical missions, based in part on his earlier experience evangelizing to Native American tribes through an interpreter, increased the awareness and participation in Christian missions, especially those conducted abroad. His legacy continues within the modern Body of Christ, as missionaries in several organizations are required to read his philosophy and apply it to their model of doctrine and practice.

Chapter 03: *Planning for Victory with Lessons from History*

John Wesley (1703 – 1791 A.D.)

John Wesley, an Anglican priest, and Christian scholar in England, was one of the principal founders of Methodism. It originated as a reform movement within the Church of England, and then evolved into its own denomination after his death. With the assistance of his brother, Charles – who is credited with writing almost 9,000 hymns – he blended superb organizational skills and a zealous approach to evangelical missions to bring the Gospel of Christ to millions of people across the globe. Although Methodism appealed to all levels of society, the movement gained initial momentum by directing its message to those on the margins of society.

Wesley's doctrine rejected predetermination, and instead stated that Salvation was available to all believers. He placed a specific emphasis on Sanctification (a progressive process), and its effects on Christian character. He also rejected the "fire and brimstone" that induced fear in the listener, choosing instead a message of joyfulness that accompanied true faith. His oratorical style was very charismatic, and the message of fulfillment and love was well-received by the population.

Wesley was an innovative reformer, a trait that propelled the movement's growth. His relationship with Calvinist reformer George Whitefield introduced him to "open air preaching," a radical concept for its time, allowed delivery of the message to thousands of listeners in every environment imaginable. This led to the creation of a lay ministry of itinerant pastors – accepted regardless of race or gender – that earned the respect and trust of average citizens. Wesley's doctrine of racial tolerance made Methodism the preferred denomination for slaves who, after emancipation, became leaders of the first "black churches."

Tradition holds that during his lifetime, Wesley preached more than 40,000 sermons and wrote more than 200 books. His efforts inspired the creation of the Salvation Army, a Methodist denomination that provides services to disadvantaged members of society. History also credits his brother, Charles Wesley, for introducing the musical worship seen today in modern services.

Chapter 03: *Planning for Victory with Lessons from History*

John Nelson Darby (1800 – 1882 A.D.)

John Darby, an Anglican pastor, and evangelist in Ireland, was a classically trained scholar and considered to be the "Father of Dispensationalism." Unlike the preceding influencers on this list, history records no record of him receiving formal theological education. Dissatisfied with the rigidity of the Anglican Church, Darby left his post to become the *de facto* leader of the Plymouth Brethren, an association of Christians that opposed the Church. The members were anti-denominational, anti-clerical, anti-creedal and followed a very conservative interpretation of Scripture. He is credited with authoring *The Darby Bible* which he translated himself from Greek and Hebrew texts, and several biblical commentaries that are currently being utilized in modern theological education.

Darby formalized the doctrine of dispensationalism, a system that teaches biblical history is best understood within the context of successive administrations of God's interactions with Man, called *dispensations*. His doctrine lists seven dispensational periods from *Genesis* to *Revelation* – Paradise, Noah, Abraham, Israel, Gentiles, Spirit, and Millennium - ending with the literal 1,000-year earthly rule of the Millennial Kingdom of Christ. He separated his doctrine from the Historical Premillennial view when he introduced the theory of *Rapture* in the 1830's.

According to Darby's End Times Doctrine – *Dispensational Premillennialism* – the Second Coming of Christ will happen in two stages. During his career, he travelled extensively in Europe, the United States, Canada, and Australia sharing his doctrine. Although Rapture Theory has been the subject of debate and criticism for many reasons, it received support and endorsement from several well-known evangelists. Afterwards, dispensational premillennialism became the view of many leading conservative evangelicals and fundamentalists and remains so in varying forms and degrees in modern Christianity.

His Rapture Theory also renewed the public interest in Bible prophecy, inspiring the book *Left Behind* by Tim LaHaye, and a movie series of the same name directed by Vic Sarin.

Chapter 03: *Planning for Victory with Lessons from History*

7 Benefits of Studying Historical Theology

The study of Historical Theology and Biblical History connects the Christian to Christ. The Bible uses genealogies to establish lineage, which establishes authority by birthright. As a Christian, you have been "born again" – grafted into God's Vine – and through the gift of Grace you will receive a birthright: an Eternal Life in God's Kingdom of Heaven with your Lord and Savior, Jesus Christ. Knowing the lineage of your divine "family tree" is meaningful, but what makes if practical? How will understanding how the Christian faith came to be help you make better decisions tomorrow, or lead you to a deeper relationship with God during the next worship service?

1. **Instruction replaces ignorance with truth**. Knowing the history is knowing the reality; it grounds Christians in fact. Assumptions – how it *may* have happened, or how it was *thought* to have happened – are an unstable platform for faith. When truth replaces ignorance, a foundation is created that's solid and unshakable, providing Christians the stability to grow and mature in their faith.

   > *They are darkened in their understanding*
   > *and separated from the life of God because*
   > *of the ignorance that is in them due to*
   > *the hardening of their hearts.*
   >
   > ~ Ephesians 4:18 ~

2. **Distinguish sound doctrine from false teaching**. The Christian faith, guided by God's Wisdom over time, has established sound doctrine (orthodoxy) and rejected false doctrines (heresy). Understanding *how* and *why* this came to be affords Christians the ability to better distinguish between the two. While it may be easy to identify patent falsehoods such as, "*Christ would approve of my drug habit,*" it is much more difficult to identify false teaching that contains an element of truth. External influences in our culture – and internal influences propagated by those who place personal gain over God's Word – have woven false

Chapter 03: *Planning for Victory with Lessons from History*

teachings into the Scripture that are believed (and quoted) by many. The saying, "*God helps those who help themselves,*" is a lie. God gave His only begotten Son because Man *cannot* help himself, and no amount of good works done by Man will *ever* change that.

> *For the time will come when people will not put up with sound doctrine. Instead, to suit their own desires, they will gather around them a great number of teachers to say what their itching ears want to hear.*
>
> ~ 2 Timothy 4:3 ~

3. **Past examples guide decisions in the present**. You read in previous pages how Polycarp, the Bishop of Smyrna, refused to renounce Christ to a Roman Proconsul even while being threatened with torture and death. If he had denied Christ, he would have lived. He did not, and he was burned alive at the stake. Modern Christians are facing increasing levels of pressure and hostility from secularists, and many young adults are choosing to leave the faith and conform to society instead of standing firm in Christ. Examples such as Polycarp can remind us to stand firm and strengthen our resolve.

> *For everything that was written in the past was written to teach us, so that through the endurance taught in the Scriptures and the encouragement they provide we might have hope.*
>
> ~ Romans 15:4 ~

4. **Protection from isolation and individualism**. The Christian faith is the Body of Christ, the "priesthood of believers," and the Word of God consistently reminds us we are "members of the Body." Interaction and fellowship reduce the opportunity for misinterpreting Scripture.

> For as the body is one and has many members, but all the members of that one body, being many, are one body, so also is Christ. For in fact the body is not one member but many.
>
> ~ 1 Corinthians 12:12,14 ~

Chapter 03: *Planning for Victory with Lessons from History*

5. **A guide to focus on the essentials of faith.** History reveals that despite theological differences, leaders in the past had the wisdom to focus on core essential teachings in agreement, while continuing to debate nonessential doctrine. That focus makes Christian fellowship cohesive.

> *Finally, brothers and sisters, whatever is true, whatever is noble, whatever is right, whatever is pure, whatever is lovely, whatever is admirable — if anything is excellent or praiseworthy — think about such things.*
>
> ~ Philippians 4:8 ~

6. **Perceive God's Truth in essential doctrine.** History reveals that despite differing interpretations of Scripture, leaders had the wisdom to be guided by the Holy Spirit and perceive core truths that Man couldn't challenge.

> *I appeal to you, brothers and sisters, in the name of our Lord Jesus Christ, that all of you agree with one another in what you say and that there be no divisions among you, but that you be perfectly united in mind and thought.*
>
> ~ 1 Corinthians 1:10 ~

7. **Identify immutable truths that form doctrine.** History reveals as the Christian faith matured; immutable truths were identified in God's Word that remained unchanged despite ecclesiastical difference. These truths are, and will continue to be for all time:

   - Scripture is the inspired, authoritative, true Word of God
   - God is eternally existing, as Father, Son, and Holy Spirit
   - Jesus Christ, the Son, is fully God and fully human
   - The Holy Spirit is fully God, and operates in our sanctification
   - The church is the people of God, the body of Christ, the temple of the Holy Spirit
   - We have hope in Christ for life after our death, Christ's return, and our resurrection

Chapter 03: *Planning for Victory with Lessons from History*

> *But you must continue in the things which you have learned and been assured of, knowing from whom you have learned them, and that from childhood you have known the Holy Scriptures, which are able to make you wise for salvation through faith which is in Christ Jesus.*
>
> ~ 2 Timothy 3:14-15 ~

A secondary benefit of studying biblical history and historical theology may not be as obvious as the seven listed above, but it is equally important – and it can save lives. Any Christian that's ignorant of truth, cannot discern false teaching, and develops heretical doctrine in isolation is a target for cults.

No one wakes up one morning and thinks to themselves, "*I think I'll join a cult today.*" No one searches Internet job boards with a heading that states, "Cult Members Wanted." Yet, many people end up in cults unknowingly, and many are *Christians*. How is that possible?

Primarily, they do not know God's Word because they do not spend enough time (if any at all), reading their Bible. They get their Scripture from a PowerPoint slide in a one-hour church service each week. They believe God's Word but are not adequately prepared to defend against the misuse of Scripture in false teachings.

They have no foundation built on historical theology to understand how heretical doctrine invades the Christian faith, how it is identified, and how leaders successfully defended the Body of Christ and eradicated it.

In the words of Martin Luther King, Jr., "*We are not makers of history; we are made by history.*" The greatest tragedy of any person joining a cult – especially a believer professing faith in Christ – is how easily it can be prevented. Combining the regular study of the Bible with biblical history and historical theology is meaningful, practical and a solid foundation for faith.

Chapter 03: *Planning for Victory with Lessons from History*

The Importance of Studying Biblical Languages

> *There are, it may be, so many kinds of languages in the world, and none of them is without significance. Therefore, if I do not know the meaning of the language, I shall be a foreigner to him who speaks, and he who speaks will be a foreigner to me.*
>
> ~ 1 Corinthians 14:10-11 ~

At a university in Georgia, a professor boldly proclaimed to his students, "*I can speak every language known to Man, except Greek.*" An exchange student from Tanzania, whose native language was Swahili, asked the professor (in Swahili) if he could speak the language. The professor replied, "*Nope, sure cannot. That's Greek to me.*" After a few chuckles the class moved on, but not before further adding to the Greek languages' reputation for being incomprehensible.

One does not need to be in Bible College or Seminary to appreciate the importance of biblical languages, nor must one be fluent in these languages to benefit from them. The original languages of the Old and New Testaments, Hebrew and Greek, can be of benefit to anyone who studies the Word of God. Why is this true, and what are the practical and immediate benefits?

The most critical consideration when approaching biblical study is *grammar* – not in translations – but in original languages of the Bible. A passage of Scripture *cannot* be interpreted in a way that the words in that passage do not support. This in no way suggests Bible translations cannot reveal God's Truth in languages other than Hebrew and Greek. However, limitations exist in Bible translations. This is not because of their quality, but the nature of the language itself.

An understanding of grammar in the original language can protect against misinterpretation and false teaching, but it can also provide a deeper understanding of God's Word as well. You can see the truth of this in the simple example below. In the Greek language, there are many, each expressing a different level of love. In this example, two words for "love" are used: *Agape* (divine and unconditional love), and *Phileo* (brotherly love). Read the Scripture below from John 21:15-17, a dialogue between Christ and Peter, and ask yourself, "*why was Peter saddened*"?

Chapter 03: *Planning for Victory with Lessons from History*

> So when they had eaten breakfast, Jesus said to Simon Peter, "Simon, son of Jonah, do you love Me more than these?" He said to Him, "Yes, Lord; You know that I love You." He said to him, "Feed My lambs."
>
> He said to him again a second time, "Simon, son of Jonah, do you love Me?" He said to Him, "Yes, Lord; You know that I love You." He said to him, "Tend My sheep."
>
> He said to him the third time, "Simon, son of Jonah, do you love Me?" Peter was grieved because He said to him the third time, "Do you love Me?" And he said to Him, "Lord, You know all things; You know that I love You." Jesus said to him, "Feed My sheep."

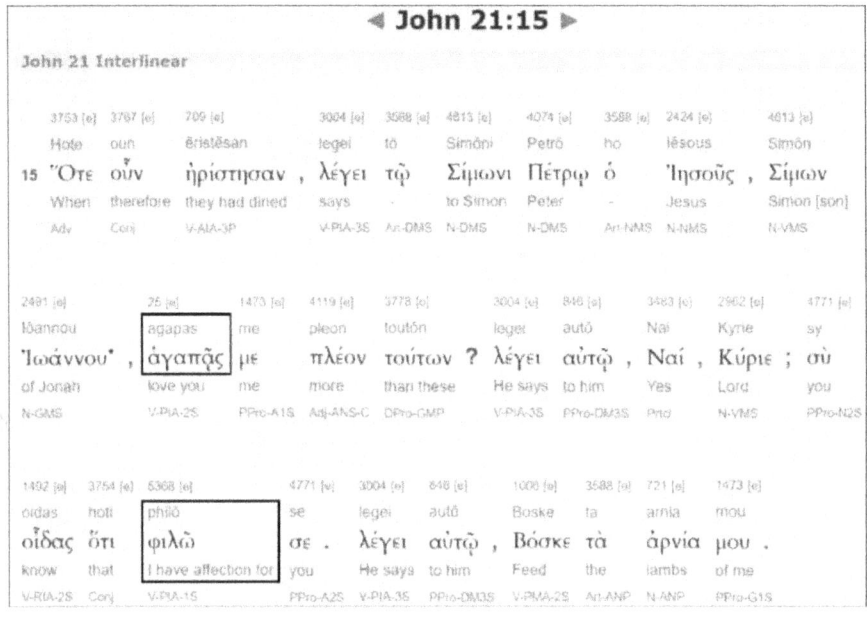

In the first exchange, Christ asked Peter, "*do you love Me*" (Agape), to which Peter replies, "*You know that I love You,*" (Phileo). The guilt Peter experienced from denying Christ three times was still evident.

Chapter 03: *Planning for Victory with Lessons from History*

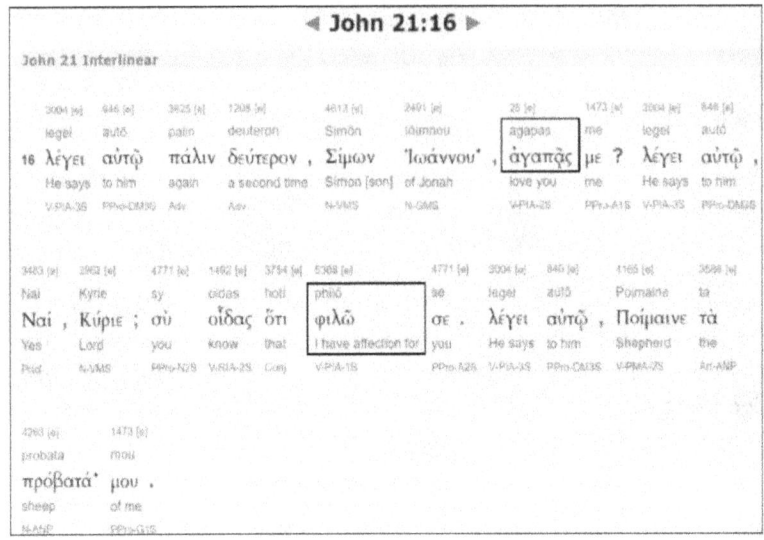

In the second exchange, Christ asked Peter, "*do you love Me*" (Agape), and Peter replies, "*You know that I love You*," (Phileo).

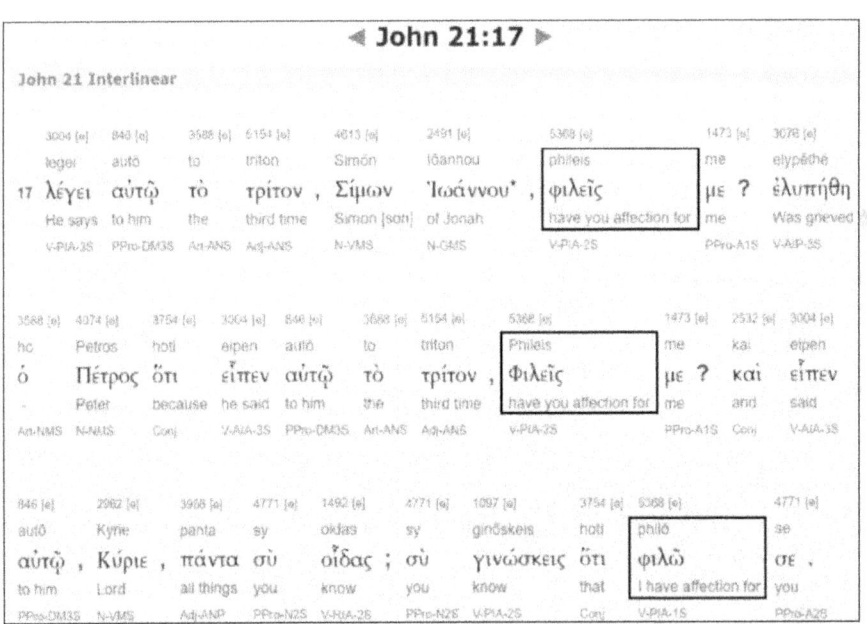

In the third exchange, Christ asked Peter, "*do you love Me*," only this time He lowered the level of the word used for "love" to *phileo*. So, why was Peter saddened?

Chapter 03: *Planning for Victory with Lessons from History*

First, the fact that Christ asked Peter three times about loving Him was a stark reminder to Peter of his three denials of Jesus at a critical moment when his faith was tested (*see* John 18).

> *So when they had eaten breakfast, Jesus said to Simon Peter, "Simon, son of Jonah, do you love Me more than these?" He said to Him, "Yes, Lord; You know that I love You." He said to him, "Feed My lambs."*
>
> ~ John 21:15 ~

Second, Christ called him by his true name (Simon), not Peter (meaning "stone" in Aramaic), causing him to self-assess his level of professed faith and commitment.

> *And I also say to you that you are Peter, and on this rock I will build My church, and the gates of Hades shall not prevail against it.*
>
> ~ Matthew 16:18 ~

> *He said to him again a second time, "Simon, son of Jonah, do you love Me?" He said to Him, "Yes, Lord; You know that I love You." He said to him, "Tend My sheep."*
>
> ~ John 21:16 ~

Finally, Christ changes the Greek word for "love" used in the dialogue from *agape* to *phileo*, to reveal to Peter the source of his wavering faith.

> *He said to him the third time, "Simon, son of Jonah, do you love Me?" Peter was grieved because He said to him the third time, "Do you love Me?" And he said to Him, "Lord, You know all things; You know that I love You." Jesus said to him, "Feed My sheep."*
>
> ~ John 21:17 ~

There are several teachings visible in this dialogue; some obvious, some subliminal, and some that could never be noticed unless the Scripture was read in the original Greek language.

Chapter 03: *Planning for Victory with Lessons from History*

Resources for Biblical Language Translation

Thankfully, there are several resources available for Christians who are passionate about studying the Word of God, but not seeking formal education in theological disciplines.

They are free to use (in their basic form), and easy to use. Several resources are listed below. The description provided by the resource was used, and their listing does not infer endorsement by the author.

BibleGateway (http://www.biblegateway.com/versions)

Bible Gateway is your rich social and personal connection to freely read, research, and reference Scripture on your desktop, laptop, tablet, smartphone . . . anywhere; in more than 200 versions and more than 70 languages!

BibleHub (http://biblehub.com/interlinear)

Bible hub is a production of the Online Parallel Bible Project. This project is privately owned and supported for the express purpose of sharing Bible study tools online. Most of our work is done by volunteers with an interest in using their technological skills to this end. Please see our contact page for additional information.

Bible Study Tools (http://www.biblestudytools.com/lexicons)

Our website offers Greek and Hebrew Interlinear for the New and Old Testament, lexicons for original Greek and Hebrew reading of Scripture, as well as popular Church history books. Use our gateway to free resources for quick verse search or to start a daily reading plan and study Scripture deeper with our library of tools.

Blue Letter Bible (http://www.blueletterbible.org)

Blue Letter Bible provides powerful tools for an in-depth study of God's Word through our free online reference library, with study tools that are grounded in the historical, conservative Christian faith.

Scripture 4 All (http://www.scripture4all.org)

The objective of Scripture4all (read "Scripture for all") is to make the original Scriptures accessible for a broad public by developing

Chapter 03: *Planning for Victory with Lessons from History*

tools to bridge the gap between the original Bible texts and Bible translations.

Chapter 03: *Planning for Victory with Lessons from History*

[THIS PAGE INTENTIONALLY LEFT BLANK]

Chapter 04

Defending Christ Against the Adversaries of God

"For the Lord your God is the one who goes with you to fight for you against your enemies to give you victory."

~ Deuteronomy 20:4 ~

Chapter 04: *Defending Christ Against the Adversaries of God*

Championing the Christian Faith in Modern Society

Faithful Christians are under spiritual and physical assault in our modern world, and their challenges are greater than at any other time in recent history.

Hostile religions, anti-faith ideology and politically correct governments are literally trying to destroy Christianity at its core. Concurrently, activists pursuing an anti-God agenda are attempting to rewrite the moral and ethical systems of our Western culture. The doctrine of the "separation of Church and State" has evolved into "Suppression of Church and Secularism of State," and contemporary Christians in the Body of Christ appear unprepared to stop the momentum of this movement.

> *If you were of the world, the world would love its own. Yet because you are not of the world, but I chose you out of the world, therefore the world hates you.*
>
> ~ John 15:19 ~

The external challenges faced by Christians are not limited to threats outside the faith; factions within the Body of Christ are having negative impacts as well. In a May 2016 interview with the Vatican's official news publication, *La Croix*, Pope Francis made the following statement in response to the reporters' question regarding Islamic terrorism:

> *"Today, I do not think that there is a fear of Islam as such but of ISIS and its war of conquest, which is partly drawn from Islam. It is true that the idea of conquest is inherent in the soul of Islam. However, it is also possible to interpret the objective in Matthew's Gospel, where Jesus sends his disciples to all nations, in terms of **the same idea of conquest***" (emphasis added).

The Pope, whether intentionally or unintentionally, claims a moral equivalency exists between Christ's Great Commission and the Islamic terrorists' goals of conquering Western culture and establishing an Islamic Caliphate. According to those words, a

Chapter 04: *Defending Christ Against the Adversaries of God*

group of students sharing the Gospel at a university is similar to radicalized men in black hoods, beheading non-believers on international television.

One of the solutions to this dilemma is training Christians in the art and skill of *Apologetics*. Christian Apologetics (ἀπολογία / *apologesia*) is a discipline of Christian theology that presents reasoned and evidential arguments for Christianity, defending it against objections. Why should Christians have an interest in this discipline? Because God's Word, the Bible, commands it.

> *But sanctify the Lord God in your hearts, and always be ready to give a defense to everyone who asks you a reason for the hope that is in you, with meekness and fear.*
>
> ~ 1 Peter 3:15 ~

The modern culture in which Christians live is a product of Enlightenment philosophies that qualify reason and evidence-based knowledge as *rational*, and faith as *irrational*. This thought has been elevated to such a position of primacy that Christian doctrines and beliefs have been barred from "rational discourse."

From a strategic perspective, it is the task of Christian Apologetics to develop and sustain a cultural environment in which the Gospel can be heard as a viable option, that can be intellectually reconciled, for rational men and women everywhere.

This reality is further complicated when well-intentioned Christian leaders make statements such as, "*No person has ever come to faith in Christ using intellectual arguments,*" as an argument against the need for Apologetics programs in all but Seminary programs.

That rationale is shortsighted, as it fails to consider the real condition of modern Christians and ignores the difference between necessity and utility.

While not necessary for the Gift of Salvation through faith in Christ – that is the sole responsibility and providence of the Holy Spirit – Apologetics is a powerful asset for demonstrating the *need* to have faith in Christ, and therefore provides substantial benefit.

Chapter 04: *Defending Christ Against the Adversaries of God*

The defense of Christianity is a responsibility shared by everyone professing faith in Christ as their Lord and Savior.

Disturbing Facts and Trends: CHRISTIAN ADULTS

The prevailing tendency in Christian churches is to assume that other members are better qualified, uniquely equipped and more mature in their faith to handle issues that entail defending the faith. The Pew Research Center (pewresearch.org / 2018) has gathered alarming statistics that clearly demonstrate why that assumption is incorrect.

- The number of self-identified **Christians** has **decreased 8%** in the last seven years
- The number of self-identified **atheists** has **increased 7%** in the last seven years
- **37%** of people who attend church every week and identify themselves as Evangelical do not give **any** money to their church
- **Fifty-six million** Americans do not observe **any** religion, the second largest community after evangelical Christians.
- An average of **47%** of the local church budget is spent on **pastors** and **programs**

Despite the best efforts of church leadership and the stated intentions of members, the real numbers reveal a frightening trend. These statistics are not addressing a problem in church participation, but adherence to the Christian faith itself.

Is it possible that believers are making a conscious decision that Hell is preferable to Heaven? A more likely explanation would be that a diluted, non-biblical *version* of the Christian faith – that is not providing answers to questions in a way that is meaningful – is leaving believers spiritually empty and asking the question, "*Why bother?*" That is a legitimate question, and the correct answer will dictate their eternal fate.

> *Inasmuch as these people draw near with their mouths and honor Me with their lips, but have removed their hearts far from Me, and their fear*

Chapter 04: *Defending Christ Against the Adversaries of God*

> *toward Me is taught by the commandment of men.*
>
> ~ Isaiah 29:13 ~

Disturbing Facts and Trends: CHRISTIAN YOUTH

The prevailing mindset of parents in Christian homes is to assume that their children, having grown up in church and exposed to the doctrines of faith, will continue in their walk with Christ after they "leave the nest." Researchers at Cross Examined (crossexamined.org / 2018) have statistics that prove why that mindset is incorrect.

- **70-75%** of Christian youth **leave the church** after high school
- More than **half** of **all** college professors view Christian students **unfavorably**, especially Evangelicals
- Most teenagers are **incredibly inarticulate** about their **faith**, and its place in their lives
- College professors are **five times more likely** to identify themselves as **atheists** than the general public
- The "**new** atheists" — Dawkins, Harris, and Hawking — are writing books and are growing in **popularity**

Christian parents are raising their children to profess faith in Christ and pursue fellowship with other believers with participation in worship services and church events. On the surface, it appears those actions would suffice.

The statistics prove otherwise. For many young adults, while they have been well-versed in *what* to believe, they have never been given an adequate understanding of *why* the doctrines they believe are true. Faced with anti-Christian hostility in a world that considers their view to be unpopular and irrational, they do not possess the resources to defend their faith properly.

It is easier to confirm to the world and "fit in" than it is to fight for faith, especially when the reasoning for the belief cannot be articulated.

Chapter 04: *Defending Christ Against the Adversaries of God*

> *But the ones on the rock are those who, when they hear, receive the word with joy; and these have no root, who believe for a while and in time of temptation fall away.*
>
> ~ Luke 8:13 ~

Disturbing Facts and Trends: CHRISTIAN PASTORS

The prevailing belief of active Christians is to assume their pastors are immersed in God's Word, strong in their faith, and beyond the "worldly needs" of non-theologians in their church. Into Thy Word Ministries (intothyword.org / 2018) has gathered statistical data, collected from practicing pastors, suggesting the prevailing beliefs are not grounded in fact.

- **75%** feel they are **unqualified** and/or poorly trained by their seminaries to **lead a church**
- **57%** said they would **leave the pastorate** if they had a better opportunity - including **secular** work
- **81%** said there was **no regular discipleship** program or effective effort of **mentoring**
- **1,500** pastors leave the ministry **each month** due to moral failure, spiritual burnout, or church conflict
- **72%** stated they **only studied the Bible when they were preparing for sermons** or **lessons**

Pastors have a variety of important tasks to manage in their church, and experience significant stress that many congregants never imagine. They are also human, a fact that is often missed, by members (and pastors themselves).

To believe the defense of the faith is the sole responsibility of pastors is to ignore God's Word and transfer a personal responsibility to a pastor who may be already overwhelmed. Imagine a church in which faith in Christ was so deeply entrenched, its pastor would be spiritually fed each week by the congregation, instead of the dynamic seen currently. It would be a church so biblically-grounded, so rooted in faith, and so confident of the Gift of Salvation from Christ that the defense of God's Promises would be a natural condition.

Chapter 04: *Defending Christ Against the Adversaries of God*

> *At that time many will turn away from the faith and will betray and hate each other, and many false prophets will appear and deceive many people. Because of the increase of wickedness, the love of most will grow cold.*
>
> ~ Matthew 24:10-12 ~

7 Benefits of Studying Biblical Apologetics

In *Acts 4*, the apostles Peter and John were arrested for preaching the Gospel of Christ to the people of Jerusalem. They were brought before a council of the Sanhedrin – leaders of the Jewish population with great authority – to face the High Priest Annas. The directive given to the apostles was clear: stop professing Christ or you will face severe penalties. Keep in mind these were the same officials that were responsible for the crucifixion of Jesus. Filled with the Holy Spirit, Peter boldly defended his faith in Christ.

> *But Peter and John answered and said to them, "Whether it is right in the sight of God to give heed to you rather than to God, you be the judge; for we cannot stop speaking about what we have seen and heard."*
>
> ~ Acts 4:19-20 ~

The two apostles received a few more threats but left the council unharmed, thanks to the Grace of the Holy Spirit and skill in Apologetics. As you read this Scripture in *Acts*, do not miss the more important message: *it was not the apostles who were on trial that day, it was Christ and His message.*

The Sanhedrin did not care about the apostles; they cared about the *message* they were sharing. They were not concerned with their preaching – it was normal practice within the Roman Empire to publicly share faith and philosophy – it was *Christ* that caused them concern. They wanted Christ – His teachings and His legacy – gone forever.

Chapter 04: *Defending Christ Against the Adversaries of God*

The benefits presented will assist individual Christians, but we do these things, not for us, but to defend and glorify Christ.

> *Whether, then, you eat or drink or whatever*
> *you do, do all to the glory of God.*
>
> ~ 1 Corinthians 10:31 ~

Obeying God's Word Establishes the Standard

The first obligation for any Christian is to obey God's Word. We are not free to selectively decide which commands to follow and which to ignore; every word in the Bible is divinely inspired, and all hold equal weight.

In *1 Peter 3:15*, God's instructions are clear: "*But sanctify the Lord God in your hearts, and always be ready to give a defense to everyone who asks you a reason for the hope that is in you, with meekness and fear.*" After years of research and study, students of the Bible have discovered the correct interpretation of this Scripture: it means **exactly** what it says in plain language.

The Bible is the inerrant, infallible Word of God, not a menu from which items are selected based on one's personal preference at that moment. In *1 Peter 3:15*, notice the words "always" and "everyone," default to a position of righteousness, and believe God means what He says, always, in all Ages.

> *For as through the one man's disobedience the many*
> *were made sinners, even so through the obedience*
> *of the One the many will be made righteous.*
>
> ~ Romans 5:19 ~

Obedience has an excellent precedent in the New Testament: Christ, Our Lord and Savior. Everything He said, taught and demonstrated was attributed to His Father in heaven. Christians cannot begin to discuss Apologetics – or progressive Sanctification, or becoming more "Christ-like," or maturity in faith – without first giving primacy to the message of obedience.

Chapter 04: *Defending Christ Against the Adversaries of God*

> *For I have not spoken on My own authority; but the Father who sent Me gave Me a command, what I should say and what I should speak.*
>
> ~ John 12:49 ~

During Jesus' earthly ministry, the Bible tells us He was followed by "multitudes" on several occasions. This happened because of what He did and said, not because of what He wrote or thought. Regardless of the calling in a Christian's life, the process starts with the individual prior to extending outward. To acknowledge the authority of Scripture and make a profession of faith is not enough; Christ expects us to establish His standard to successfully glorify Him in all we do.

> *But be doers of the word, and not hearers only, deceiving yourselves. For if anyone is a hearer of the word and not a doer, he is like a man observing his natural face in a mirror; for he observes himself, goes away, and immediately forgets what kind of man he was. But he who looks into the perfect law of liberty and continues in it, and is not a forgetful hearer but a doer of the work, this one will be blessed in what he does.*
>
> ~ James 1:22-25 ~

If you believe the Scriptures, the promises He makes for serving Him faithfully not only provide blessings to the doer of His Word, but to those around us as well. In *defending* the faith according to His Word, we obey His command and engage a world that needs His message. When Christians *walk* in the faith according to His Word, the unspoken testimony, observable to everyone, gives credibility to our verbal witness. It is been said that integrity can be defined as "*doing the right thing when no one is watching.*" To those who do not know it yet, someone is *always* watching. Admittedly, subjugating our human will to God is not easy, but Christ already told us that.

> *Enter by the narrow gate; for wide is the gate and broad is the way that leads to destruction, and there are many who go in by it. Because narrow is the gate and difficult is the way which leads to life, and there are few who find it.*
>
> ~ Matthew 7:13-14 ~

However, He *did* tell us it would be worth it.

Chapter 04: *Defending Christ Against the Adversaries of God*

> *Whatever you do, do your work heartily, as for the Lord rather than for men, knowing that from the Lord you will receive the reward of the inheritance. It is the Lord Christ whom you serve.*
>
> ~ Colossians 3:23-24 ~

Develop a Strong and Mature Faith

There is nothing more profitable for the development of a strong Christian faith than knowing and understanding the Word of God. Reading the Bible is the only way to know God's Word, and studying the Bible is the only way to understand it. It is impossible to defend something unknown, and difficult to defend something not understood. The discipline of Apologetics dictates by necessity a grounded knowledge of the Scriptures. This process does not require acceptance into Bible college; it begins in the Christian home, as early as possible. The benefits of a strong, mature Christian faith extend well beyond the physical borders of the individual.

The basics of Christian Apologetics can be learned at any age and should be studied by everyone. However, given the statistics provided previously – 70% to 75% of Christian youth leaving the church after high school – a special emphasis on exposing children to Apologetics training is warranted.

If parents are not actively and intellectually engaged with their faith, do not have reasonable arguments for Christian beliefs, and good answers to their children's questions, then Christianity runs the risk of losing its youth. It is no longer adequate to teach children Bible stories and memorize verses of Scripture. They need doctrine and Apologetics as the foundation of their faith in Christ.

Unfortunately, in many modern churches the Armor of God more closely resembles a wooden sword and a plastic helmet, rather than the spiritual armor described by Paul in Ephesians. Although the ship is off course, the Good News is that it can be righted easily with God's Word.

Chapter 04: *Defending Christ Against the Adversaries of God*

One of the challenges experienced by Christian youth is that of intellectually reconciling alleged "contradictions" in the Bible. Fortunately, there are no actual contradictions in the Bible; they can all be sourced to language translation error, lack of contextual analysis or misinterpretation on the part of the reader. For example, consider *Deuteronomy 5:16* and *Luke 14:26*:

> *Honor your father and your mother, as the Lord your God has commanded you, that your days may be long, and that it may be well with you in the land which the Lord your God is giving you.*
>
> ~ Deuteronomy 5:16 ~

This Scripture is the 5th Commandment, given to Moses by God on Mount Sinai. The fact that God directed this to be one of the Ten Commandments suggests He was serious about this topic in the Old Testament period. Now compare God's command to the Scripture found in *Luke 14:26*:

> *If anyone comes to Me and does not hate his father and mother, wife and children, brothers and sisters, yes, and his own life also, he cannot be My disciple.*
>
> ~ Luke 14:26 ~

These are the words of Christ, also God, speaking to the multitudes following Him, about the price they would have to pay to be His disciples. Do you see the issue here?

Imagine your child having a conversation with college professors – the same ones that are five times as likely to self-identify as atheists and admit they do not care for evangelical Christians – about the apparent contradiction and try to perceive the emotional stress.

Teacher: Do you believe God tells the truth, never lies, and never makes mistakes?

Your Child: Yes, I do.

Teacher: Do you believe the Bible is the inerrant, infallible, divinely-inspired Word of God?

Your Child: Yes, I do.

Chapter 04: *Defending Christ Against the Adversaries of God*

Teacher:	What would happen if God made a mistake, lied, or contradicted Himself in the Bible?
Your Child:	He could not. That is impossible.
Teacher:	Of course, it is. But for the sake of philosophical argument, if that happened, what would that make God?
Your Child:	Imperfect.
Teacher:	Correct. By definition, can God's Word be imperfect?
Your Child:	No, it cannot.
Teacher:	And if some imperfection were found in God's Word that revealed God to be imperfect, what would that make him?
Your Child:	Not God.
Teacher:	How do you explain the obvious contradiction we are both reading in these words?
Your Child:	I cannot, but there must be an explanation.
Teacher:	There is, and it is perfectly logical. Would you like to know what it is?
Your Child:	Yes, please.
Teacher:	You have been lied to; there is no "perfect God" or "infallible Word." You just proved that yourself. I just freed you from your bonds of ignorance – welcome to the real world.

That horrific scenario presents itself in universities every day, and accounts for the statistics regarding the exodus of Christian youth from the faith. The most troubling aspect of this exchange is it could have been avoided or, with proper training in Apologetics, used to discredit the teacher by exposing rampant use of logical fallacy and no real understanding of the Bible.

In a class of one-hundred students, that ability would have provided a powerful testimony for the Gospel of Christ.

Chapter 04: *Defending Christ Against the Adversaries of God*

Setting aside the logical fallacies in this dialogue, we will look at the alleged "contradiction," that is not a contradiction at all. It is a translation issue – Greek to English – resulting from the limitations of translators and the language itself.

The word "hate" in the original Greek language is **Μισέω** (mis-eh'-o). Greek words, like English words, have multiple meanings.

◄ **Luke 14:26** ►

Luke 14 Interlinear

1487 [e]	5100 [e]	2064 [e]	4314 [e]	1473 [e]	2532 [e]	3756 [e]	3404 [e]	3588 [e]	3962 [e]	1438 [e]
Ei	tis	erchetai	pros	me	kai	ou	misei	ton	patera	heautou
26 Εἴ	τις	ἔρχεται	πρός	με ,	καὶ	οὐ	μισεῖ	τὸν	πατέρα	ἑαυτοῦ*
If	any one	comes	to	me	and	not	hates	the	father	of himself
Conj	IPro-NMS	V-PIM/P-3S	Prep	PPro-A1S	Conj	Adv	V-PIA-3S	Art-AMS	N-AMS	RefPro-GM3S

Using a Greek Interlinear Bible (biblehub.com), one can identify the word (3404 [e]) and look up the definition(s).

◄ 3404. miseó ►

Strong's Concordance

miseó: to hate

Original Word: μισέω

Part of Speech: Verb

Transliteration: miseó

Phonetic Spelling: (mis-eh'-o)

Short Definition: I hate, detest

Definition: I hate, detest, love less, esteem less.

Does it translate as "hate"? Yes, but it also means "love less" and "esteem less," the proper translation given the context of Christ's teaching. Armed with the proper definition, review the Scripture in Luke 14:26 with new understanding.

> *"If anyone comes to Me and does not **love** his father and mother, wife and children, brothers and sisters, yes, and his own life also, **less than me**, he cannot be My disciple."*

Chapter 04: *Defending Christ Against the Adversaries of God*

Is there a conflict with loving your Creator more than anything in the World, even yourself? No, of course not. Does loving God more than parents contradict His 5th Commandment to "honor your father and mother"? No, of course not. Did Christ contradict the Father's Commandments when he spoke to the multitudes that day? No, of course not. This is but one of the hundreds of "contradictions" that do not exist in the Bible.

Additionally, one does not need to resort to understanding biblical languages if they understand the metaphorical context and intent. Compared to the infinite love God has for us, and the divine love (*agape*) we have for him, the most incredible worldly love that exists would look like "hate" in comparison. That is how infinitely great God's love is for all of us.

Given the facts as presented, one can see a series of tragedies in this scenario. First, a Christian student who is biblically illiterate is woefully unprepared to engage a teacher. Second, Christian students experiencing this type of exchange regularly are walking away from the faith to avoid confrontation and isolation. Third, the irony that a Scripture describing Christ's infinite love for the student is used by the teacher to turn the student away from Christ. In this case, if the Christian student chooses to join the 70% to 75% of students leaving the faith after high school, it is a proverbial "self-inflicted wound" that could have been prevented with an understanding of Apologetics.

> *As a result, we are no longer to be children, tossed here and there by waves and carried about by every wind of doctrine, by the trickery of men, by craftiness in deceitful scheming; but speaking the truth in love, we are to grow up in all aspects into Him who is the head, even Christ.*
>
> ~ Ephesians 4:14-15 ~

The benefits are not only immediate; they are long-term as well. One who stays in the faith grows in the faith, and with the understanding and foundation of God's Word, becomes strong enough in the faith to lead and defend others. A strong faith trusts God in all matters and does not let cycles of "seasons" alter the relationship with Christ. A mature faith is stable, balanced, and experiences the joy of inner-peace. One seeks fellowship, spiritual disciplines and sharing the Gospel for Christ's glory.

Chapter 04: *Defending Christ Against the Adversaries of God*

> *For I am convinced that neither death, nor life, nor angels, nor principalities, nor things present, nor things to come, nor powers, nor height, nor depth, nor any other created thing, will be able to separate us from the love of God, which is in Christ Jesus our Lord.*
>
> ~ Romans 8:38-39 ~

Confidence in Fulfilling Christ's Great Commission

When God commands Christians to obey His Word, they listen and try to submit. When the Bible tells believers to profess faith in Christ for the Gift of Eternal Salvation, they do so eagerly and rejoice. When Christ commands believers to evangelize – make disciples of all the nations – they hesitate. In many cases, they panic at thought of it. That response poses a problem for several reasons, not the least of which is telling God "NO" to a direct order, while being responsible for potentially consigning thousands of people to a fiery judgment in Hell in the process.

Does that claim sound overstated? It is not. First, look at Christ's words when He gave us The Great Commission.

> *Go therefore and make disciples of all the nations, baptizing them in the name of the Father and the Son and the Holy Spirit, teaching them to observe all that I commanded you; and lo, I am with you always, even to the end of the age.*
>
> ~ Matthew 28:19-20 ~

If one answers the Bible's call to defend the faith, they are obeying God's Word. To become proficient in Apologetics – the defense of faith – one must read, study, and understand God's Word. During this time, one develops a more intimate bond with their Savior, their faith becomes increasingly grounded and strong, and the Christian's level of spiritual maturity increases. While that may be personally enriching, it in no way acts on Christ's command, nor does it reveal the glory of God to non-believers that

Chapter 04: *Defending Christ Against the Adversaries of God*

need to hear the truth of Salvation. Some may believe that "evangelism" is not their gift or calling:

> *And He Himself gave some to be apostles,*
> *some prophets, some evangelists, and*
> *some pastors and teachers.*
>
> ~ Ephesians 4:11 ~

If your concept of evangelism is preaching to crowds of thousands in a football stadium, you may be correct about it not being your gift. That acknowledged, it would also be correct to state your concept of evangelism was *incorrect*. Sharing the Gospel is every Christian's duty and honor. It is a duty because God commands it; it is an honor in that it allows Christians to glorify the God of their Salvation. Sharing the Gospel does not have to be formal public speaking; informally sharing a testimony with friends and associates, in a one-on-one conversation, is how most Christians fulfill the Great Commission.

In some cases, a direct conversation is not required. For example, recall the dialogue between the teacher and your child. Only this time – because the child knew basic principles of Apologetics – the outcome changes significantly. For this example, assume the same scenario, using the same verses.

Teacher:	Do you believe God tells the truth, never lies, and never makes mistakes?
Your Child:	Yes, I do.
Teacher:	Do you believe the Bible is the inerrant, infallible, divinely-inspired Word of God?
Your Child:	Yes, I do.
Teacher:	What would happen if God made a mistake, lied, or ...
Your Child:	With all due respect, I know where you are going with this. I can prove to you no conflict exists in the Scripture and put this issue to rest quickly.
Teacher:	You think so?

Chapter 04: *Defending Christ Against the Adversaries of God*

Your Child: Yes, I do. The original Greek uses the word mis-eh'-o for "hate." It does mean that, but it also means to "love less" or "to hold in lower esteem." It is a translation issue based on lingual restrictions, not a contradiction as you suggest.

Teacher: I am going to have to verify that myself.

Your Child: I would encourage that. I would also respectfully suggest that a more in-depth study of the Word of God might reveal truths and insights that cannot be discovered when it is only read to prove God does not exist. You will also find that no contradictions exist in Scripture, the harmony of the Gospel is perfect, and the power of Christ's message of Salvation exists in the divinely-inspired Word of God we believers call the Bible.

Teacher: [Silence]

Be strong and courageous, do not be afraid or tremble at them, for the Lord your God is the one who goes with you. He will not fail you or forsake you.

~ Deuteronomy 31:6 ~

The child in this scenario just experienced three victories, the rewards of which may not be fully perceived immediately. First, a Christian that is strong in their faith will be continuing in their faith. Second, a teacher with an agenda will be changed forever – hopefully it results in a profession of faith in Christ – but if not, the teacher will think twice before walking into another field of spiritual landmines. Finally, the indirect witness given to the one-hundred classmates, who just watch a Christian boldly proclaim and defend their faith, may be just the gentle nudge several classmates needed to come to Christ for Salvation.

In fact, if 5 students in this class of 100 are led to Christ, that is wonderful. If those 5 students each lead another 5 people to Christ, that is a blessing. If each of those students each lead another 5 people to Christ, that is 3,750 souls saved from an eternal death. One Christian student with a knowledge of Apologetics, boldly proclaiming and defending their faith in front of 100 classmates.

Chapter 04: *Defending Christ Against the Adversaries of God*

Does that claim still sound overstated? It is not and that poses a dilemma. The potential exists, but a lack of biblical literacy almost guarantees that scenario only plays out rarely, if ever at all. Why should we care? Because when it comes to Salvation and the Great Commission, there is no "Plan B."

> *He who believes and is baptized will be saved; but he who does not believe will be condemned.*
>
> ~ Mark 16:16 ~

When discussing evangelism, a question that is frequently asked by Christians is, "*What happens to people who die without hearing the Gospel?*" That is a great question; it demonstrates the presence of compassion and conscience. The Bible does not speak to this issue directly but studying the Scriptures does provide an answer. Prior to addressing this emotional topic, Christians *must* know that God would *never* commit an act of injustice or impose an underserved judgment.

> *The Rock! His work is perfect, for all His ways are just; A God of faithfulness and without injustice, righteous and upright is He.*
>
> ~ Deuteronomy 32:4 ~

With that established to address the issue of "special exceptions" – such as infants, aborted fetuses, intellectually impaired, etc. – one can look to God's Word for answers and gain a newfound appreciation of the urgent need for sharing the Gospel and making disciples in all nations. Dr. David Platt, President of the Southern Baptist Convention's International Mission Board, and founder of the resource ministry Radical (radical.net) inspired the following points.

1. **All people KNOW God the Father**. Regardless of where people live on the planet, they sense the existence of a Creator. God has imprinted His knowability on the hearts of everyone and has revealed His Glory in the natural world of His Creation.

    > *For the wrath of God is revealed from heaven against all ungodliness and unrighteousness of men, who suppress the truth in unrighteousness, because what may be known of God is manifest in them, for God has shown it to them. For*

Chapter 04: *Defending Christ Against the Adversaries of God*

> *since the creation of the world His invisible attributes are clearly seen, being understood by the things that are made, even His eternal power and Godhead, so that they are without excuse.*
>
> ~ Romans 1:18-20 ~

2. **All people REJECT true knowledge of God the Father**. They feel more comfortable worshiping the creation, not the Creator, an act that leads to idolatry.

> *- because, although they knew God, they did not glorify Him as God, nor were thankful, but became futile in their thoughts, and their foolish hearts were darkened. Professing to be wise, they became fools, and changed the glory of the incorruptible God into an image made like corruptible man—and birds and four-footed animals and creeping things. Therefore God also gave them up to uncleanness, in the lusts of their hearts, to dishonor their bodies among themselves, who exchanged the truth of God for the lie, and worshiped and served the creature rather than the Creator, who is blessed forever. Amen.*
>
> ~ Romans 1:21-25 ~

3. **There are NO innocent people in the world**. There are those who behave better than others, but all humans are born with a fallen nature, and all of mankind has sinned.

> *What then? Are we better than they? Not at all. For we have previously charged both Jews and Greeks that they are all under sin. As it is written: "There is none righteous, no, not one; There is none who understands; There is none who seeks after God. They have all turned aside; They have together become unprofitable; There is none who does good, no, not one." "Their throat is an open tomb; With their tongues they have practiced deceit"; "The poison of asps is under their lips"; "Whose mouth is full of cursing and bitterness." "Their feet are swift to shed blood; Destruction and misery are in their ways; And the way of peace they have not known." "There is no fear of God before their eyes." Now we know that whatever the law says, it says to those who are under the law, that every*

Chapter 04: *Defending Christ Against the Adversaries of God*

> *mouth may be stopped, and all the world may become guilty before God.*
>
> ~ Romans 3:9-19 ~

4. **All people are CONDEMNED for rejecting God the Father**. Even if a person has not heard the Good News of Christ, they have still rejected knowledge of God the Father. When the question is asked, *"would God send someone to Hell just because they have not heard the Gospel?"*, the question can be asked, *"would God let someone into Heaven just because they have not heard the Gospel?"*

   If the answer to that question is "yes," what would be the worst thing a Christian could do? Share the Gospel. If a person having no knowledge of Christ was guaranteed a pass to Heaven – and a Christian shares the Gospel with them – that person must make a choice: profess faith in Christ or be condemned to eternal death. Not only does this concept contradict the Great Commission – and God does not contradict Himself – it is counterintuitive and not grounded in God's Word.

   > *Now we know that whatever the law says, it says to those who are under the law, that every mouth may be stopped, and all the world may become guilty before God. Therefore by the deeds of the law no flesh will be justified in His sight, for by the law is the knowledge of sin.*
   >
   > ~ Romans 3:19-20 ~

5. **God has made THE way for the Salvation of Man**. This is the core message of the Gospel, and the reason God sent His only begotten Son, Jesus Christ, to show us the way to God the Father. That is GOOD NEWS.

   > *But now the righteousness of God apart from the law is revealed, being witnessed by the Law and the Prophets, even the righteousness of God, through faith in Jesus Christ, to all and on all who believe. For there is no difference; for all have sinned and fall short of the glory of God, being justified freely by His grace through the redemption that is in Christ Jesus, whom God set*

Chapter 04: *Defending Christ Against the Adversaries of God*

> *forth as a propitiation by His blood, through faith, to demonstrate His righteousness, because in His forbearance God had passed over the sins that were previously committed, to demonstrate at the present time His righteousness, that He might be just and the justifier of the one who has faith in Jesus.*
>
> *~ Romans 3:21-26 ~*

6. **People cannot come to God apart from FAITH in Christ.** There are some Christians that find this fact to be unnerving; the thought of 1 BILLION people on the planet, who have never heard the Gospel, would be condemned to an eternal death. The initial emotional response tends to be, "there MUST be another way!" One might wish there was but consider for a moment what that wish would imply: Christ did not need to die on the Cross – there was another way the entire time. When one invalidates the necessity of the Cross, they have invalidated the basis of their faith in the process.

> *Where is boasting then? It is excluded. By what law? Of works? No, but by the law of faith. Therefore we conclude that a man is justified by faith apart from the deeds of the law. Or is He the God of the Jews only? Is He not also the God of the Gentiles? Yes, of the Gentiles also, since there is one God who will justify the circumcised by faith and the uncircumcised through faith. Do we then make void the law through faith? Certainly not! On the contrary, we establish the law.*
>
> *~ Romans 3:27-31 ~*

7. **Christ COMMANDS the church to make the Gospel known to ALL people.** Once Christ gave believers the Great Commission, that was a general command. He also gave Christians a specific plan – God's plan – instructing believers on the implementation of His command.

> *For "whoever calls on the name of the Lord shall be saved." How then shall they call on Him in whom they have not believed? And how shall they believe in Him of whom they have not heard? And how shall they hear without a preacher? And how shall they preach unless*

Chapter 04: *Defending Christ Against the Adversaries of God*

> *they are sent? As it is written: "How beautiful are the feet of those who preach the gospel of peace, who bring glad tidings of good things!"*
>
> ~ Romans 10:13-15 ~

Will professing faith in Christ bring Salvation? Yes. Will one who hears the message and believes call on Christ? Yes. Will God command that Christians be sent to share the Gospel? Yes. The one potential "weak link" in this plan – the one part that rests in the hands of people, not God – is the "preaching" mission given in *Romans 10:14*. If believers do their part of the mission, God handles everything else. Christ wanted believers to know that if the Gospel *stops* with us, it *dies* with us. There is no "Plan B."

The discipline of Christian Apologetics, boldly proclaiming and defending the Christian faith, has an impact that extends far beyond the believer. Armed with strong faith and the will to obey God's Word to make disciples of all nations – and knowing there are 1 billion lost souls that need to hear your voice sharing the Good News of the Gospel of Christ – you begin to understand how important your role is in God's Plan, and how one believer can impact the entire world.

> *I tell you that in the same way, there will be more joy in heaven over one sinner who repents than over ninety-nine righteous persons who need no repentance.*
>
> ~ Luke 15:7 ~

Reverse the Trend of Apostasy in the Church

Christians who believe they are living in the biblical End Times are watching for signs, such as the Antichrist, the "Mark of the Beast," and various signs revealed in Scripture. Is it possible that believers might be missing the most obvious (but least promoted) sign? It is apostasy, and the creation of the Apostate Church. A person is an apostate when – with full knowledge of the Gospel, and a full understanding of God's Word – they turn against Christ in a final act of rejection.

Chapter 04: *Defending Christ Against the Adversaries of God*

Disturbing statistics were presented earlier in this section about the percentage of Christian youth walking away from church.

Even more disturbing are the number of Christians that reject God's Word and *stay* in the church. In many cases, they are not congregants: they are *pastors*. God revealed to Christians this would happen – it is an absolute requirement for End Times.

> *Let no one in any way deceive you, for it will not come unless the apostasy comes first, and the man of lawlessness is revealed, the son of destruction.*
>
> ~ 2 Thessalonians 2:3 ~

How can Christian Apologetics be employed to combat this problem? A believer who studies and understands God's Word, and who's committed to obeying God's Word, is well-prepared to identify the signs of a person sliding into apostasy. The most obvious sign is rendering judgment on Scripture, independent from biblical history, historical theology, and Christian tradition. Left unnoticed and unaddressed, those who do not walk away from their church completely will infect the Body of Christ, like tares sown among the wheat.

> *And then many will be offended, will betray one another, and will hate one another. Then many false prophets will rise up and deceive many. And because lawlessness will abound, the love of many will grow cold.*
>
> ~ Matthew 24:10-12 ~

The Antichrist cannot operate freely in a world that is obeying the Gospel, and destroying the Christian faith directly is not an option. Satan has a plan to deal with this situation: dilute the faith of individual believers into a state of apostasy, infect the Body of Christ, and establish apostate churches with biblically illiterate members who remain unknowingly deceived. The only defense against this strategy is a knowledge of sound doctrine and a biblical interpretation of Scripture. Given the apostasy evident in many pastor's teachings, Satan would likely enjoy seeing an increase in Christian attendance at these churches. What are some characteristics of an apostate church?

1. Pastors are more concerned with a beautiful building and increasing church membership than teaching God's Word

Chapter 04: *Defending Christ Against the Adversaries of God*

2. Pastors deny established Christian doctrine: the deity of Christ, sufficiency of Scripture, authority of Scripture, etc.
3. Pastors accommodating requests from the church while knowingly violating God's Word in the process
4. Pastors supporting the ordination and marriage of homosexuals
5. Pastors not teaching why the Gospel is Good News: the bad news of sin, hell, judgment and eternal damnation

A true believer in Christ would be repulsed by these teachings and walk away from the church. An apostate would stay in the church and make more apostates. In the hands of faithful Christians who are true to God's Word, Apologetics is an effective tool to combat the infection of apostasy in the faith.

Combat the Teaching of False Doctrine

Reversing the trend of apostasy in the church is preventing believers from leaving the church completely because of "tares among the wheat." The task of combating false teaching requires the Christian believer to engage the source of the threat itself. This is done directly by identifying and revealing false teachers, and indirectly by equipping Christians to avoid the environments in which these teachers flourish.

The willingness to obey God, a thorough understanding of Scripture and a strong faith are the non-negotiable and critical components of a successful defense strategy.

> *But false prophets also arose among the people,*
> *just as there **will** also be false teachers **among you**,*
> *who **will** secretly introduce destructive heresies,*
> *even denying the Master who bought them,*
> *bringing swift destruction upon themselves.*
>
> ~ 2 Peter 2:1 ~

Two truths regarding the presence of false teachers are revealed immediately through God's Word. First, their existence is absolute; there *will* be false teachers, who *will* introduce

Chapter 04: *Defending Christ Against the Adversaries of God*

destructive heresies. Second, they are not outsiders; they are already *among you*, in the church. God knew humans would be no match for Satan on any level, so He gave us His divine protection through Christ, and a look into Satan's game plan through His Scripture as well.

The strategy is rather straightforward: the one in control, implementing the plan, is Satan, a master of deception.

> *No wonder, for even Satan disguises himself as an angel of light.*
>
> ~ 2 Corinthians 11:14 ~

Satan is also a counterfeiter. He cannot create anything, so he copies God to create a counterfeit gospel and false teachings.

> *I am amazed that you are so quickly deserting Him who called you by the grace of Christ, for a different gospel; which is really not another; only there are some who are disturbing you and want to distort the gospel of Christ.*
>
> ~ Galatians 1:6-7 ~

Satan then plants the counterfeit gospel in the minds of his false teachers. These false teachers will insert themselves in church congregations – or lead congregations – and intentionally deceive Christians with Satan's false gospel.

> *I know that after my departure savage wolves will come in among you, not sparing the flock;*
>
> ~ Acts 20:29 ~

If the false teachers are successful, their false gospel will create a new generation of false Christians. These deceived souls will be biblically illiterate, challenge the authority of Scripture, and reject the core beliefs of the Gospel of Christ.

> *They profess to know God, but by their deeds they deny Him, being detestable and disobedient and worthless for any good deed.*
>
> ~ Titus 1:16 ~

Chapter 04: *Defending Christ Against the Adversaries of God*

The false Christians then send their children into the world, to receive further false teachings from a secularist perspective (God does not exist, immoral behavior is OK, pride is required, etc.). The false secular message, mirroring the beliefs of false Christians, remains unchallenged and continues. This is not a situation in which a fellow Christian disagrees with a non-essential aspect of theological doctrine.

This is a situation in which deceived souls believe they are Christian (they are not), believe they are saved (they are not), and believe they will stand righteous in judgment before God (they will not).

> *And then I will declare to them, 'I never knew you; depart from Me, you who practice lawlessness!'*
>
> ~ Matthew 7:23 ~

How is it possible that well-meaning Christians, seeking a relationship with God, end up in this position? The answer is simple: people do not read God's Word. The deception remains because the culture does not know otherwise, and eventually it replaces God's Word as truth. Consider the following anti-Gospel deceptions many self-professed Christians believe to be true.

1. **God will not give you more than you can handle.** *Of course* He will give you more than you can handle; life is more than we can handle. If we could handle life on our own, we would not need Christ. We cannot handle it by ourselves, which is why God the Father sent Christ to an unsaved world – to allow us to have a relationship with God in which He handles it for us. This statement is false teaching and undermines God's Word.

2. **Bad things happen to good people.** Two issues arise immediately with this false teaching. First, Jesus Himself taught us there are no "good" people: *And Jesus said to him, "Why do you call Me good? No one is good except God alone"* (Luke 18:19). Second, to label something as "bad" – even if it appears to our finite minds to be so – is imposing our judgment on God's Will.

3. **God helps those who help themselves.** This false teaching is so anti-Gospel, it rises to the level of heresy.

Chapter 04: *Defending Christ Against the Adversaries of God*

Christ taught us to die to ourselves, and Salvation was a gift of Grace from faith alone. Every Christian has been blessed with gifts and talents, but they are to be used for His Glory, not ours. This message – *you start working first, and God will jump in when He thinks you have worked hard enough* – should **never** come out of a Christian's mouth.

4. **We are ALL God's children**. We were all created by God; that fact is undisputed. However, our relationship with God the Father is not by virtue of our existence. Our relationship with the Father is a result of our relationship with His Son: *For you are all sons of God through faith in Christ Jesus* (Galatians 3:26). When Christians make this statement, they are rejecting the necessity of the Cross.

These teachings are not harmless; they are anti-Scripture. If you did not know that, you now know how Satan deceives us.

There are a number of strategies Christians can employ to combat false teaching and teach others in the Body of Christ how to avoid this deception. It should come as no surprise that every strategy begins with the Bible.

1. **Study God's Word in the Bible**. Do not just read the Bible, study it. The Internet allows easy access to the writings, books and sermons of well-established Christians who are strong in their faith. Nothing replaces the study of God's Word, but access to credible leaders with the proper interpretation of biblical truth provides a significant asset to those who are serious about learning sound doctrine.

2. **Share God's Word with your family daily**. Parents whose faith is grounded in doctrine raise children whose faith is grounded in sound doctrine. Daily prayer, Bible study and devotionals strengthen the entire family, and allow the family's faith to mature together. If you do not have a worldly family with which to study the Bible, seek out your spiritual family instead: your Brothers and Sisters in Christ.

3. **Reveal false teaching to your family**. As knowledge and understanding of God's Word becomes established, expose others to false teachings that are commonly held by the culture. Stand ready to prove your message with Scripture,

Chapter 04: *Defending Christ Against the Adversaries of God*

and guide them through the process of how false doctrine enters Christian minds unknowingly.

4. **Devote yourself to fellowship in church**. Armed with the knowledge and understanding of God's Word, find a church that teaches biblical truth. Once found, immerse yourself (and your family) in fellowship with the Body of Christ. Being engaged with a church not only surrounds your family with support and collective strength, it offers the opportunity to help others as well. When parents are "doers of the Word and not just hearers," children see the example and are less likely to succumb to false teaching.

None of these strategies, practiced in isolation, will ensure no exposure to false teaching is experienced. When combined, however, they contribute to a solid foundation of sound doctrine and biblical truth. Regardless of the strategies employed, the best defense against false teaching is understanding God's Word.

Create Stronger Unity in Fellowship

The discipline of Apologetics requires a Christian to dive deeply into the Scripture, searching God's Word for revealed truth. Every time the Bible is read, a new truth is revealed. Once the truth of Christian doctrine becomes visible, new details begin to emerge on how to apply these truths to one's life.

Many Christians are surprised to learn the biblical truth regarding *fellowship*. The surprise does not stem from what the Word of God says it is but, once known, how it is currently practiced "in the church." Christian fellowship tends to be casual, and based around events such as a worship service or church dinner. God's Word reveals a startling truth: *it was never meant to be that way*.

> *They were continually **devoting** themselves*
> *to the apostles' teaching and to fellowship,*
> *to the breaking of bread and to prayer.*
>
> ~ Acts 2:42 ~

Chapter 04: *Defending Christ Against the Adversaries of God*

One would expect to see Christians *devoted* to teaching and prayer, but devoted to *fellowship*? This was not an activity to be casually enjoyed for one hour each week; it was a discipline that was passionately pursued and enthusiastically embraced. Per God's Word, it still *is* that discipline, even though the diluted brand of Christian faith experienced by most believers does not meet the standard. The Bible is very clear on the topic: being devoted to fellowship is commanded due to its critical role in maintaining unity in the Christian faith.

> *Only conduct yourselves in a manner worthy of the gospel of Christ, so that whether I come and see you or remain absent, I will hear of you that you are standing firm in **one spirit**, with **one mind** striving together for the faith of the gospel; in no way alarmed by your opponents — which is a **sign** of destruction for them, but of **salvation for you**, and that too, from God.*
>
> ~ Philippians 1:27-28 ~

Paul was telling the church at Philippi that unity in fellowship – one mind, one spirit, standing together – was a sign of Salvation to the Body of Christ. Equally important, it was a sign from God Himself to the opponents of Christianity of their guaranteed destruction. How can that be possible? The Scripture reveals Christ gave believers the answer when He prayed for His faithful elect in the Gospel of John.

> *I do not pray for these alone, but also for those who will believe in Me through their word; that they all may be one, as You, Father, are in Me, and I in You; that they also may be **one in Us**, that the world may believe that You sent Me. And the glory which You gave Me I have given them, that they may be one **just as** We are one:*
>
> ~ John 17:20-22 ~

Do not miss the two critical truths revealed in Scripture. First, the relationship Christians have with the Triune God is not proximal; there is no distance, no "God up there." Those who profess faith in Christ are **one in Them**, **just as** Christ was one with God the Father.

Second, the unity of Christian fellowship is such that we are to be one with each other, **just as** Christ and God the Father are one.

Chapter 04: *Defending Christ Against the Adversaries of God*

Why? So that Christian unity in fellowship would make the world believe that God had sent His only begotten Son.

The biblical truth of God's Word is clear. The unity of fellowship among believers is:

1. A commanded discipline to which we are to be devoted
2. A sign from God of Salvation for believers
3. A sign from God of destruction for opponents
4. The same level of unity that Christ has with God the Father

It is at this point that Christians look up from their Bibles, take a mental inventory of the fellowship practiced at church, and realize *something is not right*. What Christians grounded in biblical truth discover is what they are *seeing* does not match what they are *reading* in the Bible. When Scripture – the divinely-inspired, inerrant, infallible, timeless Word of God – is in conflict with the practices of modern Christianity, it is not the Bible that is wrong.

How does modern Christianity find its way back to biblical truth and standards? By reading and understanding God's Word, and redefining false perceptions commonly held by believers. In many gatherings, the pastor will say a prayer before having fellowship with a cup of coffee and a donut. However, the Bible says an aspect of fellowship is being devoted to prayer, to God and for each other.

> *For this reason I bow my knees to the Father of our Lord Jesus Christ, from whom the whole family in heaven and earth is named, that He would grant you, according to the riches of His glory, to be strengthened with might through His Spirit in the inner man, that Christ may dwell in your hearts through faith; that you, being rooted and grounded in love, may be able to comprehend with all the saints what is the width and length and depth and height — to know the love of Christ which passes knowledge; that you may be filled with all the fullness of God.*
>
> ~ *Ephesians 3:14-19* ~

Be honest: when was the last time someone prayed a prayer like this for their Brothers and Sisters in Christ? When Paul prayed for the Body of Christ in Ephesus, he was devoted and intent. A devotion to this level of prayer for each other is what a true reading

Chapter 04: *Defending Christ Against the Adversaries of God*

of Scripture demands. Modern society may make it difficult to attend special church functions, but it cannot inhibit our praise for God, or prayers for each other.

Military veterans that experience combat know their experience creates a sense of unity and loyalty rarely matched by other circumstances. They would sacrifice their lives for each other, but would we do the same for the Body of Christ, in the version of modern Christianity practiced today?

> *This is My commandment, that you love one another as I have loved you. Greater love has no one than this, than to lay down one's life for his friends. You are My friends if you do whatever I command you.*
>
> ~ John 15:12-14 ~

In the light of biblical truth, what can be said for attending a worship service for one hour per week, feeling uncomfortable about being "surrounded by people we do not know"? Given that mindset, following God's Word as outlined in *John 15:12-14* is not likely to happen. While that might seem a tad extreme, following God's Word and devoting oneself to fellowship *will* produce less dramatic, albeit equally important, results.

1. Christ's love becomes more visible to the world
2. Devotion demonstrates a reverence for Christ
3. Experience mutual support and encouragement
4. Benefit from the prayers of other believers
5. Apply the Grace of Salvation in service to others
6. The shared experience of Christ in a diverse group
7. Building a strong and mature Christian faith

That list represents only a few of the infinite number of benefits afforded the Body of Christ engaging in faithful service to God. When one understands the depth of the truth in God's Word, perspectives change. We come to understand that if "church" is a building – offering a variety of programs designed to attract members and build a congregation – Christians are simply consumers in search of the most appealing brand.

We come to understand that if "church" is a business – a marketing and messaging machine designed to increase our equity position in Christian market share – Christians are simply

Chapter 04: *Defending Christ Against the Adversaries of God*

competitors in a field with numerous players that must be defeated in order to allow the church to "win."

We come to understand that if "church" actually means the Body of Christ – our Brothers and Sisters with whom we are strongly united in biblical fellowship – Christians are a community of believers, and members of the same Body of which Christ is the Head. That is what Scripture, God's Word, is calling for all Christians to understand. It will be accomplished when believers become convicted, but before that happens, they need to be convinced. That requires reading and understanding the Bible.

From whom the whole body, joined and knit together by what every joint supplies, according to the effective working by which every part does its share, causes growth of the body for the edifying of itself in love.

~ Ephesians 4:16 ~

Replace Cultural Ignorance with Truth

Christianity is under assault on many fronts in our modern society. A liberal bias in the media perpetuates people of faith as "ignorant bigots." Professors in liberal universities have claimed as their mandate a responsibility to stamp faith out of the minds of their students. A politically correct culture is elevating the "separation of Church and State" to the "separation of Church and Life." Governmental agencies, hostile to the Christian faith, are using the courts to impose regulations that try to remove religious freedom from Christian-owned businesses. The role of Christian Apologetics in defense of faith – supported by a solid foundation of understanding in God's Word – seems to be obvious.

We are destroying speculations and every lofty thing raised up against the knowledge of God, and we are taking every thought captive to the obedience of Christ.

~ 2 Corinthians 10:5 ~

Chapter 04: *Defending Christ Against the Adversaries of God*

Recent scandals in Christianity have not helped the image of the faith. The very public (and very memorable) fall of several televangelists – such as Jim Bakker, Oral Roberts, and Jimmy Swaggart – have seriously undermined the public's perception of Christians. The acknowledgement of pedophilia in the Catholic Church – culminating with an apology from the Pope to affected families – cast Christianity in a very negative light. Despite these moral failures and the external forces listed above, the faith has prevailed.

While Christian Apologetics may be the obvious answer to the problem, the problem may not be as obvious as originally believed. Neither the external forces nor the occasional scandal explain the yearly decline in believers professing faith in Christ. Based on the statistics below, the same strategies used to create defenders of Christianity – who are knowledgeable in God's Word, strong in their faith, and united in biblical fellowship – may solve the problem of cultural ignorance before a strong defense is needed.

Researchers at The Barna Group (barna.com), a resource and research company considered to be a leading organization focused on the intersection of faith and culture, released results from several of their studies conducted in 2016. The results of these studies are terrifying and explain several of the problems plaguing the Christian faith in our modern culture.

- Fewer than half of all adults can name the four Gospels
- Many Christians cannot identify more than two or three of Christ's disciples
- 82 percent of Americans believe that, "*God helps those who help themselves,*" is a Bible verse
- 60 percent of Americans cannot name even five of the Ten Commandments
- 50 percent of high school students thought that Sodom and Gomorrah were husband and wife
- Many Americans believe that the *Sermon on the Mount* was preached by Billy Graham
- 12 percent of adults believe that Joan of Arc was Noah's wife

My people are destroyed for lack of knowledge. Because you have rejected knowledge, I also will reject you from

Chapter 04: *Defending Christ Against the Adversaries of God*

> *being priest for Me; Because you have forgotten the law of your God, I also will forget your children.*
>
> ~ Hosea 4:6 ~

When the *Book of Hosea* was written almost 2,740 years ago, the prophet was speaking against the widespread habit of engaging in religious ceremony, without a genuine commitment of the heart to serve God. It seems that history's unlearned lessons reappear to teach mankind what it missed the first time. When parents are not actively and intellectually engaging children in the truth of God's Word, and churches sacrifice Bible study to entertain congregants, the result will be alarmingly predictable.

> *But if the watchman sees the sword coming and does not blow the trumpet and the people are not warned, and a sword comes and takes a person from them, he is taken away in his iniquity; but his blood I will require from the watchman's hand.*
>
> ~ Ezekiel 33:6 ~

The Biblical Basis for a Well-Reasoned Faith

A modern, secularist culture argues that faith and reason cannot coexist; they are diametrically opposed. Faith, it is argued, is based on belief, not fact, and therefore irrational. The Bible is a collection of stories, believed because God commands it, accepted on blind faith by non-intellectual Christians.

Despite what secularists claim, does the Scripture demand unquestioned adherence to an irrational dogma, based on blind faith, apart from reason? Setting aside the assumptions of both secularism and *fideism* – "*God said it, that settles it, and I do not need any reason to back it up!*" – the wisdom of God's Word reveals His desire for Man to embrace faith and reason simultaneously.

> *The unfolding of Your words gives light.*
> *It gives understanding to the simple.*
>
> ~ Psalm 119:130 ~

Chapter 04: *Defending Christ Against the Adversaries of God*

God's Word speaks definitively on understanding and the use of reason throughout Scripture, and while divine wisdom is a gift God imparts to mankind through the Holy Spirit, it is not a license to forego the use of the Christian's mind. Our minds – finite, fallen and prone to ungodly thoughts as they may be – remain a necessary component in the process of coming to faith in Christ, and building the mature faith that is required to lead others to Him for their Salvation. A well-reasoned faith needs:

1. **Knowledge** of the Old Testament prophecies, and the facts surrounding Christ's birth, earthly ministry, death, burial, resurrection, and ascension
2. **Reasoning** to discern the meaning of those facts, and how they apply to the Salvation of fallen souls
3. **Confirmation** of the truth of God's Word, and agreement of the role this truth plays in Eternal Life and,
4. **Trust** in God's promise that Christ is Lord and Savior

Combining God's gift of reason with the discernment of the Holy Spirit allows us to boldly defend the Christian faith.

7 Logical Fallacies Used to Discredit Christian Testimony

In philosophy, a logical fallacy is a pattern of reasoning that is makes an argument invalid because of flaws in its logical structure. The ability to perceive these fallacies is critical to the discipline of Christian Apologetics. To have a thorough understanding of Scripture, and then have a powerful testimony "discredited" by false logic, is a missed opportunity to lead people to Christ. It is also preventable if one can recognize the structure of these arguments and how they are used. Listed below are seven common logical fallacies that serve as the foundation for many of the arguments Christians will experience when sharing the Gospel.

> *But examine everything carefully.*
> *Hold fast to that which is good.*
>
> ~ 1 Thessalonians 5:21 ~

Chapter 04: *Defending Christ Against the Adversaries of God*

1. **Argumentum Ad Hominem** (Attacking the Person)

    This is a logical fallacy in which an argument against a premise is made by attacking the person asserting the premise (character, motive, etc.) instead of the premise itself.

    > † Have you heard the Gospel of Christ?
    > ☺ No. Christians are judgmental bigots.
    > † That sounds judgmental, but it does not sound like the Gospel. I'll be happy to tell you why …

    The method for defeating this argument is to redirect the conversation back to the premise (the Gospel). Once a defense of the person (Christians) is advanced, the premise (the Gospel) becomes secondary.

2. **Ad Hominem Tu Quoque** (Hypocrisy Invalidates Truth)

    This is a logical fallacy in which an argument tries to discredit the truth of a premise by showing the person's failure to act in accordance with the truth of the premise.

    > † You shouldn't get drunk; the Bible says drunkards will not inherit the Kingdom of Heaven.
    > ☺ Thanks for sharing. Now, why were you so late for work this morning?
    > † I had a bad hangover; sorry about that.

    Christians do not invalidate the truth of God's Word by not living up to His perfect standards. We are all sinners with a fallen nature; that is the reason we need the Gospel for our Salvation. On a practical level, Christians who live biblically according to God's Word have a testimony that is more valid than those who do not.

3. **Argumentum Ad Ignorantiam** (Appeal to Ignorance)

    This is a logical fallacy in which an argument tries to discredit the truth of a premise by asserting a contrary argument is true because it has not (or cannot) be proven to be false. In this context, "ignorance" is defined as *a lack of contrary evidence*.

    > ☺ Evolution proves that Man originated from monkeys, not God.

Chapter 04: *Defending Christ Against the Adversaries of God*

- † What evidence supports that position?
- ☻ There is no scientific evidence that proves me wrong.

A lack of contrary evidence does not confirm (or invalidate) the truth of a premise. In the absence of absolute proof, an argument based on reason – showing the most probable explanation – is the best means for supporting the premise.

4. **Argumentum Ad Populum** (Proof by Majority Opinion)

   This is a logical fallacy in which an argument tries to discredit the proof of a premise by asserting a contrary premise is true because a majority believes it to be so.

   - ☻ I had sex with 10 different people last month.
   - † The Scripture teaches immoral behavior is a sin.
   - ☻ Everyone does it and no one cares. Your Bible is wrong.

   History is filled with examples of a majority of people believing a fact to be true, only to be proven false later by a minority later. Christ revealed that in *Matthew 7:13* when He taught: *"Enter by the narrow gate; for wide is the gate and broad is the way that leads to destruction, and there are many who go in by it."*

5. **Post Hoc, Ergo Propter Hoc** (Cause and Effect)

   This is a logical fallacy that assumes because an event occurred after another event, it must have occurred because of it. The flaw is the result of assuming a causal relationship instead of a sequential relationship.

   - ☻ Praying to God is a waste of time; He does not listen to your prayers.
   - † Why do you believe God does not listen to prayers?
   - ☻ I used to pray all the time before tests in school, but I still failed.
   - † Did you ever study?
   - ☻ If God listened to prayers, I shouldn't have to study.

   When cause and effect get confused – *"God does not listen because I failed my tests"* – correlation cannot logically prove causation. This type of reasoning is most obvious in arguments such as, "If God were "A," then "B" would (or would not) happen.

6. **Non-Sequitur** (Does Not Follow)

    This is a logical fallacy in which the conclusion does not logically follow from the premise of the argument.

    > ☺ All Christian pastors are greedy; all they care about is taking people's money.
    > † Why do you believe that?
    > ☺ The pastor I saw on TV bragged about his big house and fancy cars. Then he said, "If you send money to my ministry, God will bless you with the wealth you deserve."

    All truthful arguments must have a conclusion that logically follows from the asserted premise. This type of logical fallacy tends to be the foundation of over-generalization and is typically the easiest to recognize.

7. **Onus Probandi** (Burden of Proof)

    This is a logical fallacy in which the burden of proof for proving (or disproving) the truth of a premise is placed on the wrong side of the argument.

    > † Have you heard the Good News of Jesus Christ?
    > ☺ You Christians believe in an imaginary God that does not exist.
    > † What makes you believe God does not exist?
    > ☺ I do not have to prove anything to you. You are the one who believes in an imaginary God, not me.

    This type of fallacy assumes that the rejection of one premise does not need the affirmation of an alternative premise. Logic demands a premise rejected as truth must concurrently be affirmed as false. In this case, the person asserting the premise, "*God does not exist,*" has shifted the obligation to prove the asserted premise.

There are dozens of logical fallacies, many which fall beyond the scope of this writing. However, the seven fallacies presented

Chapter 04: *Defending Christ Against the Adversaries of God*

form the foundation for 90% of the arguments levied against the Christian faith.

> *"Come now, and let us reason together," says the Lord, "Though your sins are like scarlet, they shall be as white as snow. Though they are red like crimson, they shall be as wool."*
>
> ~ Isaiah 1:18 ~

In the next section, *7 Common Arguments Against God and Christianity*, try to find the fallacy (or combination of fallacies) employed to support the premise. Knowing these fallacies, and understanding how they are used, allows believers engaged in the discipline of Christian Apologetics to formulate preemptive strategies in advance. Remember: it is not you that is on trial, it is God, and His only begotten Son, Jesus Christ.

> *Prepare yourself and be ready, you and all your companies that are gathered about you; and be a guard for them.*
>
> ~ Ezekiel 38:7 ~

7 Common Arguments Against God and Christianity

There are several well-established arguments for the existence of God available to Christians, ontological, teleological, cosmological, and Christological, to name a few. All of them are sufficient to undermine irrational claims atheists use to "prove" that God does not exist. The atheist's argument proves to be nothing more than "a house of cards." In the words of Dr. Frank Turek, Christian Apologist and author, *"atheists have to sit on God's lap to slap Him in the face."* In the end, arguments formulated to disprove God must presuppose various elements confirming His existence.

The purpose of this section is to give readers an overview of common arguments directed at Christians sharing the Good News of Jesus Christ. It is also meant to encourage Christians to study

Chapter 04: *Defending Christ Against the Adversaries of God*

the topic in-depth, learn more, and take advantage of the vast amount of available resources in print and online.

1. **There is no evidence of God's existence.** Existence is evidence of God's existence, and arguments that attempt to disprove God as the originator fail to meet a logical standard. Despite their best efforts, all the atheists' arguments to explain the reality we experience must originate with First Cause. To suggest "everything has always existed" does not consider the constant change that is occurring in a unified and structured manner.

    To argue for an infinite amount of time in the past cannot be reconciled in a temporal space, as "today" – a finite point in time that is occurred – could theoretically never be reached given the infinite points in time that must precede it. Finally, ascribing existence to "chance" is a fallacy in the form of a categorical error: chance is a descriptor of statistical probability, not a cause in and of itself.

2. **If God created everything, what created God?** This question is frequently asked by those opposing the concept of God, but it fails to take into account the classical models of theism and leads only to infinite regression with no solution. The technical term for the solution to this objection is *efficient causality*, and it is based on the following model.

    All things need a cause to exist. If a person is playing the piano, the music that is heard is caused by the pianist. If the pianist stops, the music stops; everything (such as music) that exists calls for a cause to exist, separate from itself.

    If the chain of causes is regressed to nothing – the "No God" argument – then nothing could be caused and existence would be nothing. If that sounds irrational, it is. When the chain of efficient causation is regressed to its point of origin – given the choice between nothing and God – God is the only rational solution.

3. **God is not all-powerful if there is something He cannot do, which means He's not God.** This argument against God tends to begin with questions such as, "*If God*

Chapter 04: *Defending Christ Against the Adversaries of God*

is all-powerful, can He make a square circle? Can He "will" Himself out of existence? The Bible says He cannot be wicked, evil or lie. A limited God cannot be God at all."

This objection to God does not consider the Christian ontological view of God and one of its primary components: free will. God can do anything He chooses, which means He can choose *not* to do something as well.

The flaw in this line of reasoning is the misconception that if God *does not* do something, it is because He *cannot* do it. The truth is if God does not do something – resulting from His perfect free will – it is because He choose not to. A second flaw exists in the expectation that God would make an irrational choice.

Based on the order, structure, coherence and efficiency of our temporal environment – all a reflection of God's perfection and rationality – it would be illogical to expect God to act illogically.

Can God cause Himself to cease to exist, make a square circle or lie? Yes. However, that type of irrationality – now the exclusive providence of Man – would disrupt existence and reduce everything that is known into unknowable absurdities. Only a human being could ever be that absurd and be so brazen as to believe God would disorder the rational universe for amusement.

4. **Believing in God is the same as believing in fairy tales**. Fairy tales, regardless of origin, have a common denominator: they are created to amuse children, and have no value separate and distinct from that purpose. Trying to compare God to a fairy tale does not work for many reasons.

    First, fairy tales have no evidence – such as historical, bibliographical, textual, or experiential – to confirm they are anything but children's stories. Human history has evidence, including those listed above, that offers testimony to God's existence.

    The Christian ontological and theological systems provide value that extends beyond the words, in both temporal and eternal realms. Fairy tales were written *by* Man, *for* Man, for a *worldly* purpose; God is the divine inspiration behind all that is been revealed, spoken, and written about Him. Tinker Bell has never inspired acts of unimaginable bravery, martyrdom, or inspired the moral and ethical systems of nations.

Humpty Dumpty never shaped a human spirit, moved a person to compassion or freed a fallen soul from the sins of their past. This argument makes a better bedtime story for children than a valid objection to the existence of God.

5. **If God really existed, evil would not exist**. This argument fails at once and serves as a great example of "sitting in God's lap to slap Him in the face." Assumed in this argument is an objective standard of "good and evil," that transcends relative morals created by Man. If an objective standard for Evil exists – the basis for the objection – then an objective standard for Good exists as well.

   An objective standard for Evil that transcends time and circumstance, such as "torturing babies is wrong," must exist separately from Man. The same applies to an objective standard of Good.

   That attribute can only be attributed to God, and to apply the judgment of a finite mind on the actions of an infinite God is irrational. A stalk of wheat mourns the loss of "one of its own" during the harvest, without ever knowing it is part of a plan to feed starving children in sub-Saharan Africa. Assume that God decided to remove Evil (and its source) from existence right now. What would change?

   There would be no free will; what would be the need, if making the choice between right and wrong was removed?

   There would be no virtues, as all the opportunities to act virtuously would not exist. Why need courage in the absence of fear and danger? Finally, there would be no mankind, fallen and prone to sin. Do you believe Evil should have never existed? It is God's universe, He does things *His* way. You may have a better way, but *you* do not have a universe.

Chapter 04: *Defending Christ Against the Adversaries of God*

6. **Science has dismissed the need for God**. There are many that believe mankind invented the concept of God to answer questions science had not yet resolved. This is the "God in the Gap" argument: where there are gaps in knowledge, the concept of God gives an explanation until science discovers the "real" answer.

   Eventually, when science answers all the questions – or "fills in all the gaps" – there will no longer be a need for God. The flaw in this reasoning is science does not tell us anything; scientist do, and they filter data through their own perception and bias.

   Science cannot answer questions that are existential or philosophical, yet it is these non-scientific qualities of the human mind that drive scientific discovery. It is also non-qualifiable human traits that interpret the data. During the last decade, science has moved closer to proving the existence of God than disproving Him. Scientists widely accept the "Big Bang" theory as the origin of existence, a fact that supports *the ex nihilo* argument (something from nothing).

   They have also confirmed the outward expansion of the universe, acknowledging a beginning with the origin at the center. Science and God are not mutually exclusive, and the value of science is clear: it will fill the gaps in Man's faith until enough evidence exists to prove what Christians already know. God exists.

7. **Christianity originated in ancient times for ignorant people**. Christianity originated the Roman Empire, the most scientifically advanced culture on earth at the time. The invention of concrete led to innovations such as paved roads, architecture, aqueducts, and ship harbors, all of which needed advanced knowledge in mathematics and engineering. Roman astronomers gave society the 7-day week and solar calendar.

   Agricultural innovations included wheeled plows, grinding millstones, greenhouses, and genetic enhancement of crops through cross-breeding. These were the "ignorant people of antiquity" who came to faith in Christ in Jerusalem, a thriving and culturally-diverse metropolis of approximately 600,000 residents. They understood the science of procreation; why else would a Virgin Birth have been miraculous?

They had knowledge of medicine: how many diseases appear in the Bible, and why was Christ's healing power considered miraculous? This objection to God is rooted in ignorance and is easily defeated with a Bible and history texts.

Objecting to God: Atheists or Antichrists?

In the words of Sun Tzu, Chinese general and philosopher, "*Know thy self, know thy enemy. A thousand battles, a thousand victories.*" The Apologist preparing to boldly proclaim and defend the Christian faith would do well to heed this sage advice.

The Oxford Dictionary defines an atheist as "*a person who disbelieves or lacks belief in the existence of God or gods.*" To an atheist, the Father, Son, and Holy Spirit – along with fairies, leprechauns, and ghosts – do not exist. They are not real.

If silly "Bible Thumpers" want to waste their time in some fantasy land, let them. *Who cares; just leave me alone.*

> *Who is the liar but the one who denies that Jesus is the Christ? This is the antichrist, the one who denies the Father and the Son.*
>
> ~ 1 John 2:22 ~

Atheists do not hate God. They dislike the concept of God being "imposed" on them, but they cannot hate something that does not exist. This is important for Christians to know as they use the word "atheist" in their conversations.

A new movement is emerging that hates God and all He represents. They want Him removed from collective consciousness, sanctioned in public discourse, and banished from progressive society.

Chapter 04: *Defending Christ Against the Adversaries of God*

Supporters of this movement *are not* atheists, they are *antichrists*, and Scripture gives us a clear warning about them in advance:

> *For many deceivers have gone out into the world who do not confess Jesus Christ as coming in the flesh. This is a deceiver and an antichrist.*
>
> ~ 2 John 1:7 ~

If you are a general maneuvering military forces through a country, it helps to know if that country is friendly, neutral, or hostile. If you expect neutral, and encounter hostile instead, it will not end well.

The Oxford Dictionary defines an antichrist as "*a person or force seen as opposing Christ.*" Know the difference.

Chapter 05

The Priority of Prayer in the Christian Mission

"Do not deprive one another except with consent for a time, that you may give yourselves to fasting and prayer; and come together again so that Satan does not tempt you because of your lack of self-control."

~ 1 Corinthians 7:5 ~

The Right of Prayer in the Christian Mission

Chapter 05: *The Priority of Prayer in the Christian Mission*

Learning to Pray: It is Always the Perfect Time

Prayer is a spiritual discipline widely practiced by Christians during worship services, church events and in many Christian homes. However, while all believers acknowledge its importance, many are unaware of the role God intended prayer to serve in their lives.

Many Christians are hesitant to ask questions about prayer for fear of embarrassment, wrongly believing the answers should be "obvious" to them. Would one who spends years attending a church be comfortable asking the following questions?

1. *Why has no one ever taught me how to pray?*
2. *Is there a "right and wrong way" to approach prayer?*
3. *Does God hear me every time I pray?*
4. *Are there certain times I should pray during the day?*

These questions are valid, necessary, and the answers – from a biblical perspective – may not be as obvious as they seem. Those who grow up in church environment take for granted the way they practice prayer is the way God intended. Those who come to Christ later in life may not receive instruction on the role of prayer in a new believers' biblical life. If you grew up in a Christian home with parents that recognized the importance of prayer as a spiritual discipline – *Glory to God!* – the biblical insights presented in this chapter will allow for an increased understanding of the role of prayer in a Christian's life.

> *You, however, continue in the things you have learned and become convinced of, knowing from whom you have learned them, and that **from childhood you have known the sacred writings** which are able to give you the wisdom that leads to salvation through faith which is in Christ Jesus.*
>
> ~ 2 Timothy 3:14-15 ~

To answer any question about prayer, one must first understand the nature of the God to whom we pray.

Chapter 05: *The Priority of Prayer in the Christian Mission*

7 Scriptural Truths that Reveal God's Nature

As modern Christianity has moved away from its biblical roots – softening its message for broader appeal, and diluting God's Word to appease church members – the respect afforded to the Creator has diminished proportionally. Despite proclaimed reverence for God the Father, the actions and attitudes displayed by much of believers suggest they have a much different view of God than the image of Him portrayed in the Bible. Sermons preached from pulpits across America resonate with the message of God's love, mercy, and grace for mankind – an unquestionable, absolute truth – but neglect the attributes that cause us to fear and revere Him.

Contemporary art and culture portrays Jesus as meek and emaciated, with effeminate features, and a passion for hugging cuddly sheep. Christians that profess faith in Christ as Lord and Savior have a disturbing tendency to view Him as a genie in a bottle and fashioned in an image suitable to the individual needs of the believer. A comparison between Scripture and the views held by believers regarding Christ reveals a startling fact: *God takes Himself **much** more seriously than many Christians take Him.*

That proves to be problematic for several reasons. In the following pages, it will be clear that God's active role in the Christian's life, as it is throughout all of Scripture, is conditional and fluid. Nothing happens apart from God. Purposeful prayer appeals to God's Will to act, and prayer with the power to inspire God rests on a foundation of unshakable faith. That level of faith – which manifests supernatural and miraculous intervention – can only be achieved through fear and reverence of the King of kings, Lord of lords, and Creator of everything: Almighty and Holy God.

> *I am the vine, you are the branches; he who abides in Me and I in him, he bears much fruit, for apart from Me you can do nothing.*
>
> ~ John 15:5 ~

Chapter 05: *The Priority of Prayer in the Christian Mission*

The Power and Presence of a Holy God

Christians sleep well at night in the knowledge that God, who loved us so much He gave His only begotten Son to pay the debt for our sin, is listening to our prayers. *Proverbs 9:10* tells us, *"The fear of the Lord is the beginning of wisdom, and the knowledge of the Holy One is understanding."* In prayer, we have God's attention; take that seriously. Our God that forgives sin, gives Salvation, defeats Satan and creates everything is a God to be feared, and always respected.

1. **God dwells in unapproachable light**. Walking into a nuclear blast would instantly disintegrate a human body; the light, heat, wind, and power is unimaginable. Imagine the same experience in God's presence, but infinitely more powerful. A Christian's glorified body will reign with Christ in this Light. Being in the presence of God is no less serious to *Him* than the gift of Salvation is to *you*.

    > *He who is the blessed and only Potentate, the King of kings and Lord of lords, who alone has immortality, dwelling in unapproachable light, whom no man has seen or can see, to whom be honor and everlasting power.*
    >
    > ~ 1 Timothy 6:15-16 ~

2. **God's presence overwhelms the human mind**. Coming in the presence of a spiritual being, such as an angel, is a terrifying experience that overwhelms the finite human mind. When studying the Bible, one discovers many instances in which an angel encounters man, and the angel's first words are the same: *"Do not be afraid!"* How much more so the experience would be when it is God the Father.

    > *His head and His hair were white like white wool, like snow; and His eyes were like a flame of fire. His feet were like burnished bronze, when it has been made to glow in*

Chapter 05: *The Priority of Prayer in the Christian Mission*

> *a furnace, and His voice was like the sound of many waters. In His right hand He held seven stars, and out of His mouth came a sharp two-edged sword and His face was like the sun shining in its strength. When I saw Him, I fell at His feet like a dead man.*
>
> ~ Revelation 1:14-17 ~

3. **The angels that terrify Man tremble before God.** When angels come into the presence of God's Light, it so overwhelms them they must cover their body and face with their wings, turn their head away and proclaim, "*Holy! Holy! Holy!*" in fear and reverence. The fact that Christians will talk about "Guardian Angels" with honor and reverence, while at the same time taking the Lord's name in vain, is inexcusable.

> *I saw the Lord sitting on a throne, high and lifted up, and the train of His robe filled the temple. Above it stood seraphim; each one had six wings: with two he covered his face, with two he covered his feet, and with two he flew. And one cried to another and said: "Holy, holy, holy is the Lord of hosts. The whole earth is full of His glory!"*
>
> ~ Isaiah 6:1-3 ~

4. **God's power extends throughout Heaven.** When Christ revealed Himself to John in the *Book of Revelation*, there was much activity in Heaven. One can sense the energy in the text: everything was pulsating with the power of God. Even the spot where God sits – the White Throne of Judgment – emits lightening, thunder, and a host of heavenly voices. In front of the throne are seven lamps burning with pillars of flame. The unimaginable power of our omniscient God extends everywhere.

> *And from the throne proceeded lightnings, thunderings, and voices. Seven lamps of fire were burning before the throne, which are the seven Spirits of God.*
>
> ~ Revelation 4:5 ~

Chapter 05: *The Priority of Prayer in the Christian Mission*

5. **God's presence demands that you think before you speak.** In ancient times, a kings' son had access to the royal court and could speak freely with his father. Even so, hasty speech – such as insubordination, inappropriate demands, insults, and rebellious remarks – met with severe consequences. A son could face banishment from the kingdom, or face execution. In God's Kingdom, the first (banishment) results at once in the second (eternal death). Choose your words wisely in the presence of your Creator.

> *Do not be hasty in word or impulsive in thought to bring up a matter in the presence of God. For God is in heaven and you are on the earth; therefore let your words be few.*
>
> ~ Ecclesiastes 5:2 ~

6. **God demands full payment for promises.** When Man violates worldly vows, God's redemptive plan allows Christ to intercede on Man's behalf to God the Father. When Man violates vows to God the Father and Christ, who can stand in defense? God takes promises seriously – He never goes back on His Word – and He demands we honor promises made to Him.

   When Christians foolishly say, "*God, I promise I'll do __ if You do __,*" then do not keep their word once the trouble passes, rest assured He does not take that lightly. The trouble that prompts the impulse to make a hollow promise to God is temporary. The penalty for making an empty promise to God lasts infinitely longer.

> *When you make a vow to God, do not be late in paying it; for He takes no delight in fools. Pay what you vow! It is better that you should not vow than that you should vow and not pay.*
>
> ~ Ecclesiastes 5:4-5 ~

7. **God makes the choice between Heaven and Hell.** In the Roman Empire, an accused person facing judgment would stand in the Colosseum, surrounded by thousands of spectators waiting for Caesar to rule on their fate. If the Emperor gave a "thumbs up," the accused would live. If the

Emperor gave a "thumbs down," the accused would be put to death. In both cases, the verdict and sentence would be swift and carried out at once. The accused had no power or control over their fate and were at the mercy of Caesar. If that scenario sounds unnerving, consider standing before a Holy God in front of the White Throne of Judgment. Unlike Caesar, God the Father is just, merciful, and loving. Unlike Caesar's court, the accused are given representation – Christ Jesus – to act as an intercessor with God the Father.

Despite that assurance, be mindful of these truths. First, the verdict and sentence will be swift, and carried out at once. Second, you have no power or control over your fate. Only a fear and respect for God the Father, and a profession of faith in His Son, Christ Jesus, offer any hope on the Day of Judgment.

> *Do not fear those who kill the body but are unable to kill the soul; but rather fear Him who is able to destroy both soul and body in hell.*
>
> ~ Matthew 10:28 ~

Honesty Does Not Create Reality – It Reveals It.

Understanding the true nature of God does not change His relationship with us; His love, promises and gift of Salvation continues to be eternal and unchanging. However, it should change the relationship *we* have with *Him*.

In our worldly environment, the way we perceive those around us dictates the way we interact with them. If one wants to stay employed, it is wise not to curse at the CEO of the company. If one wants to stay married, it is wise not to lie to the spouse. If one wants to make friends, it is wise not to be insulting when first introduced to people.

If one wants a good relationship with the Creator, and keep communion with Him through purposeful prayer, it is wise to approach and treat Him in a manner worthy of His title: GOD.

Chapter 05: *The Priority of Prayer in the Christian Mission*

The Role of Prayer in Christian Life

To the apostles of the early church, prayer was not an obligation, ritual or requirement; it was the driving force behind every word spoken and action undertaken. Prayer was as much of a necessity as food, water, and oxygen.

Scripture teaches in Acts 2:42, *"They were continually devoting themselves to the apostles' teaching and to fellowship, to the breaking of bread and to prayer."* The early church knew they were dependent on God's power, purpose, and Grace.

> *"Is anyone among you suffering? Then he must **pray**. Is anyone cheerful? He is to sing **praises**. Is anyone among you sick? Then he must call for the elders of the church and they are to **pray** over him, anointing him with oil in the name of the Lord; and the **prayer** offered in faith will restore the one who is sick, and the Lord will raise him up, and if he has committed sins, they will be forgiven him. Therefore, confess your sins to one another, and **pray** for one another so that you may be healed. **The effective prayer of a righteous man can accomplish much**"* (James 5:13-16).

Modern Christianity has shifted its focus away from prayer as the central focus of worship services, replacing it with uplifting music, charismatic sermons, and PowerPoint presentations. The early believers viewed prayer as fundamental to their faith, while many Christians in America today view it only as a supplemental activity. Why should Christians living in Western culture – secure, affluent, and not lacking necessities – spend so much of their time devoted to prayer? The mindset needed to ask that type of question is evidence of how far believers have strayed from God's Word.

It is believed in certain circles that in the absence of the level of persecution experienced by the apostles, the priority of prayer is reduced. Beware of that theory's logical conclusion: if Christians will not pray without persecution, and Scripture teaches us to pray, God can arrange situations that guarantee prayer.

Chapter 05: *The Priority of Prayer in the Christian Mission*

Christians that embrace purposeful prayer as fundamental to their relationship with God have access to His blessings and intercessory power. Scripture reveals prayer to be the cause of every miraculous effect experienced by the early church. Every victory described in Scripture is the result of intentional prayers offered by righteous servants of God. Consider these examples taken from the *Book of Acts*:

1:4   The apostles and disciples gathered in the upper room of a home after Christ's Ascension. They are not planning, creating marketing materials, or writing sermons – they are continually devoting themselves to prayer. While they are praying, the Holy Spirit comes upon each of them.

2:41   They preach with boldness, speak in tongues, and on that day 3,000 souls came to Christ. Glory to God!

3:1   Peter and John are walking to the temple to pray, and they heal a lame beggar along the way. The people gather together in amazement, which gives Peter another chance to proclaim Christ as Lord.

4:4   They preach with boldness, and on that day 5,000 souls came to Christ. Glory to God!

4:24   Peter and John get arrested, then released, and return to tell everyone what happened to them. Upon hearing the news, everyone raised their voice and prayed to God for boldness with such devotion the room shakes.

5:19   An angel rescues the apostles from prison, and they go to the temple to preach Christ. Glory to God!

6:4   The apostles appoint deacons to handle administrative issues so they could stay devoted to prayer.

6:7   God's Word spread, the number of disciples increased daily, and many of the Jewish priests were professing faith in Christ. Glory to God!

10:9   Peter is on the rooftop praying, fell into a trance, and has a vision from God.

10:44   Gentiles receive the Good News of Christ. Glory to God!

These are but a few of the many examples that reveal a pattern in Scripture: *prayer precedes the growth of the church.*

Chapter 05: *The Priority of Prayer in the Christian Mission*

"Our Father": The Model for Christian Prayer?

Christians often recite *Our Father* (The Lord's Prayer) as part of their worship service. In some instances, pastors will direct believers to this in response to the question, "*How should I pray?*" Some Christians believe this prayer to be a requirement, while others argue using this teaching as a prayer violates the spirit of Christ's lesson to His disciples. This section will discuss both perspectives, and speak to the most important aspect underlying this issue: *what lesson was Christ teaching His disciples?*

> *"This, then, is how you should pray: 'Our Father in heaven, hallowed be Your name, Your kingdom come, Your will be done, on earth as it is in heaven. Give us today our daily bread, and forgive us our debts, as we also have forgiven our debtors. And lead us not into temptation, but deliver us from the evil one'"* (Matthew 6:9-13).

During His earthly ministry, the disciples asked Jesus to teach them *how* to pray. The Scripture above was His response, and His teaching became a corporate prayer most Christians can recite from memory. Arguments against the use of this Scripture as a corporate prayer originate in the preceding verse, *Matthew 6:7*.

> *And when you pray, do not use vain repetitions as the heathen do. For they think that they will be heard for their many words.*
>
> ~ Matthew 6:7 ~

When a congregation stands to recite this passage, in unison and from memory, most Christians are more concerned with matching the cadence of speech to those around them, than focusing on the words they are reciting. This reduces the prayer to the thing His message was teaching against - meaningless and vain repetitions. The intent of Christ's lesson was to teach His disciples *how* to pray, not *what* to say. Those who support this position argue that structured prayer, recited from memory,

Chapter 05: *The Priority of Prayer in the Christian Mission*

reduces His teachings to an exercise of religious, ritualistic display. The second challenge originates in the *Gospel of Luke*, in which Scripture presents a different account of the same event:

> *Father, hallowed be Your name. Your kingdom come. Give us each day our daily bread. And forgive us our sins, for we ourselves also forgive everyone who is indebted to us. And lead us not into temptation.*
>
> ~ Luke 11:2-4 ~

If God commands Christians to recite this passage as a prayer, which version should we use?

The argument in support of reciting *Our Father* (The Lord's Prayer) finds its origin in the *Book of Acts*:

> *They were continually devoting themselves to the apostles' teaching and to fellowship, to the breaking of bread and to prayer.*
>
> ~ Acts 2:42 ~

The foundation of this argument does not become clear until one reads the text in the original language (Greek):

◀ **Acts 2:42** ▶

Acts 2 Interlinear

1510 [e]	1161 [e]	4342 [e]		3588 [e]	1322 [e]	3588 [e]	652 [e]	2532 [e] 3588 [e]
ēsan	de	proskarterountes		tē	didachē	tōn	apostolōn	kai tē
ἦσαν	δὲ	προσκαρτεροῦντες		τῇ	διδαχῇ	τῶν	ἀποστόλων ,	καὶ τῇ
they were	moreover	steadfastly continuing		in the	teaching	of the	apostles	and -
V-IIA-3P	Conj	V-PPA-NMP		Art-DFS	N-DFS	Art-GMP	N-GMP	Conj Art-DFS

2842 [e]	3588 [e]	2800 [e]	3588 [e]	740 [e]	2532 [e]	3588 [e]	4335 [e]
koinōnia	tē	klasei	tou	artou	kai	tais	proseuchais
κοινωνίᾳ ,	τῇ	κλάσει	τοῦ	ἄρτου ,	καὶ	ταῖς	προσευχαῖς .
in fellowship	the	breaking	of the	bread	and	the	prayers
N-DFS	Art-DFS	N-DFS	Art-GMS	N-GMS	Conj	Art-DFP	N-DFP

Most English translations exclude the direct article ("the") from the text, leaving the impression the prayer life of the early church was unplanned and improvisational. While spontaneous prayer occurs throughout Scripture, it is clear structured prayer – most

Chapter 05: *The Priority of Prayer in the Christian Mission*

likely read and/or spoken in unison from the Old Testament – was an integral part of worship for the apostles and disciples.

The Value of Christ's Teachings on Prayer

Although disagreement about the application of this Scripture exists, most Christians would agree the value of Christ's teachings are clear. The focus must be on the importance of the Word, not the way it is spoken.

Jesus was teaching His disciples about prioritizing prayer, the relationship with God the Father, and placing the glory of Eternal Life above earthly needs. If you have never studied the text of this Scripture in detail, the following section should offer a deeper understanding of, and appreciation for, God's Word.

> *"Our Father who is in heaven, Hallowed be Your name. Your kingdom come. Your will be done, on earth as it is in heaven. Give us this day our daily bread, and forgive us our debts, as we also have forgiven our debtors. And do not lead us into temptation, but deliver us from evil. For Yours is the kingdom and the power and the glory forever. Amen"* (Matthew 6:9-13).

1. **Our Father who is in heaven**: There is no hesitation to address God as "Father" in modern Christian culture; it is a common occurrence believers take for granted. The model of prayer Jesus taught His disciples was radical for its day and considered by religious leaders in the Jewish faith to be heretical. The concept Jesus was teaching – *to have an intimate relationship with the Creator as His children* – provoked shock and awe. Pious Jews would not say God's name, or write it on paper, as a demonstration of their reverence.

    A High Priest would enter the innermost part of the temple once a year to act as a mediator between God and His people. Jesus rejects that and teaches His disciples to address God as "Father" (Ἀββᾶ / AH-bah). Imagine standing before God the Father – angels hiding their faces,

Chapter 05: *The Priority of Prayer in the Christian Mission*

unapproachable light, pillars of fire erupting in front of the White Throne of Judgment – and say to Him, "*Father, it is me, your child!*" Jesus taught His disciples the importance of intimate relationships, and the value they serve in God's redemptive plan. Those involved in an intimate relationship, who are madly in love, do not think about themselves. An intimate relationship with God overrides Man's self-centered nature. Man's values and priorities change in intimate relationships as well.

> *For you have not received a spirit of slavery leading to fear again, but you have received a spirit of adoption as sons by which we cry out, "Abba! Father!"*
>
> ~ Romans 8:15 ~

2. **Hallowed be Your name**: The word "hallowed" means *holy*, *revered*, and *sacred*. Christians understand God's name is holy, but the meaning behind Jesus' teaching go deeper. People's names are not just their identity; it speaks to their character and reputation as well. When believers protect their "good name," they are protecting character and reputation. When you profess faith in Christ and become a child of God, you become a part of an intimate relationship.

   Would you risk everything to protect the image, character, and reputation of a stranger? Maybe, maybe not; but what if that person was not a stranger, but your father instead? Intimacy changes many things. Intimacy with God the Father changes everything.

   > *You shall not profane My holy name, but I will be sanctified among the sons of Israel; I am the Lord who sanctifies you.*
   >
   > ~ Leviticus 22:32 ~

3. **Your kingdom come**: Jesus taught His disciples to pray for the Day of the Lord, Christ's Second Coming, and show through faith and deed they looked forward to it. Many Christians today are terrified of the "End Times," thinking only of the tribulation and not of the glorious Second

Chapter 05: *The Priority of Prayer in the Christian Mission*

Coming of Christ. When you pray these words, you are praying for the Day of the Lord. Have you done anything this week that you would not do standing before the White Throne of Judgment? The *Book of Revelation* gives all who profess Christ as Lord and Savior reason to look forward to that Day with hope and anticipation.

Christians whose faith is strong, and actions are righteous, should pray these words every day. As for everyone else, as the saying goes, *"be careful what you pray for."* God hears and answers the prayers of the righteous; just be aware of the meaning of the words you speak before God.

> Then the seventh angel sounded; and there were loud voices in heaven, saying, "The kingdom of the world has become the kingdom of our Lord and of His Christ, and He will reign forever and ever."
>
> ~ Revelation 11:15 ~

4. **Your will be done, on earth as it is in heaven**: Jesus taught His disciples there is a standard to live up during time spent in this world: *as it is in heaven*. That is a high standard to set and difficult to meet, but Christ had good reasons for these words. God's Kingdom is in heaven, Satan's kingdom is the world, and Scripture reveals in Luke 4:6 Satan has dominion over his kingdom: "And the devil said to Him, "I will give You all this domain and its glory; for it has been handed over to me, and I give it to whomever I wish."

When Christians subjugate their will to God, they bring glory to the Father. Their obedience also takes authority away from Satan in his earthly kingdom, a fact that drives him insane with rage. God's purpose for us is to join with Him in perfect accord. Until then, Christians can bring heaven closer to the world.

> And all the angels were standing around the throne and around the elders and the four living creatures; and they fell on their faces before the throne and worshiped God, saying, 'Amen, blessing and glory and wisdom and

> *thanksgiving and honor and power and might,
> be to our God forever and ever. Amen.'*
>
> ~ Revelation 7:11-12 ~

5. **Give us this day our daily bread**: It is difficult for Christians living in Western culture, especially those in America, the thought of going hungry. That was not the case 2,000 years ago, when meals were not guaranteed. The message of Jesus' teaching goes beyond food and speaks to total dependency on God for all things in life. It is easy for Christians to forget everything they take for granted can disappear in an instant; nothing in life exists apart from the gift and Grace of God's Will.

> *Therefore do not be anxious, saying, 'What
> shall we eat?' or 'What shall we drink?' or
> 'What shall we wear?' For the Gentiles seek
> after all these things, and your heavenly
> Father knows that you need them all.*
>
> ~ Matthew 6:31-32 ~

6. **And forgive us our debts, as we also have forgiven our debtors**. In this verse, Matthew uses the word "debt," while the *Gospel of Luke* (11:4) uses the word "sin." Many Christians are not aware those words are synonymous. God's Word is clear about forgiveness: "*For if you forgive others their trespasses, your heavenly Father will also forgive you*" (Matthew 6:14). However, believers do not always understand how critical Jesus' teaching is on this issue, and how it applies to their life. Imagine a world in which people have unlimited lines of credit, with no questions asked.

They spend recklessly, indulge every desire, and never consider consequences. Unexpectedly, a bill arrives demanding payment, and the person realizes they cannot pay the bill. That is how sin works in the lives of Christians. We accumulate debt (sin) we are never capable of repaying, and stare in horror when the bill arrives. Profession of faith in Christ paid your debts before the bill arrived and saved you from Hell.

Chapter 05: *The Priority of Prayer in the Christian Mission*

> *But because of your stubbornness and unrepentant heart you are storing up wrath for yourself in the day of wrath and revelation of the righteous judgment of God, who will render to each person according to his deeds:*
>
> ~ Romans 2:5-6 ~

7. **And do not lead us into temptation**: When Jesus taught this verse to His disciples, He was not telling them they would never face temptation. Jesus faced temptation in the wilderness for 40 days at the hand of Satan, and He prevailed. When Christians pray this passage, they are asking God to protect them from *giving in* to temptation; the ability not to *yield* to it. Everyone experiences temptation at some point in life, and it is unrealistic (and unbiblical) to ask God to remove it.

   God gives Man desires (good), and Satan tempts Man at the crossroads of his desires (bad). Satan and desires both serve God's purpose in this realm; they are here to stay until Christ's Second Coming. However, Christians can praise God knowing He will never cause them to yield to their fallen nature. God always gives His children a "way out."

   > *For since He Himself was tempted in that which He has suffered, He is able to come to the aid of those who are tempted.*
   >
   > ~ Hebrews 2:18 ~

8. **But deliver us from evil**: As said above, Christ taught His disciples the promises of God are eternal. He gives us a way to avoid yielding to temptation – if we choose to rely on His strength – which delivers us out of Satan's hands.

   > *But the Lord is faithful, and He will strengthen and protect you from the evil one.*
   >
   > ~ 2 Thessalonians 3:3 ~

9. **For Yours is the kingdom and the power and the glory forever. Amen**: There is no hidden message in this verse; it means what it says. Jesus taught His disciples to praise

the glory and honor of God in everything they did. After all you do – and before starting anything – thank God for His blessing and His presence in your life.

> *Now to the King eternal, immortal, invisible, the only God, be honor and glory forever and ever. Amen.*
>
> *~ 1 Timothy 1:17 ~*

The Right Way to Approach God in Prayer

Scripture reveals the importance of a proper mindset, and a proper condition of the Christian heart, when we come before God in prayer. It is not a matter of the words we speak, the posture we assume, or the place we choose to pray. The approach to prayer considers our reverence, obedience, and desire to do God's Will. The Bible provides clear instructions and examples for the believer to follow. It also reveals why the superficial approach to prayer promoted by many pastors – the "name it and claim it" method of prayer – is patently false.

> *Draw near to God and He will draw near to you. Cleanse your hands, you sinners; and purify your hearts, you double-minded.*
>
> *~ James 4:8 ~*

When Jesus taught His disciples how to pray, several basic premises were established as fact. First, they were desperate for God's Grace and the promise of eternal Salvation. Second, they had obedient hearts committed to serving God's Will. Third, they were dependent on God's Providence for everything in their lives.

Finally, they were consumed with the mission of joining Christ, and God the Father, in the Kingdom of Heaven. The thought of petitioning God for the things of the world – more money, fancier things, or elevated status – never entered into their prayer life.

Chapter 05: *The Priority of Prayer in the Christian Mission*

His disciples understood they had been created by God, in His image, to serve Him and glorify His name. This message is repeated throughout Scripture, yet some Christians still believe God is a genie in a bottle to be summoned for personal gain. This perspective underlies the doctrine of the "prosperity gospel," and teaches a false approach to prayer that weakens our ability to communicate with our Creator.

Instead of approaching God as a sinner, unworthy of His Grace and pleading for His mercy, we come with a list of self-centered demands with the hope of glorifying ourselves before Man. By adjusting perspective and subjugating our will to His, Christians have the opportunity to experience the power of God in their lives.

7 Components of Purposeful Prayer

When Jesus told His disciples in *John 16:23*, *"Truly, truly, I say to you, if you ask the Father for anything in My name, He will give it to you,"* they knew asking in His name **also** meant asking according to His Will. They also knew that asking according to His Will meant anything glorifying God. That point is often overlooked. That does not mean God will not provide for the benefit of individual Christians – He does – but only when the benefit serves to glorify Him at the same time.

Prayers to God can be structured or spontaneous, long or short, spoken or thought. Every Christian needs time each day to be alone with God's Word, and to communicate with Him. The seven components listed below are not a model for what to say, but are meant to be a guide – based on biblical example – for things to consider when communicating with your Creator.

1. **Focused Introspection**: Scripture teaches us to "think before we speak" (Ecclesiastes 5:2), and spending a few moments in quiet meditation allows us to gather our thoughts. A series of deep, controlled breaths – breath in *the Holy Spirit, breath out the world* – often helps to put the body and mind at peace before prayer.

Chapter 05: *The Priority of Prayer in the Christian Mission*

> *Let the words of my mouth and the meditation*
> *of my heart be acceptable in Your sight,*
> *O Lord, my rock and my Redeemer.*
>
> ~ Psalm 19:14 ~

2. **Deserved Exaltation**: Honoring God's presence and priority in your life acknowledges the reason you choose to pray. His omnicience, omnipresence and role as the originator of your existence are responsible for your faith, and complete dependency on Him for everything.

> *Worthy are You, our Lord and our God, to*
> *receive glory and honor and power; for*
> *You created all things, and because of*
> *Your will they existed, and were created.*
>
> ~ Revelation 4:11 ~

3. **Repentant Confession**: A prevalent theme throughout Scripture is approaching God with a spirit of humility and repentance. Repenting is not just apologizing; it is the act of confessing sin and turning away from it altogether. If one apologizes for sin, and continues to commit the same sin, any apology offered to God lacks genuine sincerity.

> *Have mercy upon me, O God, according to Your*
> *lovingkindness; According to the multitude*
> *of Your tender mercies, blot out my*
> *transgressions. Wash me thoroughly from*
> *my iniquity, and cleanse me from my sin.*
>
> ~ Psalm 51:1-2 ~

4. **Obedient Petition**: God will provide anything for His children, as long as they are consistant with His Word. Throughout Scripture, prayers that demonstrated an obedience to serve His Will and glorify His name are answered. In the process of answering those prayers, God provided worldly blessings as well.

A Christian who is indwelt with the Holy Spirit will not petition God in prayer for anything that undermines His Word. Imprecatory prayers – those that call for evil or a

Chapter 05: *The Priority of Prayer in the Christian Mission*

curse against a person – are not consistent with Christ's teaching and would not be considered obedient petitions.

> *If you abide in Me, and My words abide*
> *in you, ask whatever you wish, and*
> *it will be done for you.*
>
> ~ John 15:7 ~

5. **Thankful Recognition**: One of the most significant differences between God the Father and false gods of other faiths is His involvement in our life: He listens to, and answers, our prayers. Christians have many reasons to thank God and recognize the role He plays in our life.

> *Let them give thanks to the Lord*
> *for His lovingkindness, and for His*
> *wonders to the sons of men! For He has*
> *satisfied the thirsty soul, and the hungry*
> *soul He has filled with what is good.*
>
> ~ Psalm 107:8-9 ~

6. **Empethetic Intercession**: Scripture commands Brothers and Sisters in Christ pray for each other, and to pray for those that seek to cause us harm. Offering intercessory prayer for a person from a sense of obligation, without sincerity and empathy, is hollow and offensive to God. It is difficult to pray for someone you dislike.

However, you will discover over time that it is difficult to dislike a person for whom you pray. When genuine empathy is demonstrated for anyone seeking to cause you harm, the Holy Spirit becomes evident and God is glorified as a result.

> *Do nothing from selfishness or empty conceit,*
> *but with humility of mind regard one another as*
> *more important than yourselves; do not merely*
> *look out for your own personal interests, but*
> *also for the interests of others.*
>
> ~ Philippians 2:3-4 ~

7. **Glorifying Praise**: All Christians should include praise in their prayer life that calls for the glory of God to be known

to all nations. God the Father created Man in His image, for His purpose of glorifying Him. That is the reason we exist. Christians that pray for God's Word to be spread, the glory of His promises to be known, and the Salvation of souls through a profession of faith in Christ, are offering the type of prayer God responds to in miraculous ways.

> *For the earth will be filled with the knowledge of the glory of the Lord, as the waters cover the sea.*
>
> ~ Habakkuk 2:14 ~

There is no "right and wrong" way to pray to God the Father; He knows our thoughts and gives words to unspoken thoughts. However, Scripture reveals the way we approach our Creator – in heart mind, and spirit – does make a difference.

The Wrong Way to Approach God in Prayer

Are there times when God does not listen to our prayers? The instinctual response tends to be "NO," but a study of Scripture reveals otherwise. This is a sensitive topic for many Christians, and a difficult point to accept, given the "name it and claim it" mentality of diluted versions of Christianity. In instances in which God chooses not to listen to prayers, it is typically the result of improper mindset and misguided motivation. God warns double-minded Christians, whose actions betray their claims of faith, not to expect *anything* from Him.

That is important, and Christians need to be aware God takes His Word seriously.

> *But he must ask in faith without any doubting, for the one who doubts is like the surf of the sea, driven and tossed by the wind. For that man ought not to expect that he will receive **anything** from the Lord, being a double-minded man, unstable in all his ways.*
>
> ~ James 1:6-7 ~

Chapter 05: *The Priority of Prayer in the Christian Mission*

One of the most prominent charges non-believers make against Christians is the appearance of hypocrisy: quoting God's Word, but not following their own rules. Scripture reveals God does not care for hypocrisy either; Christians who practice this behavior experience negative impacts on their prayer life.

> *You husbands in the same way, live with your wives in an understanding way, as with someone weaker, since she is a woman; and show her honor as a fellow heir of the grace of life, so that your prayers will not be hindered.*
>
> ~ 1 Peter 3:7 ~

When Jesus taught His disciples "to ask, and they will receive," it was with the understanding their prayers would be consistent with His Will. Unlike believers in modern Christianity, His disciples knew it would be pointless to ask otherwise. Scripture reveals the motivation driving the prayer request is a factor in whether God answers prayers or ignores them.

> *When you ask, you do not receive, because you ask with wrong motives, that you may spend what you get on your pleasures.*
>
> ~ James 4:3 ~

One of the worst ways to approach God in prayer is through confidence in "good works." God's gift of Salvation is not given *by* good works, but *for* good works. The good things we do are an extension of our faith in Christ. However, placing too much confidence and trust in good works causes Christians to:

1. **Place appearance above righteousness**: Your outward appearance, including image and reputation, will mean nothing on the Day of the Lord. When Christ's pronounces His judgment, nothing will be hidden in your heart. Your faith and obedience to God will be all that matters.

> *Woe to you, scribes and Pharisees, hypocrites! For you are like whitewashed tombs which indeed appear beautiful outwardly, but inside are full of dead men's bones and all*

> *uncleanness. Even so you also outwardly appear righteous to men, but inside you are full of hypocrisy and lawlessness.*
>
> ~ Matthew 23:27-28 ~

2. **Compare themselves to Man instead of God**. The only standards that matter are those God sets for us; on the Day of Judgment, worldly standards do not matter. To compare our deeds against those in a fallen world serves no purpose. It will not be Man granting us Salvation.

   > *For we dare not class ourselves or compare ourselves with those who commend themselves. But they, measuring themselves by themselves, and comparing themselves among themselves, are not wise.*
   >
   > ~ 2 Corinthians 10:12 ~

3. **Glorify themselves and feel superior to others**. Pride is the primary sin, the sin that caused Satan to fall from Heaven, and a sin God refers to as an *abomination*. When Christians place too much faith in their good works, they risk the same fate as the Pharisee in this Scripture. While the Pharisee prayed, he referred to himself five times, and only referred to God once. That is not the kind of heart Christians want to have on the Day of Judgment.

   > *The Pharisee stood and prayed thus with himself, 'God, **I** thank You that **I** am not like other men — extortioners, unjust, adulterers, or even as this tax collector. **I** fast twice a week; **I** give tithes of all that **I** possess.'*
   >
   > ~ Luke 18:11-12 ~

4. **Place more faith in themselves than in God**. A cursory review of biblical history shows us what happens when Man elevates himself above God: *it never ends well for Man*. Christians live in a culture that not only promotes self-glorification, it considers it a virtue. The pursuit of self-gratification is natural, efficient, and instantaneous.

Chapter 05: *The Priority of Prayer in the Christian Mission*

Social media has become a mecca for Christians who choose to worship the newest idols: themselves. The accuracy of the Scripture below is disturbing, and clearly predicted the result of Man becoming a "lover of self," the sin that leads to all others that follow in the passage.

> *But know this, that in the last days perilous times will come: For men will be lovers of themselves, lovers of money, boasters, proud, blasphemers, disobedient to parents, unthankful, unholy, unloving, unforgiving, slanderers, without self-control, brutal, despisers of good, traitors, headstrong, haughty, lovers of pleasure rather than lovers of God, having a form of godliness but denying its power. And from such people turn away!*
>
> ~ 2 Timothy 3:1-5 ~

Even more disturbing than the accuracy of this Scripture is that Paul was referring to the Body of Christ, not unbelievers.

7 Reasons Why Christians Pray Every Day

Scripture reveals prayer was a vital and fundamental part of the early church. Although many churches offer Bible study programs, only a few offer "prayer study" programs to believers. Studying the Bible – the inerrant, infallible Word of God – is extremely important in Christian life.

However, prayer is equally as important, as both serve as lines of communication between the believer and God. Additionally, nothing strengthens a Christian's faith like having their prayers answered in a way only God the Father can make it happen. That said, there are seven reasons why Christians must make prayer a priority in their daily regimen.

1. **The Bible commands believers to pray**. God's Word instructs Christians to pray, every day, unceasingly and with intentionality. In many cases Christians only pray

Chapter 05: *The Priority of Prayer in the Christian Mission*

when there is a crisis and they are in trouble, not realizing the crisis may never have happened had they been in daily communication with God.

> *Then you will call upon Me and go and pray to Me, and I will listen to you.*
>
> *~ Jeremiah 29:12 ~*

2. **Christ Jesus, our role model, prayed regularly.** The Bible instructs us to grow in faith and become more like Christ. Scripture reveals Jesus prayed regularly and unceasingly, *"So He Himself often withdrew into the wilderness and prayed"* (Luke 5:16), which means we must pray in the same manner as He did.

> *Therefore be imitators of God as dear children. And walk in love, as Christ also has loved us and given Himself for us, an offering and a sacrifice to God for a sweet-smelling aroma.*
>
> *~ Ephesians 5:1-2 ~*

3. **Prayer is how we communicate with God.** Prayer is a two-way communication between the believer and the Creator, and we know from worldly experience when communication breaks down, things fall apart. If there is someone in your life you love dearly, would you refuse to speak to them for days, or even weeks? Consider how much more that applies to your love of Christ, the source of your faith and eternal Salvation.

> *Now this is the confidence that we have in Him, that if we ask anything according to His will, He hears us. And if we know that He hears us, whatever we ask, we know that we have the petitions that we have asked of Him.*
>
> *~ 1 John 5:14-15 ~*

4. **Prayer is how we take part in God's work.** Although God can do things on His own or through His angels, He tends to work through Man most of the time. The Bible teaches we receive instruction from God by way of the Holy Spirit, *"when He, the Spirit of truth, has come, He will guide*

Chapter 05: *The Priority of Prayer in the Christian Mission*

you into all truth" (John 16:13), and prayer is the way the Holy Spirit gives us our mission from God.

> *Most assuredly, I say to you, he who believes in Me, the works that I do he will do also; and greater works than these he will do, because I go to My Father.*
>
> ~ John 14:12 ~

5. **Prayer keeps us humble before God.** Scripture reveals pride to be one of the sins God hates most, and humility is one the virtues God exalts most. Kneeling before God, and professing dependency on Him, destroys our pride.

> *If My people who are called by My name will humble themselves, and pray and seek My face, and turn from their wicked ways, then I will hear from heaven, and will forgive their sin and heal their land.*
>
> ~ 2 Chronicles 7:14 ~

6. **Answered prayers strengthen our faith.** Scripture reveals God is the source of our strength, and prayer is how we communicate with Him. When a believers' prayer is answered, in a supernatural way only God could have made happen, our faith is strengthened significantly.

This can happen directly or indirectly; when we witness the prayers of other believers being answered, it serves as a source of strength and inspiration for the entire Body of Christ. The more we pray, the more opportunity exists to see prayers answered. Praying to God daily increases the potential to experience God's blessing exponentially.

> *I will worship toward Your holy temple, and praise Your name for Your lovingkindness and Your truth; For You have magnified Your word above all Your name. In the day when I cried out, You answered me, and made me bold with strength in my soul.*
>
> ~ Psalm 138:2-3 ~

7. **Prayer strengthens unity in fellowship**. Scripture reveals Christian fellowship is an integral part of healthy spiritual bonds. However, individual daily prayer strengthens unity as well. This benefit is supplemental, and not meant as an alternative to physical fellowship with our Brothers and Sisters in Christ. You read in an earlier section, *7 Components of Purposeful Prayer*, "empathetic intercession" is one of God's commandments.

When intercessory prayers are answered, and powerful testimony of God's blessing is known to everyone, the sense of unity within the body of believers grows stronger. Additionally, when Christians pray daily for unity within the church, God responds to the call. Those are the type of "obedient petitions" God wills us to pray each day for each other.

> *And let us consider how to stimulate one another to love and good deeds, not forsaking our own assembling together, as is the habit of some, but encouraging one another; and all the more as you see the day drawing near.*
>
> ~ Hebrews 10:24-25 ~

Biblical Fasting in Support of Purposeful Prayer

Fasting is a spiritual discipline and a critical part of prayer, yet it is ignored by many Christians in modern culture. Scripture reveals clearly the role and importance of fasting, and its power to change history when combined with prayer.

In *Matthew 17*, a father asks Jesus to heal his child after His disciples were unable to cast out the demon. Jesus rebukes His disciples and heals the child at once. The disciples, embarrassed and confused, ask Jesus why they could not heal the child. Jesus' answer was clear: "*But this kind does not go out except by prayer and fasting.*" These disciples loved God, obeyed Scripture and followed Jesus – the demon knew this – and yet, their prayers were insufficient for the task.

Chapter 05: *The Priority of Prayer in the Christian Mission*

Biblical fasting serves many purposes, the most important of which is humbling ourselves before God. It also shows self-discipline and spiritual dedication, both of which, the Bible tells us, get God's attention. It heightens spiritual alertness and prepares us to be more receptive to God's answer through the Holy Spirit.

It expresses a sense of urgency, conveying the message that we are so serious about engaging Him in prayer, we are willing to forego nourishment in exchange for His attention.

It increases our dependency on God, and places Him above everything else we need. If God's Word *did not* command us to fast, obvious benefits would inspire us to practice fasting anyway.

Some Christians believe Jesus never commanded His disciples to fast and set aside the practice as an Old Testament ritual that is no longer needed. Technically that is correct, but Jesus never commanded His disciples to breath either for the same reason: it was obvious to Christ they were going to do it without His instruction.

In *Matthew 6:5-6*, Jesus teaches His disciples how to approach prayer:

"When you pray, you are not to be like the hypocrites; for they love to stand and pray in the synagogues and on the street corners so that they may be seen by men. Truly I say to you, they have their reward in full. But you, when you pray, go into your inner room, close your door and pray to your Father who is in secret, and your Father who sees what is done in secret will reward you."

Jesus warns them against the incorrect way, *"When you pray, do not ...,"* then teaches them the correct way, *"But you, when you pray, ..."* Christ did not say *if*, He said *when*. It was a certainty His disciples were going to pray, just as Christians accept it today.

In *Matthew 6:16-18*, Jesus uses the identical structure and method to teach His disciples how to approach fasting:

"Whenever you fast, do not put on a gloomy face as the hypocrites do, for they neglect their appearance so that they will be noticed by men when they are fasting. Truly I say to you, they have their reward in full. But you, when you fast, anoint your head and wash your face so that

Chapter 05: *The Priority of Prayer in the Christian Mission*

your fasting will not be noticed by men, but by your Father who is in secret; and your Father who sees what is done in secret will reward you."

Jesus warns them against the incorrect way, *"Whenever you fast, do not ...,"* then teaches them the correct way, *"But you, when you fast, ..."* Christ did not say *if*, He said *when*. It was a certainty His disciples were going to fast. Believers that obey God's Word cannot deny Christ expects us to fast any less than He expects us to pray.

It is likely Christians committed to obeying God's Word, who do not practice, have not had the opportunity to study its biblical basis in Scripture. Many Christians also view fasting as an act of "suffering for God," instead of what it is intended to be: *the way to **destroy pride**.*

Everyone proud in heart is an abomination to the Lord; Though they join forces, none will go unpunished.

~ Proverbs 16:5 ~

Imagine standing before God's Throne of Judgment, and the Creator turns His face from you in disgust saying, *"You are an abomination to Me, I cannot stand the sight of you."* If you predict that meeting will not end well, you are correct. If pride can remove an angel from Heaven (Satan), how much worse will it be for us?

God hates pride, and His only begotten Son, Jesus, warned His disciples repeatedly in His teaching: *"For whoever exalts himself will be humbled, and he who humbles himself will be exalted"* (Luke 14:11). Most Christians know pride is a sin and pray to God for humility. What they may not understand is God does not "make" a believer humble; Christ tells His believers to humble themselves, and set the standard God uses to judge mankind.

And being found in appearance as a man, He humbled Himself and became obedient to the point of death, even the death of the cross. Therefore God also has highly exalted Him and given Him the name which is above every name.

~ Philippians 2:8-9 ~

In the original language of the New Testament, the Greek word **Ταπεινόω** (tah-pie-NAH-oh), has two meanings. It means *to*

Chapter 05: *The Priority of Prayer in the Christian Mission*

humble, when imposed on ourselves, and *to afflict as a discipline* (humiliate), when imposed on us by God. The same is true for the original language of the Old Testament.

The Hebrew word עָנָה (ah-NAH) means *to humble*, when imposed on ourselves, and *to afflict as a discipline* (humiliate), when imposed on us by God. Christ does not want the Father to impose that on His Children, so He commands us to impose it on ourselves.

> *Humble yourselves in the sight of*
> *the Lord, and He will lift you up.*
>
> ~ James 4:10 ~
>
> *Therefore humble yourselves under the mighty*
> *hand of God, that He may exalt you in due time.*
>
> ~ 1 Peter 5:6 ~

In *Leviticus 16:29-31*, God commanded His people to afflict themselves prior to the High Priest's offering on *Yom Kippur*, the holiest day in the Jewish religion. The Father made it clear His people would not benefit from the sacrifice if they did not meet His conditions first.

> "This shall be a statute forever for you: In the seventh month, on the tenth day of the month, you shall afflict your souls, and do no work at all, whether a native of your own country or a stranger who dwells among you. For on that day the priest shall make atonement for you, to cleanse you, that you may be clean from all your sins before the Lord. It is a Sabbath of solemn rest for you, and you shall afflict your souls. It is a statute forever."

Why would God command His people to afflict their soul? The soul controls our *intelligence* (**I** think), our *will* (**I** want), and our *emotions* (**I** feel). Humility removes our self-centered focus and turns our thoughts to God instead. When Christians fast, they humble themselves before God, and in the absence of pride God's miraculous intervention has changed the course of biblical history. Consider the following examples of the power of fasting and prayer listed below.

Chapter 05: *The Priority of Prayer in the Christian Mission*

Ezra 8:21-23

Ezra led thousands of Jewish people out of captivity in Babylon and guiding them back safely to Jerusalem to rebuild the city. Their travels took them through very dangerous territory and exposed them to high levels of risk. Ezra had to make a choice: trust the *world's* way, or trust *God's* way.

> *"Then I proclaimed a fast there at the river of Ahava, that we might humble ourselves before our God, to seek from Him the right way for us and our little ones and all our possessions. For I was ashamed to request of the king an escort of soldiers and horsemen to help us against the enemy on the road, because we had spoken to the king, saying, "The hand of our God is upon all those for good who seek Him, but His power and His wrath are against all those who forsake Him." So we fasted and entreated our God for this, and He answered our prayer."*

The Jewish people made it safely to Jerusalem and began the process of rebuilding their destroyed temple and city. That is how God responds to the power of fasting and prayer.

Esther 4:16

Although Jews could leave the land of their captivity and return to Jerusalem, many chose to stay and assimilate into the Persian culture. Esther chose to stay and eventually became Queen; her husband, the King, did not know she was Jewish. One of the King's high-ranking officers planned to have all the Jews in the kingdom exterminated, putting Esther and her family at risk. Esther had to make a choice: trust the *world's* way, or trust *God's* way.

> *"Go, assemble all the Jews who are found in Susa, and fast for me; do not eat or drink for three days, night or day. I and my maidens also will fast in the same way. And thus I will go in to the king, which is not according to the law; and if I perish, I perish."*

The Jews did not perish: the officer planning the mission was executed instead, and the King issued a decree exalting the Jewish people in the Persian kingdom. That is how God responds to the power of fasting and prayer.

Chapter 05: *The Priority of Prayer in the Christian Mission*

1 Kings 21:25-29

King Ahab was the wickedest king in the history of the Jewish people. He and his wife, Jezebel, provoked God's anger to such an extent that God planned to "utterly sweep him away" and destroy every generation of the king's family. God tasked the prophet Elijah with delivering His message to the wicked king. King Ahab had to make a choice: trust the *world's* way, or trust *God's* way.

> *"Surely there was no one like Ahab who sold himself to do evil in the sight of the Lord, because Jezebel his wife incited him. He acted very abominably in following idols, according to all that the Amorites had done, whom the Lord cast out before the sons of Israel. It came about when Ahab heard these words, that he tore his clothes and put on sackcloth and fasted, and he lay in sackcloth and went about despondently. Then the word of the Lord came to Elijah the Tishbite, saying, "Do you see how Ahab has humbled himself before Me? Because he has humbled himself before Me, I will not bring the evil in his days;"*

The wicked King Ahab, the person most deserving of God's wrath, avoided utter annihilation by trusting Elijah's message and subjugating his will to God's Will. That is how God responds to the power of fasting and prayer. It is clear from these biblical examples how we approach God in prayer is extremely important.

Fasting destroys our pride, puts our focus on God, and shows we are serious about our relationship with Him. As these examples show, *"With God all things are possible"* (Matthew 19:26).

7 Reasons Why Christians MUST Practice Fasting

In the *Gospel of Matthew*, we read an account in Chapter 26 of Jesus praying in the Garden of Gethsemane. He went there with His disciples to pray, but told them to stay in one location while He went *a little further*.

He instructed three of His closest disciples to come with Him, but then told them to stay in one location while He went *a little further*. Jesus' example

Chapter 05: *The Priority of Prayer in the Christian Mission*

of "leading from the front" is evident: *He always went a little further*. The spiritual discipline of biblical fasting, combined with prayer, shows your commitment to Christ and His example.

It is a way to tell the Father you are willing to go *a little further*. As you read the historical accounts in Scripture, you realize the benefits of fasting with prayer are temporal, as well as eternal.

1. **Fasting is a spiritual discipline**. Spiritual disciplines are acts of devotion that strengthen faith, increase spiritual growth and enhance the power of prayer. They show God you are serious about having a relationship with Him; it is experiential Christianity in action. Unlike "good works" seen in the world, the motivation behind fasting cannot be mistaken: it is all about God. It also serves as a test of spiritual resolve and self-discipline. If your will cannot exert its influence over your stomach, how can it exert influence over anything in your life?

    > *Whoever has no rule over his own spirit is like a city broken down, without walls.*
    >
    > ~ Proverbs 25:28 ~

2. **Christ expected us to fast**. Jesus knew fasting was a necessity, as did His disciples. With the exception of one Gentile (Luke), all of the divinely-inspired authors of Scripture were Jewish, and were adherents of the Law. In the lives of the apostles, fasting was as natural as prayer.

    > *And Jesus said to them, "Can the friends of the bridegroom mourn as long as the bridegroom is with them? But the days will come when the bridegroom will be taken away from them, and then they will fast.*
    >
    > ~ Matthew 9:15 ~

3. **Fasting extends God's blessing to others**. When Christians pray, they do not just pray for themselves. Intercessory prayer – praying for others – is how we bring the blessings of God to others in need of them. Fasting not only benefits the believers' relationship with God but invites Him into the lives of everyone who needs Him.

Chapter 05: *The Priority of Prayer in the Christian Mission*

> *So when they had appointed elders in every church, and prayed with fasting, they commended them to the Lord in whom they had believed.*
>
> ~ Acts 14:23 ~

4. **Fasting shows God we are serious about Him**. The Scriptures make it clear God takes Himself seriously, and He also takes His relationship with us seriously. When we are willing to forego nourishment – and tell God we are relying only on His sufficiency to sustain us – the Bible tells us God pays attention to our prayers.

> *"Now, therefore," says the Lord, "Turn to Me with all your heart, with fasting, with weeping, and with mourning."*
>
> ~ Joel 2:12 ~

5. **Fasting is a private act only God can see**. Scripture makes it clear that God rewards openly those who fast privately. No worldly motivation can exist for an activity known only be the believer and God. The righteousness of the believer's motivation is a force multiplier in prayer, increasing God's involvement in our life, and the chance to give Him the glory for it.

> *But you, when you fast, anoint your head and wash your face, so that you do not appear to men to be fasting, but to your Father who is in the secret place; and your Father who sees in secret will reward you openly.*
>
> ~ Matthew 6:17-18 ~

6. **Fasting makes us focus exclusively on God**. Many believers do not realize how much time they dedicate to food. Preparing meals, driving to restaurants, and thinking about food in between consumes a lot of time. Imagine spending that same amount of time focused on God, and then imagine the potential of your prayer life. Every time your stomach growls, it is a reminder to pray.

> *They reward me evil for good, to the sorrow of my soul. But as for me, when they were*

Chapter 05: *The Priority of Prayer in the Christian Mission*

> *sick, my clothing was sackcloth; I humbled myself with fasting; And my prayer would return to my own heart.*
>
> ~ Psalm 35:12-13 ~

7. **Fasting must be practiced in righteousness**. Fasting is a double-edged sword for the believer; if it is done with a proper heart it is rewarded, but it angers God if it is done for the wrong reasons. God sees and judges the hearts of His believers and fasting opens a wider channel between God and your heart. When a fasting believer prays, it catches God's attention, and He expects to see humility, righteousness, and dependency when He tests your heart. If He finds pride, selfishness or any motivation not aligned with His Will, your increased access will work against you.

> *Is this not the fast that I have chosen: to loose the bonds of wickedness, to undo the heavy burdens, to let the oppressed go free, and that you break every yoke? Is it not to share your bread with the hungry, and that you bring to your house the poor who are cast out; When you see the naked, that you cover him, and not hide yourself from your own flesh?*
>
> ~ Isaiah 58:6-7 ~

Christians pray to God with the hope He will go *a little further* for them. Fasting shows God we are grateful He answers prayers, and we are willing to go *a little further* for Him to prove it.

12 Tips for Successful Biblical Fasting

Maturing faith by practicing spiritual disciplines is like any activity in which we hope to become proficient: start slow, practice often and refine when necessary. We must make realistic assessments of our capabilities and limitations, while also considering our environmental conditions. Just as we do not rush into prayer with hasty words, we do not rush into a fast before planning. That requires self-discipline.

Chapter 05: *The Priority of Prayer in the Christian Mission*

1. **Honestly assess your physical condition**. If you have special needs or medical issues, do not ignore them.

2. **Determine the spiritual focus of the fast**. Why are you fasting? Having proper focus guides your prayer life.

3. **Determine the item(s) to be fasted**. What foods, fluids and activities will you forego during the fast?

4. **Establish a daily prayer schedule**. When will you pray, what Scripture will you read, and where will you do it?

5. **Only tell people that need to know**. Fasting is private, but those involved with your meal schedule need to know.

6. **Remove caffeine from your body slowly**. If caffeine is on the list, cut down slowly for weeks before fasting.

7. **Disconnect from non-essential people**. Fasting is a means to an end: time with God. Make the time count.

8. **Disconnect from non-essential media**. God does not answer prayers through social media or television.

9. **Post visual cues wherever practical**. Place notes with Scripture everywhere possible to motivate yourself.

10. **Manage your emotions and expectations**. Be aware fasting changes moods, and unrealistic goals fail.

11. **Determine how fasting will impact others**. If your job requires "meal meetings," plan accordingly and wisely.

12. **Be prayerful and focus on God constantly**. When not praying or reading Scripture, God is always on your mind.

NOTE: Consult a Physician Prior to Fasting

Regular fasting is not always without risk, even for healthy individuals. Some dietary recommendations are healthy to the majority of people but potentially harmful to others. You should always consult with a physician or healthcare provider before beginning any long-term fasting regimen.

Chapter 05: *The Priority of Prayer in the Christian Mission*

[THIS PAGE WAS LEFT INTENTIONALLY BLANK]

Chapter 06

Forging Spiritual Strength with Testing and Trials

"Behold, I have refined you, but not as silver; I have tested you in the furnace of affliction."

~ Isaiah 48:10 ~

Chapter 06: *Forging Spiritual Strength with Testing and Trials*

Discerning the Sources of Testing and Trials

All Christians believe in God; they profess Jesus Christ as their Lord and Savior. Most Christians believe in Hell and Satan, although modern worship services tend to avoid discussing the topic, favoring instead sermons that focus on "positive messaging." Few Christians believe in the active, ongoing presence of spiritual warfare in their lives. When the term *spiritual warfare* evokes images stemming from modern movies and not biblical teaching – such as *The Exorcist*, *The Omen* and *The Devil's Advocate* – it is easy to understand why Christians do not take the topic seriously. Most people have never (and will never) experience Satan in such a blatant manner.

Satan is a master of deception, the father of lies, and very subtle in his actions. He does not want Christians to believe in him or his fallen angels: spinning heads and contracts signed in blood are too high-profile, and counterproductive to his mission. While his methods are subtle, the results of his influence are easy to recognize in the souls he claims as his own. Scripture reveals several visible signs of his influence in believers and non-believers alike:

> *"But realize this, that in the last days difficult times will come. For men will be lovers of self, lovers of money, boastful, arrogant, revilers, disobedient to parents, ungrateful, unholy, unloving, irreconcilable, malicious gossips, without self-control, brutal, haters of good, treacherous, reckless, conceited, lovers of pleasure rather than lovers of God, holding to a form of godliness, although they have denied its power; Avoid such men as these"* (2 Timothy 3:1-5).

Christians with biblical awareness need not look far to see Satan's influence in modern society. Our culture promotes *self-esteem* (pride) and elevates it to the level of a virtue. Business schools teach the value of *personal branding* (idolatry of self), offering courses to students to create the "perfect image." Those in social sciences encourage *self-acceptance* (relative morality) and dismiss the concept of guilt that results from artificial standards (such as faith) externally imposed. Our modern society now accepts self-glorifying social media pages to be normal, despite biblical teaching to the contrary: *"Let another praise you, and not your own mouth; A stranger, and not your own lips"* (Proverbs 27:2).

This cultural shift is the focus of several sociological studies that scientifically confirm the obvious: our society has become more self-absorbed and narcissistic today than at any other time in recorded history. Satan has been hard at work, and the members of "Generation ME" are the newest temporal pawns in his spiritual war against God.

> *"But even if our gospel is veiled, it is veiled to those who are perishing, whose minds the god of this age (Satan) has blinded, who do not believe, lest the light of the gospel of the glory of Christ, who is the image of God, should shine on them"* (2 Corinthians 4:3-4).

Dr. Jean M. Twenge and Dr. W. Keith Campbell, authors of *The Narcissism Epidemic* (Atria Books, 2010), discussed several disturbing trends discovered in their research. *"In data from 37,000 college students,"* says Twenge, *"narcissistic personality traits rose just as fast as obesity from the 1980s to the present."*

They attribute this trend to inadequate parenting styles, fixation on celebrity culture, Internet and media, and an entitlement mindset resulting from underserved credit and praise. The study noted that *"young adults raised with a "participation award" mentality are more likely to have deluded expectations of themselves, their peers, and their authority figures."*

> *"Do nothing from selfishness or empty conceit, but with humility of mind regard one another as more important than yourselves; do not merely look out for your own personal interests, but also for the interests of others"* (Philippians 2:3-4).

The *Narcissistic Personality Inventory*, a standardized test that measures participants for narcissistic tendencies, reveals several common traits in "Generation ME": an elevated sense of authority and self-sufficiency – a belief that one has achieved everything on their own – superiority, exhibitionism, exploitive nature, vanity, and entitlement.

Chapter 06: *Forging Spiritual Strength with Testing and Trials*

Young adults with these traits are more likely to value money, image and fame over community, affiliation, and self-acceptance.

"The idols of the nations are but silver and gold, the work of man's hands. They have mouths, but they do not speak; They have eyes, but they do not see; They have ears, but they do not hear, nor is there any breath at all in their mouths. Those who make them will be like them, yes, everyone who trusts in them" (Psalm 135:15-18).

Satan's use of his temporal pawns does not stop there. In a published Gallup Poll, *Same-Sex Marriage Support Solidifies Above 50% in U.S.*, a comprehensive survey revealed the extent to which the moral fabric of society is eroding in this spiritual war.

Nearly all U.S. subgroups are more likely to favor gay marriage now than in the past. One factor pointing to continued expansion of gay marriage support in the future is that young Americans are more likely than older Americans to favor it. That difference by age has always been clear, and it persists today even though support has increased among all age groups over time. Americans are divided between saying legal gay marriage will have no effect on society (40%) or will make it worse (39%). Presently, fewer say gay marriage will make things worse than did so in 2003 and 2010.

Support for Legal Same-Sex Marriage by Age, 1996, 2010, and 2013

	% Should be legal, 1996	% Should be legal, 2010	% Should be legal, 2013	Change, 1996-2013 (pct. pts.)
18 to 29 years	41	52	70	+29
30 to 49 years	30	53	53	+23
50 to 64 years	15	40	46	+31
65+ years	14	28	41	+27

GALLUP

gallup.com/poll/162398/sex-marriage-support-solidifies-above.aspx

Chapter 06: *Forging Spiritual Strength with Testing and Trials*

> *"Now the deeds of the flesh are evident, which are: immorality, impurity, sensuality, idolatry, sorcery, enmities, strife, jealousy, outbursts of anger, disputes, dissensions, factions, envying, drunkenness, carousing, and things like these, of which I forewarn you, just as I have forewarned you, that those who practice such things will not inherit the kingdom of God"* (Galatians 5:19-21).

Randi Kreger, author and owner of Borderline Personality Disorder (bpdcentral.com/narcissistic-disorder), provides readers with an even more disturbing picture of the "Generation ME" narcissists.

According to Kreger, they are preoccupied with fantasies of unlimited success, power, brilliance, beauty, and ideal love. They lack any degree of empathy and are unwilling to recognize or identify with the feelings and needs of others.

They tend to have a grandiose sense of self-importance, exaggerate personal and professional achievements and talents, and expect to be recognized as superior without commensurate achievements. Additionally, they have unreasonable expectations of especially favorable treatment, and demand automatic and absolute compliance with their false expectations.

> *"Behold, the Lord's hand is not so short that it cannot save; Nor is His ear so dull that it cannot hear. But your iniquities have made a separation between you and your God, and your sins have hidden His face from you so that He does not hear"* (Isaiah 59:12).

Faithful disciples in the Body of Christ must understand that spiritual warfare is a reality. Consider spiritual warfare within the same context as the laws of physics: they are unable to scientifically prove the existence of cold (absence of heat) and darkness (absence of light), yet we know they exist, and we observe and experience their affects. Christians must reject a Hollywood image, and embrace biblical understanding instead.

> *And that they may come to their senses and*
> *escape the snare of the devil, having been*
> *taken captive by him to do his will.*
>
> *~ 2 Timothy 2:26 ~*

Chapter 06: *Forging Spiritual Strength with Testing and Trials*

The Biblical Version of the Spiritual Realm

Is the spiritual realm important, and should Christians believe it exists? The answer is "yes;" it is a topic worthy of study that believers can apply to their daily lives. Scripture reveals God takes this issue seriously, making the Bible the best point to begin: *"All Scripture is given by inspiration of God, and is profitable for doctrine, for reproof, for correction, for instruction in righteousness, that the man of God may be complete, thoroughly equipped for every good work"* (2 Timothy 3:16-17).

By its nature, the spiritual realm is not physical; scientific method can neither prove it nor measure it. However, we know science cannot prove the existence of cold or darkness, either, yet we experience both often. An article published in *Popular Science* magazine, *Animals that Hover* (Ransford, 2008), described the baffling characteristics of the hummingbird: *"The hummingbird is an animal that by all rights shouldn't be able to fly. But not only can this bird fly, it is the only bird able to fly forwards, backward, up, down, sideways, upside down, and even hover."* Science has limitations; if it cannot prove a fact to be true, that does not make it false. Such is the case with the spiritual realm.

Scripture reveals the spiritual realm exists, both good and evil, in Heaven and on the earth:

> *"He is the image of the invisible God, the firstborn of all creation. For by Him all things were created, both in the heavens **and on earth**, visible and **invisible**, whether thrones or dominions or rulers or authorities—all things have been created through Him and for Him"* (Colossians 1:15-16).

The Bible lists many examples of angels and Holy Ones that often interact with Man. They tend to be good, acting on God's orders, and for His purpose. Scripture also reveals a darker side to the spiritual realm – fallen angels that support Satan's mission – and the humans that manifest them in the temporal world. God commanded us to beware of them:

Chapter 06: *Forging Spiritual Strength with Testing and Trials*

> "There shall not be found among you anyone who makes his son or his daughter pass through the fire, or one who practices witchcraft, or a soothsayer, or one who interprets omens, or a sorcerer, or one who conjures spells, or a medium, or a spiritist, or one who calls up the dead. For all who do these things are an abomination to the Lord, and because of these abominations the Lord your God drives them out from before you" (Deuteronomy 18:10-12).

If God the Father knows this realm exists and considers it important enough to warn His children, Christian's would do well to pay attention to God's Word. The spiritual realm is a continual theme in both the Old and New Testaments.

In an example from the Old Testament, the king of Syria was at war with Israel. Unfortunately, the Israelites always knew his plans. While searching for the traitor, he discovered God was revealing his plans to the prophet Elisha, who then told Israelite commanders. The king sent warriors on chariots to surround the prophet; when Elisha's servant saw the king's forces, he was terrified. The prophet Elisha – aware of the powerful spiritual realm – asked God to show his servant why he was confident:

> "Now when the attendant of the man of God had risen early and gone out, behold, an army with horses and chariots was circling the city. And his servant said to him, "Alas, my master! What shall we do?" So he answered, "Do not fear, for those who are with us are more than those who are with them." Then Elisha prayed and said, "O Lord, I pray, open his eyes that he may see." And the Lord opened the servant's eyes and he saw; and behold, the mountain was full of horses and chariots of fire all around Elisha" (2 Kings 6:15-17).

In a humorous example from the New Testament, the apostle Paul was teaching his disciples in Ephesus, and doing many miraculous works. Sceva, the Jewish High Priest in Ephesus, had seven sons who believed they could imitate the apostles' miracles by invoking the names of Paul and Christ. That did not end well for them; imagine the seven sons of the Jewish High Priest running at full speed, naked and bleeding, down the middle of Main Street, Ephesus:

Chapter 06: *Forging Spiritual Strength with Testing and Trials*

> *"Then some of the itinerant Jewish exorcists took it upon themselves to call the name of the Lord Jesus over those who had evil spirits, saying, "We exorcise you by the Jesus whom Paul preaches." Also there were seven sons of Sceva, a Jewish chief priest, who did so. And the evil spirit answered and said, "Jesus I know, and Paul I know; but who are you?" Then the man in whom the evil spirit was leaped on them, overpowered them, and prevailed against them, so that they fled out of that house naked and wounded"* (Acts 19:13-16).

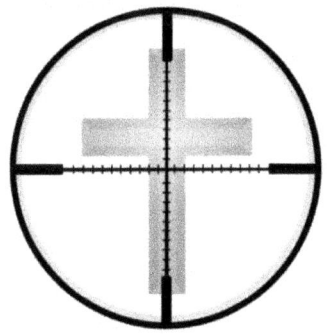

The Bible warned us about difficult days in the last times, and Scripture clearly reveals the existence of a spiritual realm. This realm has agents of good and evil, and both sides are active in the temporal world.

Why should this concern Christians, and what makes this important to all believers? Because professing faith in Christ makes you the target of those in the spiritual realm who oppose Him. The physical elements in the temporal world are not a problem; the forces that animate, control and direct them are the issue. Christians are God's children. If the world has a conflict with God, the world is against us as well.

> *"I have given them Your word; and the world has hated them, because they are not of the world, even as I am not of the world. I do not ask You to take them out of the world, but to keep them from the evil one. They are not of the world, even as I am not of the world"* (John 17:14-16).

There are no neutral parties in this conflict, and there is no place to go unnoticed. As you will discover later in the chapter, the worst place to be is "on the fence." The more you know, the better prepared you will be to defeat those seeking to defeat you.

> *Do you not know that friendship with the world is hostility toward God? Therefore whoever wishes to be a friend of the world makes himself an enemy of God.*
>
> ~ James 4:4 ~

Chapter 06: *Forging Spiritual Strength with Testing and Trials*

The Biblical Perspective of Spiritual Warfare

Before Christians can win spiritual battles, they need to acknowledge there is a war in progress. Once the believer grasps the broader view, the strategies and tactics of the smaller battles become easier to understand.

Spiritual battles, like their worldly counterparts, fluctuate constantly. Changes in the degree of intensity, terrain (spirit, heart and will), and weaponry (temptation, sin, and doubt) will alter how believers approach spiritual battles in their life. Listed below are three common battles Christians fight daily on differing terrain.

1. **Battles within the HEART**: These battles typically pit the Spirit against the flesh. The mind knows certain actions are sin, but the heart is a powerful force to control. However, the heart – with its desires, yearnings, and emotions – is no match for the Holy Spirit. When the Holy Spirit fills the Christian's heart, the power of God stands ready to guide and control formerly unrestrained desires.

    > *But I say, walk by the Spirit, and you will not carry out the desire of the flesh. For the flesh sets its desire against the Spirit, and the Spirit against the flesh; for these are in opposition to one another, so that you may not do the things that you please.*
    >
    > ~ Galatians 5:16-17 ~

2. **Battles within the MIND**: These battles typically put human reason in opposition with choice. Most Christians know they should read the Bible daily – Satan will inspire 1,000 reasons not to read it – and the believer makes a choice. Secular excuses are no match for a Holy Spirit that imparts wisdom and understanding from God. When Satan gives a believer 1,000 reasons to make bad decisions, the Holy Spirit only needs to give Christians one reason to make the correct decision – and defeat the adversary.

Chapter 06: *Forging Spiritual Strength with Testing and Trials*

> *And do not be conformed to this world, but be transformed by the renewing of your mind, so that you may prove what the will of God is, that which is good and acceptable and perfect.*
>
> ~ Romans 12:2 ~

3. **Battles within the WORLD**: To a non-believer, many of the decisions faithful Christians make every day do not make much sense. Younger believers – especially those experiencing a university or career for the first time – face an enormous amount of pressure to conform and belong. When Satan puts friendships at risk because of faith, the Holy Spirit reminds believers they have the only friend that matters: Christ Jesus. God is also a provider to those strong in their faith; opportunities taken away by Satan are nothing compared to heavenly opportunities, and they always arrive with eternal benefits for the believer.

> *You are of God, little children, and have overcome them, because He who is in you is greater than he who is in the world.*
>
> ~ 1 John 4:4 ~

God knows every Christian will face these three types of battles daily, and He has not left them unprepared or without protection. In his epistle to the church at Ephesus, the apostle Paul revealed a means of protection – available to all faithful believers professing faith in Christ – that is able to withstand any threat posed by Satan and his demonic forces.

The protection Scripture describes in *Ephesians 6:10-18* is nothing less than the full Armor of God.

> "Finally, my brethren, **be strong in the Lord** and in the power of His might. Put on the whole armor of God, that you may be able to stand against the **wiles** of the devil. For we do not wrestle against flesh and blood, but against principalities, against powers, against the rulers of the darkness of this age, against spiritual hosts of wickedness in the heavenly places. Therefore take up the whole armor of God, that you may be able to withstand in the evil day, and having done all, to stand."

Chapter 06: *Forging Spiritual Strength with Testing and Trials*

> *"Stand therefore, having girded your waist with truth, having put on the breastplate of righteousness, and having shod your feet with the preparation of the gospel of peace; above all, taking the shield of faith with which you will be able to quench all the fiery darts of the wicked one. And take the helmet of salvation, and the sword of the Spirit, which is the word of God; praying always with all prayer and supplication in the Spirit, being watchful to this end with all perseverance and supplication for all the saints"* (Ephesians 6:10-18).

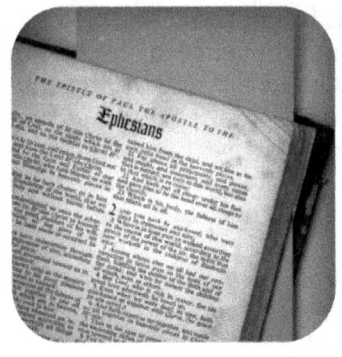

Elements of this Scripture will be discussed in further detail later in the chapter. For the time being, believers must understand the nature of the Armor of God to employ it effectively.

Putting on the Armor of God is a spiritual discipline – like prayer and studying God's Word – and must be done every day. No one can do it for the believer; it cannot be prayed on by others or placed on with a will other than your own. Without the Armor of God, we are easy prey for Satan and his forces of evil. Without this daily spiritual discipline of preparation, Christians simply cannot stand.

In the very first line of this Scripture, *"Finally, be strong in the Lord and in the strength of His might"* (Ephesians 6:10), it is critical to understand the meaning of *"be strong in the Lord."* In the original language of the New Testament, the word "strong" (**ἐνδυναμόω** / en-doo-ah-MAH-oh) means "empowered," or "fill with power." Empowerment is a personal responsibility; it is not *given*, it is *taken*. The words *"in the Lord"* mean in fellowship with Christ. This is strength you receive *with* the Lord, not just *by* the Lord.

Christians must also know in the original language of the New Testament, the word "wiles" (**μεθοδεία** / meh-thah-DYE-yah) means "expertly organized evildoing"; the devil is a master of deception. This is far more than simple *trickery*: the enemy you face is very real, and he is an expert at his craft. When it comes to enemies, none is more formidable than Satan.

Chapter 06: *Forging Spiritual Strength with Testing and Trials*

The 4 Satanic Entities of Spiritual Warfare

Before you can *defeat* an enemy, you must first be able to *define* the enemy. Scripture reveals Christians face four primary entities in spiritual warfare: *Principalities*, *Powers*, *Rulers of Darkness of This Age*, and *Spiritual Hosts of Wickedness in Heavenly Places*. When you know the nature of an adversary, you know its capability. When you know its capability, you learn how to defeat it. The Bible clearly defines the entities Christians face; further study of Scripture reveals how believers will fight – and defeat – their adversaries.

1. Principalities

In the New Testament, principalities (ἀρχή / Ahr-CHAY) denote different orders of angelic beings, both good and evil. In the forces of Satan, principalities are demons denoted by rank and purpose. The organization of Satan's principalities have three primary missions: *Moral Impurity*, *Anger*, and *Worldly Values*.

- A. **Moral Impurity**: Moral impurity is a sin against God that defiles the soul of the human host.

  "What comes out of a man, that defiles a man. For from within, out of the heart of men, proceed evil thoughts, adulteries, fornications, murders, thefts, covetousness, wickedness, deceit, lewdness, an evil eye, blasphemy, pride, foolishness. All these evil things come from within and defile a man" (Mark 7:20-23).

- B. **Anger and Bitterness**: A constant theme throughout Scripture in both the Old and New Testaments is how anger builds a barrier between the believer and God. It is a cancer that consumes Christians from the inside out, and makes prayer, sacrifice and supplication powerless in the sight of God.

  "Looking diligently lest any man fail of the grace of God; lest any root of bitterness springing up trouble you, and thereby many be defiled" (Hebrews 12:15).

- C. **Worldly Values**: The value system of a fallen world run counter to the Word and Will of God. It is impossible for a

Chapter 06: *Forging Spiritual Strength with Testing and Trials*

believer to hold worldly and biblical values in equal esteem. Examples of worldly values are wealth, power, pride, and conquest.

> *"Do not love the world nor the things in the world. If anyone loves the world, the love of the Father is not in him"* (1 John 2:15).

When Satan ranks and organizes his principalities, he is copying the structure he learned from God before his fall from Grace. Satan (and evil forces) cannot create anything original; they are parasites that copy and corrupt the pure creations of God.

> *"And the great dragon was thrown down, the serpent of old who is called the devil and Satan, who deceives the whole world; he was thrown down to the earth, and his angels were thrown down with him"* (Revelation 12:9).

Satan does not do battle against Christians alone; he has powerful back-up, and plenty of it. Satan will never be too busy – or lack enough evil forces – to overlook any individual believer in the world.

> *"Then another sign appeared in heaven: and behold, a great red dragon having seven heads and ten horns, and on his heads were seven diadems. And his tail swept away a third of the stars of heaven and threw them to the earth"* (Revelation 12:3-4).

Christians have the authority and power to battle against principalities of all ranks and purpose. Believers derive this authority through their faith and relationship with Christ, who extends individuals that authority.

> *"Having disarmed principalities and powers, He made a public spectacle of them, triumphing over them in it"* (Colossians 2:15).

The power God extends to Christians is cumulative; the capability and strength of the Body of Christ is increased through fellowship, accountability, and faith in numbers.

> *"You will chase your enemies, and they shall fall by the sword before you. Five of you shall chase a hundred, and a hundred of you shall put ten thousand to flight; your enemies shall fall by the sword before you"* (Leviticus 26:7-8).

Chapter 06: *Forging Spiritual Strength with Testing and Trials*

2. Powers

In the New Testament, powers (ἐξουσία / ex-ooh-SEE-yah) stand for delegated authority, influence, or control. This can apply to temporal rulers, or, in the context of spiritual warfare, a hierarchy of good and evil angelic entities. God delegated His authority to Satan to rule the temporal world, and Satan does the same with his demonic forces.

> *"And the devil said to Him, "All this authority I will give You, and their glory; for this has been delivered to me, and I give it to whomever I wish"* (Luke 4:6).

Satan has an enormous amount of authority over the temporal world, but Christ has been given complete authority over those powers. This can be seen in Satan's temptation of Christ above; when Satan stated his authority over the temporal world, Jesus did not question or deny it.

> *"... which He worked in Christ when He raised Him from the dead and seated Him at His right hand in the heavenly places, far above all principality and power and might and dominion, and every name that is named, not only in this age but also in that which is to come"* (Ephesians 1:20-21).

Christians have the authority and capability to battle against powers, regardless of the entity, rank, and purpose. Christ has authority over powers, and believers derive this authority due to their faith and relationship with Christ.

> *"Behold, I give you the authority to trample on serpents and scorpions, and over all the power of the enemy, and nothing shall by any means hurt you. Nevertheless do not rejoice in this, that the spirits are subject to you, but rather rejoice because your names are written in heaven"* (Luke 10:19-20).

3. Rulers of the Darkness of this Age

Christians need to know the true meaning of two important words that describe this entity. In the New Testament, the word "ruler" (**κοσμοκράτωρ** / kahz-mah-KRAH-tor) means "ruler of this world asserting independence from God." It is not simply an

Chapter 06: *Forging Spiritual Strength with Testing and Trials*

authority figure; it is one who exercises authority separate from God. The second word, "darkness" (**σκότους** / SKAH-tahs), means "moral darkness," the foundation of sin.

> *"The eye is the lamp of the body; so then if your eye is clear, your whole body will be full of light. But if your eye is bad, your whole body will be full of darkness. If then the light that is in you is darkness, how great is the darkness!"* (Matthew 6:22-23).

Darkness infers the absence of God, and those qualities and characteristics that represent Him: Light, Truth, and Hope. Living in darkness means living without access to these qualities.

> *"These will pay the penalty of eternal destruction, away from the presence of the Lord and from the glory of His power"* (2 Thessalonians 1:9).

Ignorance of the truth empowers this entity. If a person lacks knowledge – ignorance of the truth – they are easy to lead astray and deceive.

> *"My people are destroyed for lack of knowledge. Because you have rejected knowledge, I also will reject you from being My priest. Since you have forgotten the law of your God, I also will forget your children"* (Hosea 4:6).

The most common tools of deception are *secrecy* and *rumors*. Of course, not all secrecy is negative; confidentiality serves a vital role in a Christian's personal and professional life. However, secrecy that conceals falsehoods protects it from the transparency of the truth. It is this type of secrecy that allows rumors to survive and thrive.

> *"A fool's mouth is his ruin, and his lips are the snare of his soul. The words of a whisperer are like dainty morsels, and they go down into the innermost parts of the body"* (Proverbs 18:7-8).

While God's Word and His promises are timeless and eternal, every Age has its own area of darkness. Satan is very creative and highly adaptable; his methods of deception evolve as society evolves. Although the phrase "rulers of this Age" was written

Chapter 06: *Forging Spiritual Strength with Testing and Trials*

almost 2,000 years ago, Christians need to read it in the present tense.

> "And this is the condemnation, that the light has come into the world, and men loved darkness rather than light, because their deeds were evil. For everyone practicing evil hates the light and does not come to the light, lest his deeds should be exposed" (John 3:19-20).

For this reason, God's Word – and the warnings contained within it regarding Satan and spiritual warfare – are particularly relevant to contemporary issues, problems, and situations. This fact also applies to any Age in the future.

> "... far above all rule and authority and power and dominion, and every name that is named, not only in this age but also in the one to come" (Ephesians 1:21).

4. Spiritual Hosts of Wickedness in Heavenly Places

Of the four entities described in this passage of Scripture, this one is the most important to Christians studying the nature of spiritual warfare, and it is the one most often overlooked. The two key concepts in this passage are *hosts of wickedness* and *heavenly places*.

In the Old Testament, the word "host" (צָבָא / tsah-VAH) means "army," "war," and "warfare." In the New Testament, the word "host" (**πνευματικός** / new-mah-tee-KAHS) means "spiritual things" or "spiritual forces." The significance of this word is easy to miss in the English language.

The phrase "*spiritual hosts of wickedness*" does not mean "bad angelic beings that entertain guests." It describes an evil, demonic army of fallen angels – under the control of Satan – engaging in spiritual warfare, fierce battles, and targeted attacks. These attacks, against believers and non-believers alike, are planned and executed with military precision. One would expect nothing less from an army whose commander is **the** master of expertly-planned evil ("wiles" / **μεθοδεία** / meh-thah-DYE-yah).

This is an army (host) of fallen angels, loyal to Satan and his mission, that God and His archangels cast out of Heaven prior to the creation of Man.

Chapter 06: *Forging Spiritual Strength with Testing and Trials*

> *"And war broke out in heaven: Michael and his angels fought with the dragon; and the dragon and his angels fought, but they did not prevail, nor was a place found for them in heaven any longer. So the great dragon was cast out, that serpent of old, called the Devil and Satan, who deceives the whole world; he was cast to the earth, and **his angels** were cast out with him"* (Revelation 12:7-9).

Scripture refers to archangels as *princes* in both the Old and New Testaments. This is important for Christians to know as they consider the phrase "heavenly places." In Hebrew, the word "prince" (שׂר / SAYR) means "prince" or "chief ruler." In Greek, the word "prince" (ἄρχων / AHR-khon) means the same. The Bible assigns the term "king" to human leaders, and "prince" to angelic leaders.

> *"... in which you once walked according to the course of this world, according to the prince of the power of the air, the spirit who now works in the sons of disobedience"* (Ephesians 2:2).

Contrary to popular culture, Satan does not exist in an underground cave, surrounded by flames. He, like all angelic beings, exists in heavenly places: *the spiritual realm*. In the *Book of Daniel*, the prophet Daniel prays to God for help. God hears his prayers on the first day, but it takes the angel Gabriel twenty-one days to fight his way **down to earth** to help Daniel.

Even so, he was only able to defeat Satan's forces with the help of the most powerful archangel, Michael. Satan, like Michael, was an original archangel; Christians must never take his presence lightly, and never underestimate his power and reach.

> *"Then he said to me, "Do not be afraid, Daniel, for from the first day that you set your heart on understanding this and on humbling yourself before your God, your words were heard, and I have come in response to your words. But the prince of the kingdom of Persia was withstanding me for twenty-one days; then behold, Michael, one of the chief princes, came to help me, for I had been left there with the kings of Persia"* (Daniel 10:12-13).

Chapter 06: *Forging Spiritual Strength with Testing and Trials*

The Seasons and Cycles of Spiritual Warfare

The seasons and cycles of our planet are foreseeable; we understand this and plan accordingly. The same holds true for the cycles of our life. Times of abundance follow seasons of scarcity, seasons of pleasure follow times of discomfort. Christians that accept this reality plan for it and, in so doing, are prepared. The same concept applies to spiritual warfare, and Scripture reveals this truth when believers study words carefully. Consider the Bible's warning to Christians: "*For we do not **wrestle** against flesh and blood*" (Ephesians 6:12).

When one thinks of warfare, images of intense conflict fill the mind. There is a starting point, a fight, and a conclusion – at which point the forces separate for a period. However, Scripture does not use the word *fight*; it uses the word "wrestle" (**πάλη** / PAH-lay). Spiritual warfare resembles a wrestling match more than it does a boxing match. The opponents stay in contact during periods of intense maneuver, and during times of rest. Wrestling matches are not a quick fight; they are a prolonged struggle and an ongoing battle. Christians that understand the nature of this type of battle can plan their strategy accordingly.

Spiritual warfare is also cyclical; it comes and goes with the same degree of certainty as worldly seasons. The Bible gives an account of Satan tempting Jesus during His earthly ministry. Jesus prevailed (of course), but notice how the story ends:

The King James Bible tells us, "*And when the devil had ended all the temptation, he departed from him for **a season**"* (Luke 4:13, KJV). The New King James Bible tells us, "*Now when the devil had ended every temptation, he departed from Him until **an opportune time**"* (Luke 4:13, NKJV). Despite a small variation in words, the message is the same, and it is important.

A *season* reveals two immediate realities: it is a finite, temporary span of time, and it **will** return in the future. It also tells us Satan will return at "*an opportune time*" … for **him**. Satan's opportune time will always be the *worst* time for us. Christians that accept this will plan for, not pity, themselves.

Chapter 06: *Forging Spiritual Strength with Testing and Trials*

Satan: A Profile of the Christian's Adversary

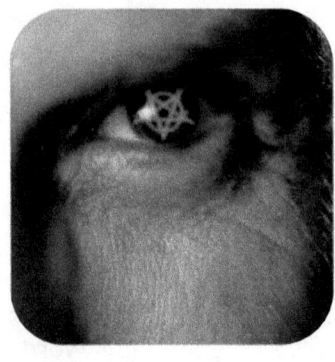

During WWII, U.S. General Patton and German Field Marshal Erwin Rommel read each other's writings. They were fierce adversaries opposed in warfare, but each respected the other's capability and skill. However, both dedicated themselves to defeating the other. That is the mindset modern Christian's must embrace with respect to their adversary, Satan. The apostle Paul had the same mindset when he wrote his second epistle to the church at Corinth: *"... so that no advantage would be taken of us by Satan, for we are not ignorant of his schemes"* (2 Corinthians 2:11).

In the modern age of science and technology, believers often dismiss Satan as a primitive myth. In the modern age of positive messaging, some pastors do not discuss Satan for fear of upsetting the mood of their congregants. Many Christians do not discuss Satan, fearing the mention of his name invites demonic presence into their life. Some reject God entirely – hating His authority and restrictions – and choose to worship Satan instead.

To those who fall into any of those four categories, Satan says, "thank you," and sends his regards. Why? Your adversary wants you to deny him, obey him, fear him, or worship him. Each of those four categories of believer serves his purpose and grand design. That does not mean Christians should admire Satan, but they must respect his capability and skill. To ignore him is to conceal him – his goal in the world – which allows him to destroy and deceive without blame or credit.

Forget Satan's caricature – red suit, pitchfork, tail, and a fiery cave deep underground – and turn to Scripture for a better understanding of the adversary Christians face daily.

In the original language of the Old Testament, the word "Lucifer" (הֵילֵל / hay-LAYL) meant "the morning star." He was God's first (and most powerful) cherub, the highest of all classes of angels. He was the symbol of perfection, wisdom, and beauty. God anointed Lucifer to serve with Him, but his pride led to a war in Heaven, and Lucifer's fall to earth.

Chapter 06: *Forging Spiritual Strength with Testing and Trials*

> *"And war broke out in heaven: Michael and his angels fought with the dragon; and the dragon and his angels fought, but they did not prevail, nor was a place found for them in heaven any longer. So the great dragon was cast out, that serpent of old, called the Devil and Satan, who deceives the whole world; he was cast to the earth, and his angels were cast out with him"* (Revelation 12:7-9).

Contrary to popular belief, Lucifer was not cast out of Heaven and into Hell; he and his fallen angels – a full third of the angels in Heaven that followed him – were cast down to the earth. His glorifying name, *the morning star*, was replaced by more disparaging names. In this passage, he is called "the dragon" (**δράκων** / DRAH-kohn), a fitting name. The ancient Greeks believed dragons had extraordinary insight, and could find prey anywhere, no matter where they hid.

> *"How you have fallen from heaven, O star of the morning, son of the dawn! You have been cut down to the earth, you who have weakened the nations! But you said in your heart, "I will ascend to heaven; I will raise my throne above the stars of God, and I will sit on the mount of assembly in the recesses of the north. I will ascend above the heights of the clouds; I will make myself like the Most High"* (Isaiah 14:12-14).

Although Lucifer lost his heavenly realm, he did not lose his capabilities and skills. Scripture reveals several of the traits and characteristics he has, before and after his fall.

> *"Thus says the Lord God: "You were the seal of perfection, full of wisdom and perfect in beauty. You were in Eden, the garden of God; Every precious stone was your covering: The sardius, topaz, and diamond, beryl, onyx, and jasper, sapphire, turquoise, and emerald with gold. The workmanship of your timbrels and pipes was prepared for you on the day you were created. You were the anointed cherub who covers; I established you; You were on the holy mountain of God; You walked back and forth in the midst of fiery stones."*

> *"You were perfect in your ways from the day you were created, till iniquity was found in you. By the abundance of your trading you became filled with violence within, and*

Chapter 06: *Forging Spiritual Strength with Testing and Trials*

> *you sinned; Therefore I cast you as a profane thing, out of the mountain of God; And I destroyed you, O covering cherub, from the midst of the fiery stones. Your heart was lifted up because of your beauty; You corrupted your wisdom for the sake of your splendor; I cast you to the ground, I laid you before kings, that they might gaze at you"* (Ezekiel 28:12-17).

In the language of the New Testament, "Satan" (**Σατανᾶς** / sah-tah-NAHS) means "adversary," his current title and primary mission against God and His children. Many Christians believe God and Satan are mortal enemies, ready to "fight on sight" if the occasion ever arises. However, Scripture runs contrary to popular belief. God counts Satan among the "sons of God" (angels) and gives Satan direct access to Heaven.

> *"Now there was a day when the sons of God came to present themselves before the Lord, and Satan also came among them. And the Lord said to Satan, "From where do you come?" So Satan answered the Lord and said, "From going to and fro on the earth, and from walking back and forth on it"* (Job 1:6-7).

Satan is an active part of God's divine plan, which explains why he has direct access to the Throne of God as well.

> *"Again there was a day when the sons of God came to present themselves before the Lord, and Satan came also among them to present himself before the Lord. And the Lord said to Satan, "From where do you come?" Satan answered the Lord and said, "From going to and fro on the earth, and from walking back and forth on it"* (Job 2:1-2).

Based on these passages, Christians can be sure of two things. First, spiritual forces are heavenly by nature, no matter where they exist. Second, Satan's primary mailing address is not hell, it is earth.

Although Satan respects God's power and authority, the Bible clearly shows he has no respect for God's values or vision for Man. Consider Satan's response to God when discussing the faithful servant Job; the Lord said Job could lose everything and still have faith, while Satan believed possessions were the reason Job had any faith in God at all.

Chapter 06: *Forging Spiritual Strength with Testing and Trials*

> *"Satan answered the Lord and said, "Skin for skin! Yes, all that a man has he will give for his life. However, put forth Your hand now, and touch his bone and his flesh; he will curse You to Your face"* (Job 2:4).

In biblical Hebrew and Aramaic, the phrase "skin for skin" (עוֹר בְּעַד־ עוֹר / or bih-AD or) inferred a concept like *quid pro quo*, or "this for that." Satan told God in very clear terms that Job would sell his own skin to save his own skin. Satan, of course, was wrong, but his pride will not let him learn from his mistakes.

Scripture reveals Satan is prideful, powerful, and local. He was God's first cherub, above all others, before He cast him from Heaven. Now that he is here with Man, what's his position in the grand design? Scripture's answer is clear:

> *"And even if our gospel is veiled, it is veiled to those who are perishing, in whose case* **the god of this world** *has blinded the minds of the unbelieving so that they might not see the light of the gospel of the glory of Christ, who is the image of God"* (2 Corinthians 4:3-4).

In the case of mankind, Christ is sovereign, but Satan is directing. Satan is also busy; Christians need to recognize this and rise to the challenge of this spiritual war. We know from our reading of Scripture that Satan is infiltrating houses of worship and creating the framework for the Apostate Church.

> *"For such men are false apostles, deceitful workers, disguising themselves as apostles of Christ. No wonder, for even Satan disguises himself as an angel of light. Therefore it is not surprising if his servants also disguise themselves as servants of righteousness, whose end will be according to their deeds"* (2 Corinthians 11:13-15).

Satan is deceiving believers and non-believers alike. If we are going to defeat him, we need to know his capabilities. He is not going away if we ignore him. This is spiritual warfare.

> *"You are of your father the devil, and the desires of your father you want to do. He was a murderer from the beginning, and does not stand in the truth, because there is no truth in him. When he speaks a lie, he speaks from his own resources, for he is a liar and the father of it"* (John 8:44).

Chapter 06: *Forging Spiritual Strength with Testing and Trials*

Our Example: Satan's Temptation of Jesus

The *Gospel of Luke* gives a detailed account of Satan's temptation of Jesus that serves as a model of excellence for every Christian. After 40 days of prayer in the wilderness, weakened by fasting, Jesus went head-to-head with the master of temptation: Satan. The account is rich with practical content, and deeper study reveals symbolism offering a comparison between Adam (Father of Man) and Jesus (Redeemer of Man). This Scripture compares and contrasts Adam and Jesus, Israelites (Children of God) and Christ (Son of God), and Original Sin with God's redemptive plan.

Questions naturally arise when reading this passage. Could Jesus really be tempted? Could He have sinned? What do the temptations signify, and what is the meaning of Jesus' answers (beyond the obvious)? How can the lessons of this Scripture benefit Christians in their battles against temptation?

Although a detailed treatment of the text is beyond the scope of this writing, the information presented in this section will enlighten readers, clearly show the power of Christ over sin, and reveal how Christ's authority over sin can be harnessed by Christians in their lives. Listed below is the text of the passage, followed by answers to the questions every believer needs to know. The Scripture quoted is from *Luke 4:1-13*, NJKV:

> *"Then Jesus, being filled with the Holy Spirit, returned from the Jordan and was led by the Spirit into the wilderness, being tempted for forty days by the devil. And in those days He ate nothing, and afterward, when they had ended, He was hungry.*
>
> *And the devil said to Him, "If You are the Son of God, command this stone to become bread."*
>
> *But Jesus answered him, saying, "It is written, 'Man shall not live by bread alone, but by every word of God.'"*
>
> *Then the devil, taking Him up on a high mountain, showed Him all the kingdoms of the world in a moment of time. And the devil said to Him, "All this authority I will give*

Chapter 06: *Forging Spiritual Strength with Testing and Trials*

You, and their glory; for this has been delivered to me, and I give it to whomever I wish. Therefore, if You will worship before me, all will be Yours."

And Jesus answered and said to him, "Get behind Me, Satan! For it is written, 'You shall worship the Lord your God, and Him only you shall serve."

Then he brought Him to Jerusalem, set Him on the pinnacle of the temple, and said to Him, "If You are the Son of God, throw Yourself down from here. For it is written: 'He shall give His angels charge over you, to keep you,' and, 'In their hands they shall bear you up, lest you dash your foot against a stone.'"

And Jesus answered and said to him, "It has been said, 'You shall not tempt the Lord your God."

Now when the devil had ended every temptation, he departed from Him until an opportune time."

Satan's 3 Temptations and Jesus' 3 Victories

When reading this account in the Bible, Christians must keep several thoughts in mind. First, the type of temptations Jesus faced were the same as those believers face daily. Second, although Jesus could have relied on His own authority as the Son of God, He chose instead to rely on the power and authority of God the Father. Third, in response to Satan's powerful temptations rooted in pride, Jesus had more strength in His powerful responses, rooted in humility. Finally, each of Satan's temptations presupposed the existence of doubt in God – "*If you are the Son of God*," – the same type of doubt Satan uses to preempt his temptation of every believer.

1. **Self-Gratification**: The first temptation – "*command this stone to become bread*" – was subliminally posing the question, "*Is your Father not providing for you?*" We are all tempted to fulfill our desires outside of God's Will, and even more so during periods of need. The desires God puts in us are good: hunger, thirst, joy, and sexual pleasure. Satan

takes good desires given by God, alters their function, and tempts us to alter the application of His desires to the point of making them a sin (evil).

Jesus' response, *"Man shall not live by bread alone,"* did rebuke Satan, but it also reminded him He was victorious in the same type of situation that caused the Israelites to fail their test. During their 40-year period, the Israelites worried they would starve, and God gave manna from the Heavens to sustain them. They survived 40-years in the wilderness, with no bread, solely by the grace of God and His Will.

> *"So He humbled you, allowed you to hunger, and fed you with manna which you did not know nor did your fathers know, that He might make you know that man shall not live by bread alone; but man lives by every word that proceeds from the mouth of the Lord"* (Deuteronomy 8:3).

2. **Self-Exaltation**: The second temptation – *"worship before me, all will be Yours"* – tried to convince Jesus to "claim His prize without pain and suffering." We are all tempted to look for shortcuts, hacks, and avoid the learning curve we need to grow and mature. We are tempted to assert ourselves in the world, claim credit for accomplishments, and deprive God of our worship and His glory. Pride is the root cause for this human tendency.

Jesus' response, *"You shall worship the Lord your God, and Him only you shall serve,"* rebuked Satan, and reminded him He was victorious in the same type of situation that caused the Israelites to fail their test. During their 40-year period, the Israelites repeatedly turned to false gods and idols, despite the miracles they saw with their own eyes. After their journey ended, God bound them in a promise to reject false gods and worship Him alone.

> *"You shall fear the Lord your God and serve Him, and shall take oaths in His name"* (Deuteronomy 6:13).

3. **Self-Protection**: The third temptation – *"throw Yourself down from here"* – was subliminally posing the question, "Is God really here to protect you?" We are all tempted to

doubt God and ask for signs or proof that He exists before we commit to His Word. When believers doubt, they tend to rely on human knowledge and pride for the solution to their problem, instead of trusting that God will be there when they need Him the most.

Jesus' response, *"You shall not tempt the Lord your God,"* rebuked Satan, and reminded him He was victorious in the same type of situation that caused the Israelites to fail their test. The Israelites, lacking an adequate supply of water, bitterly contended with Moses. Moses prayed to God for help and was instructed to strike a large rock with his staff. Water flowed freely, their needs were satisfied, and the Israelites stopped complaining for a short while. In his frustration, Moses named the place of that miracle "Temptation" (מַסָּה / mah-SAW) and "Contention" (מְרִיבָה / mayr-ree-VAH), as a reminder in history of their question, *"Is God with us, or not?"*

> *"You shall not tempt the Lord your God as you tempted Him in Massa"* (Deuteronomy 6:16).

Does God Tempt Man to Sin?

If Man is tempted to sin by Satan, and God is responsible for creating Satan, is God ultimately responsible for causing Man to sin? The answer is a definitive "NO." God is sovereign, Satan is subordinate, and their goals are diametrically opposed.

God tests Man to strengthen faith and create reliance on Him for Man's benefit. Satan tempts Man to weaken faith and create doubt in God's existence – to encourage Man's fall from God's Grace. Scripture makes this known to Christians in plain language:

> *"Let no one say when he is tempted, "I am tempted by God"; for God cannot be tempted by evil, nor does He Himself tempt anyone"* (James 1:13).

The presence of Satan, temptation and sin in the life of the Christian – sanctioned, but not endorsed, by God – yields positive

Chapter 06: *Forging Spiritual Strength with Testing and Trials*

results in a believers' life, in the present and in the future. The apostle Paul discussed one of these benefits in his second epistle to the church at Corinth:

> "And lest I should be exalted above measure by the abundance of the revelations, a thorn in the flesh was given to me, a messenger of Satan to buffet me, lest I be exalted above measure" (2 Corinthians 12:7).

God uses this type of testing with Christians to reinforce the supremacy of His strength, and the sufficiency of His Grace. When the believers' faith is strong – and reliance shifts from "self" to God – the reward for this decision is tangible, and yields results that far exceed those they may have experienced without God's active intervention.

> "Joseph said to them, "Do not be afraid, for am I in the place of God? But as for you, you meant evil against me; but God meant it for good, in order to bring it about as it is this day, to save many people alive" (Genesis 50:19-20).

Could Jesus have Yielded to Temptation and Sinned?

This is an interesting question asked by many Christians and tends to lead to other important questions of equal importance. "Could Jesus have sinned? If not, how could He sympathize with human weakness? If not, what would be the point of Satan tempting Him? If He could sin, how could He be God, if God cannot sin?" Those are all valid questions, and the answers do have a significant impact on believers' lives. Scripture reveals the answer to these questions, but Christians must realize two things in advance of the answer.

First, "*Could Jesus really be tempted and sin?*" is not one question, it is two questions. Experiencing temptation and sinning are different issues. Second, temptation happens in two ways: externally and internally. This distinction is important.

Chapter 06: *Forging Spiritual Strength with Testing and Trials*

One can be tempted by an external force without the possibility of it leading to sin. For example, if a person suggested you join them to murder someone for fun, it is a safe assumption your answer would be "no." Murder is a sin and the temptation was real – you were asked to take part – but there was never a chance you would agree to do it.

However, one can be tempted by an internal force, with a very real possibility of it leading to sin. That is the result of the fallen nature of Man. For example, if a person suggested you join them for a night of partying – and you are a recovering addict prone to that temptation – there may be a chance (*God forbid!*) you would agree to do it.

With this in mind, Scripture reveals Satan's temptation of Jesus was real (Jesus was fully human), and Jesus' rejection of Satan's temptation was equally as real (Jesus was fully God). The explanation of this reality – based solely in Scripture – is outlined below.

1. **God became flesh in Jesus**: Jesus was not a man posing as God, nor was He God pretending to be a man. God took human form in Jesus as part of His redemptive plan for mankind. To believe otherwise invalidates God's effort and mission.

   "And the Word became flesh and dwelt among us, and we beheld His glory, the glory as of the only begotten of the Father, full of grace and truth" (John 1:14).

2. **Jesus was fully MAN**: When God took human form in Jesus (Incarnation), He was subjected to the experience of humanity in its entirety. Jesus was born of a physical mother, experienced emotion (marvel, wonder, anger), experienced need (hunger, thirst, exhaustion), and experienced sensation (pain, suffering, humiliation).

   "The Jews answered Him, saying, 'For a good work we do not stone You, but for blasphemy, and because You, being a Man, make Yourself God'" (John 10:33).

3. **Jesus was fully TEMPTED**: Because Jesus was subjected to the full range of human experience – emotions, needs, sensations, and physical existence – His humanity made Him vulnerable to Satan's temptations, just as any human would be tempted in a similar situation.

   "For we do not have a High Priest who cannot sympathize with our weaknesses, but was in all points tempted as we are, yet without sin" (Hebrews 4:15).

4. **Jesus is fully GOD**: Jesus was one person with two distinct natures: human and divine. They coexisted in one physical form, each equally present in Jesus. Just as His human nature allowed Him to be subjected to the human experience, His divine nature allowed Him to perform miracles and be without sin.

   "Looking for the blessed hope and glorious appearing of our great God and Savior Jesus Christ" (Titus 2:13).

5. **God will not commit SIN or EVIL**: Many Christians mistakenly believe God cannot sin or commit evil; that limitation would invalidate His omniscience. God does not sin or commit evil – not because He cannot – but because He will not. He chooses not to, the ultimate expression of His divine righteousness and free will.

   "For I know the thoughts that I think toward you, says the Lord, thoughts of peace and not of evil, to give you a future and a hope" (Jeremiah 29:11).

6. **Jesus is human and divine nature COMBINED**: Although Jesus took human form and subjugated His will to God the Father, He nonetheless kept His divine nature in the process.

   "Who, although He existed in the form of God, did not regard equality with God a thing to be grasped, but emptied Himself, taking the form of a bond-servant, and being made in the likeness of men" (Philippians 2:6-7).

7. **Human nature has the capacity to SIN**: All people have the capacity to sin because of our fallen nature. To deny that capacity in human nature – the same nature Jesus took in earthly form – would deny the Word of God.

   "If we say that we have no sin, we are deceiving ourselves and the truth is not in us" (1 John 1:8).

8. **Divine nature will not take part in SIN**: Scripture tells us God is righteous, just, and refuses to take part in sin.

   "For My thoughts are not your thoughts, nor are your ways My ways," declares the Lord. "For as the heavens are higher than the earth, so are My ways higher than your ways and My thoughts than your thoughts" (Isaiah 55:8-9).

9. **Human Capacity vs. Divine Outcome**: Jesus, in His fully human and peccable form, had the same capacity to take part in sin as the rest of mankind. Because Jesus was fully God and impeccable, refused to forego righteousness and take part in sin during His earthly experience.

   "No temptation has overtaken you except such as is common to man; but God is faithful, who will not allow you to be tempted beyond what you are able, but with the temptation will also make the way of escape, that you may be able to bear it" (1 Corinthians 10:13).

Having the capacity to sin is different from having a propensity to sin. Experiencing a tangible external temptation is different from considering a potential internal temptation. Jesus, both fully Man and fully God, understood and experienced both these realities. Jesus did not need to sin to understand sin; His divine nature ensures He understands everything, about everything. He was tempted, He defeated Satan, He overcame death, and He is empowered *you* to follow His example.

> *For in that He Himself has suffered, being tempted, He is able to aid those who are tempted.*
>
> ~ Hebrews 2:18 ~

Chapter 06: *Forging Spiritual Strength with Testing and Trials*

The Reality of Sin in Christian Life

The concept of sin exists beyond theory and practice; it is an integral part of human nature. There is no escape from this reality. Given the choice to obey God's Will or pursue our own, human nature forces mankind to rebel against God. In the wise words of King Solomon, *"For there is not a just man on earth who does good and does not sin"* (Ecclesiastes 7:20). As with all aspects of spiritual warfare, one cannot defeat an enemy if one cannot define the enemy. We are born into sin - *"Behold, I was brought forth in iniquity, and in sin my mother conceived me"* (Psalm 51:5) – there is no escaping it. For this reason, Christians must understand it and face it head on.

1. **Sin's scope is UNIVERSAL**: From the fall of Adam until Christ's Second Coming, everyone is born into imputed sin. While some may view this as unjust, consider that Christ's righteousness is imputed to us as well.

    "There is none righteous, no, not one; There is none who understands; There is none who seeks after God. They have all turned aside; They have together become unprofitable; There is none who does good, no, not one" (Romans 3:10-12).

2. **Sin's nature is LAWLESSNESS**: When we sin, we violate God's law. When we knowingly sin, we are telling God *"your laws do not apply to me; I'm superior to them."*

    "All we like sheep have gone astray; We have turned, every one, to his own way; And the Lord has laid on Him the iniquity of us all" (Isaiah 53:6).

3. **Sin's origin is SATAN**: Everyone sins, it is imputed to us at birth, and Satan's responsible. That is why spiritual warfare exists, and why Christians cannot hide from it.

    "The one who practices sin is of the devil; for the devil has sinned from the beginning" (1 John 3:8).

Chapter 06: *Forging Spiritual Strength with Testing and Trials*

Christ Came to Defeat the Works of Satan

Christians know God sent His Son, Christ Jesus, to fulfill His redemptive mission for mankind. Jesus' sacrifice of His sinless essence on the Cross imputed His righteousness to mankind: *"You know that He appeared in order to take away sins; and in Him there is no sin"* (1 John 3:5). Many Christians are unaware that Jesus had a second mission – involving Him, Man, and Satan – that bind us together in realms of intense spiritual warfare: *"For this purpose the Son of God was manifested, that He might destroy the works of the devil"* (1 John 3:8). Our loyalty to God mandates our active participation.

When Christians fall into sin, they do not stay there. They confess, ask forgiveness, and repent. Our faith in Christ makes the thought of persistent sin inconceivable, and our rebirth in Him makes intentional sin impossible. To consider oneself saved, while continuing in habitual sin, runs counter to the tenets of biblical Christianity.

To profess faith in Christ is to view life through His eyes: to want and believe what Christ wants and believes. This applies to both our eternal Salvation, and pursuing a righteous lifestyle, a Christ-like lifestyle, here and now.

> *No one born of God makes a practice of sinning, for God's seed abides in him; and he cannot keep on sinning, because he has been born of God.*
>
> ~ 1 John 3:9 ~

God sent Jesus to us 2,000 years ago, to destroy the works of the Devil. He has not finished the mission yet; it is still ongoing. Christ is coming again to finish it once and for all. What Christians do in the interim to honor Christ in defeating sin – and how they respond to Satan's ongoing temptations – will dictate how they fare in front of God's Great White Throne of Judgment.

> *Now, little children, abide in Him, so that when He appears, we may have confidence and not shrink away from Him in shame at His coming.*
>
> ~ 1 John 2:28 ~

Chapter 06: *Forging Spiritual Strength with Testing and Trials*

Every Christian Experiences Temptation

Satan has a vast arsenal at his disposal to lead Christians off the path of righteousness, the most lethal of which is *temptation*. Unfortunately for believers, it is also the most common.

Temptation is not bad; giving in to a temptation leading to sin is the issue. Satan knows every desire, fantasy and dream in the minds of believers; if it lures a believer away from God, Satan knows about it. Every prominent person featured in Scripture – kings, prophets, apostles, and disciples – contended with the lure of Satan's temptations.

> *For what I am doing, I do not understand; for I am not practicing what I would like to do, but I am doing the very thing I hate ... Wretched man that I am! Who will set me free from the body of this death?*
>
> ~ Romans 7:15, 24 ~

Fighting temptation is an ongoing, difficult battle, but it can be won with the power of God, and faith in Christ. The apostle Paul described this struggle – and the ability to be victorious – in his epistle to the church in Ephesus: *"Among them we too all formerly lived in the lusts of our flesh, indulging the desires of the flesh and of the mind, and were by nature children of wrath, even as the rest"* (Ephesians 2:3).

When Christians succumb to temptation, and allow the sin to continue unabated, they may eventually fall prey to *addiction*. An entrenched enemy is more difficult to defeat, and seemingly impossible to defeat at times, but nothing is impossible for God.

Chris Hodges, Founding Pastor at Church of the Highlands in Alabama (churchofthehighlands.com), presented an interesting approach to dealing with temptation leading to addiction. Pastor Hodges knows before an enemy can be defeated, the enemy must be defined. The following section was inspired by the wonderful work Pastor Hodges does daily at Church of the Highlands.

Chapter 06: *Forging Spiritual Strength with Testing and Trials*

Satan's temptation leads Christians to sin; unconfessed sin is rationalized by the mind and becomes more acceptable. "Acceptable" sin (an oxymoron) becomes habitual sin and, if left unaddressed – with confession, prayer, and repentance – becomes an addiction. An addiction, according to Pastor Hodges, is *an action or activity we do, that we do not want to do, that we keep doing anyway*. That sums up the situation without needing a journal of confusing medical definitions. To understand why the cycle of temptation, sin, and addiction is difficult to defeat, one must honestly define the nature of the cycle.

1. **The sin becomes part of our identity**. Those suffering with habitual sin (addiction) plan their lives around that sin. This level of planning is necessary to conceal the sin from those around them, and to decrease the external impact they know this sin will have on their life. Habitual sin, in any form it takes, will eventually become part of their identity. This creates an internal conflict; believers know in their hearts God never intended this identity for them.

> *God created man in His own image, in the image of God He created him. Male and female He created them.*
>
> ~ Genesis 1:27 ~

2. **When we try to quit – and fail repeatedly – we become increasingly hopeless**. Despite motivational posters to the contrary, failure is a miserable experience. A person in this position has rejected God's strength and continues to fight under their own power. Eventually the fight becomes exhausting and has an emotional impact.

> *The righteous cry, and the Lord hears and delivers them out of all their troubles. The Lord is near to the brokenhearted and saves those who are crushed in spirit.*
>
> ~ Psalm 34:17-18 ~

3. **Any threat to the sin becomes a threat to the person.** Once Satan aligns the addiction with a believers' identity, and in the absence of God's strength, the person begins to defend the sin itself. Phrases such as *"this is just the way I am,"* or *"God made me this way"* often go with this stage. Contrary to popular belief, the person suffering from this level of habitual sin is not in a stage of *denial*; they are in a stage of *acceptance*. This makes the problem far more difficult to discuss.

> *Be gracious to me, O God, be gracious to me, for my soul takes refuge in You; And in the shadow of Your wings I will take refuge until destruction passes by.*
>
> ~ Psalm 57:1 ~

4. **We begin to lose focus and question the meaning of our life.** Habitual sin has the ability to simultaneously put the believers' life on autopilot and destroy the onboard navigation system. The believer has put God on "stand-by," Satan is navigating the course, and the sin becomes so distracting that nothing productive is done. Phrases such as *"life was not meant to be this way,"* and *"what's the point of all this?"* tend to go with this stage.

> *The Lord will accomplish what concerns me; Your lovingkindness, O Lord, is everlasting. Do not forsake the works of Your hands.*
>
> ~ Psalm 138:8 ~

5. **We ease the psychological pain by engaging in the habitual sin.** The cycle starts again from step #1.

> *All things are lawful for me, but not all things are profitable. All things are lawful for me, but I will not be mastered by anything.*
>
> ~ 1 Corinthians 6:12 ~

To break the cycle of habitual sin (addiction), the believer needs a change of heart, not behavior. Many people do not want a change of heart; they only want to change their circumstances. They need a better plan than that, and it *must* include God.

Chapter 06: *Forging Spiritual Strength with Testing and Trials*

The Nature of Habitual Sin is Idolatry

Christians living in Western society are immersed in a culture of idolatry. The idols have evolved over time; they no longer take the shape of mythical figures, surrounded by sacrifice and incense. The "Rulers of Darkness of this Age" realize that age has passed; the new idols are much subtler, and much more prevalent. Idolatry in modern society can be defined as *an extreme admiration, love, or reverence for something or someone, who holds a higher priority than God.*

"All who fashion idols are nothing, and the things they delight in do not profit. Their witnesses neither see nor know, that they may be put to shame. Who fashions a god or casts an idol that is profitable for nothing?" (Isaiah 44:9-10).

Idolatry includes anything that holds a higher position than Christ in a persons' heart. It can take the form of *pride* (social media, careers, or authority), *materialism* (wealth, possessions, or debt), *naturalism* (science, technology, or bio-engineering), and *self-aggrandizement* (hobbies, pastimes, or pleasures). None of these components are intrinsically bad; they each add to our quality of life. However, when they cause a believer to subjugate God to their authority and influence, idolatry is present.

"Therefore consider the members of your earthly body as dead to immorality, impurity, passion, evil desire, and greed, which amounts to idolatry" (Colossians 3:5).

Christians can apply three, simple tests to anything in their life to decide if it rises to the level of idolatry. If it does, they must reassess their priorities in accordance with God's Will.

1. **Time and Attention**: How much time and attention is devoted to the item or activity in question? A Christian who does not smoke or drink – but spends 12-hours per day on social media and follows professional sports teams religiously – may have issues in need of reconciliation.

2. **Public Testimony and Devotion**: People prove their faith publicly using symbols, clothing, and behavior. They publicly proclaim their loyalties, ensuring everyone knows which side they represent. If a Christian decorates the walls of their home with professional sporting items – but nothing can be found in sight that publicly professes faith in God, they may have issues to consider.

3. **Comparative Devotion and Loyalty**: If you are a believer professing faith in Christ, and openly proclaim Him to be the most important aspect of your life, there is an easy way to test that for truth. Conduct an inventory of all items, activities, and interests, then arrange them in the order of time and/or money spent pursuing them. The highest priority at the top of the list should be Christ. If God comes second or third on the list, you may have some issues to consider.

That may turn out to be an uncomfortable test for many who are unaware of the idolatry in their lives. Christians need to remember that honesty does not create reality, it reveals it. It is better to self-correct your path to righteousness than to have God do it for you.

> *"You shall not make for yourself an idol, or any likeness of what is in heaven above or on the earth beneath or in the water under the earth. You shall not worship them or serve them; for I, the Lord your God, am a jealous God, visiting the iniquity of the fathers on the children, on the third and the fourth generations of those who hate Me"* (Exodus 20:4-5).

Idolatry – in the form of addiction, habitual sin, or an obsession – can come into a believers' life unnoticed. God's Word should be the only thing in a Christian's heart; the presence of anything else de-throne's Him. What we place above Him, we worship. That which we worship, we serve. That which we serve, enslaves us. Anything other than a slave to Christ is idolatry.

> *It shall come about if you ever forget the Lord your God and go after other gods and serve them and worship them, I testify against you today that you will surely perish.*
>
> ~ Deuteronomy 8:19 ~

Chapter 06: *Forging Spiritual Strength with Testing and Trials*

12 Tips for Defeating Satan's Temptation

Defeating temptation hinges upon a single choice: do you want to follow in the footsteps of Christ, or would you prefer to follow the world? After all, the temptations of Satan are enticements to coerce Christians to act against God's Will. God and Satan both want you to make a choice and, despite their spiritual power, the ultimate power to decide is in your hands. Satan wants you to decide quickly and impulsively; he wants Christians to be uninformed. God wants you to decide quickly as well; however, He wants Christians to be well-informed, biblically literate and make choices based on a strong faith. The twelve tips listed below will help you in making the wise choice: God the Father, and His Son, Christ Jesus.

1. **Realize God does not tempt Man.** God will never tempt mankind; Satan is solely responsible for temptation in our life. God will test us, but always with a righteous purpose, and for a noble end. Satan's goal in tempting man is to destroy him, and his relationship with God.

    "Let no one say when he is tempted, "I am being tempted by God," for God cannot be tempted with evil, and he himself tempts no one" (James 1:13).

2. **Realize God understands temptation.** God knows the feeling and impact of temptation; despite His omniscience, He went through temptation Himself in fully human form. The fact He was tempted by Satan, emerged victorious, and was crucified to remove the burden of your sins is proof He loves you enough to understand your pain.

    "For since He Himself was tempted in that which He has suffered, He is able to come to the aid of those who are tempted" (Hebrews 2:18).

3. **Realize God will not let Satan break your limits.** God will never let any temptation you face push you beyond your capacity to deal with the situation. He knows you have limitations, and He will always give you an escape route.

Chapter 06: *Forging Spiritual Strength with Testing and Trials*

Jesus died on the Cross to remove the penalty of your sin; the last thing God wants is for you to fail in sin. Remember that everything – including temptation – is cyclical and comes in seasons. Temptations are always temporary. However, the choices we make when faced temptation are eternal.

> *"No temptation has overtaken you but such as is common to man; and God is faithful, who will not allow you to be tempted beyond what you are able, but with the temptation will provide the way of escape also, so that you will be able to endure it"* (1 Corinthians 10:13).

4. **Realize you need God to fight Satan**. Lucifer, the first cherub, has immense power and authority in the world; You are no match for him. However, you have the power of God through your faith in Christ, and Satan is no match for God. God wants you to want Him in this fight, and He will step in as soon as you pray for His help. You would not bring a toothpick to a gunfight; do not make the mistake of bringing your finite capabilities to a God fight.

> *"But put on the Lord Jesus Christ, and make no provision for the flesh in regard to its lusts"* (Romans 13:14).

5. **Realize God has a plan to protect you**. God is omniscient; all-powerful, all-knowing, and aware of everything, always. Satan and his fallen angels are not. God has given you access to Him, the Armor of God, and all His forces in the heavenly realm to help you in your battle with temptation. Trust the nature of the God you serve, and the righteousness of His plan to protect you.

> *"Finally, be strong in the Lord and in the strength of His might. Put on the full armor of God, so that you will be able to stand firm against the schemes of the devil"* (Ephesians 6:10-11).

6. **Realize Satan knows God wants to help you**. There are no secrets in Heaven, and it is no secret God wants to protect His children from Satan's temptation. Satan knows this and will do anything to convince Christians that God does not care; that He is an "absentee landlord" with more

Chapter 06: *Forging Spiritual Strength with Testing and Trials*

important things to do than protect you. Scripture reveals Satan's deception to be a blatant lie – shown by the fact that God gave His only begotten Son so we could have eternal life in Heaven. Do not doubt for a second that Satan will try to subvert you. However, do not doubt for a second that God will subvert Satan when you ask for His help.

> *"For such men are false apostles, deceitful workers, disguising themselves as apostles of Christ. No wonder, for even Satan disguises himself as an angel of light. Therefore it is not surprising if his servants also disguise themselves as servants of righteousness, whose end will be according to their deeds"* (2 Corinthians 11:13-15).

7. **Turn quickly to God's Word**. There are many passages of Scripture that speak directly to your weakness, and to the specific temptation you face. Research them, find them, write them down, and memorize them. Have a Bible with you whenever possible for this very purpose. There is no temptation Satan can direct at you that has not already been defeated by God in Scripture.

> *"Or the grace of God has appeared, bringing salvation to all men, instructing us to deny ungodliness and worldly desires and to live sensibly, righteously and godly in the present age"* (Titus 2:11-12).

8. **Realize victories strengthen your faith**. Achieving victories over temptation with God's help strengthens your faith, and your confidence in God's willingness to help. The impacts of those victories build up over time and degrade Satan's ability to deceive you.

> *"Blessed is a man who perseveres under trial; for once he has been approved, he will receive the crown of life which the Lord has promised to those who love Him"* (James 1:12).

9. **Remove yourself from the source of evil**. Once you have found a weakness Satan can use as a door to temptation, shut the door by removing yourself from the environment. Satan will lose a chance to tempt you, and

Chapter 06: *Forging Spiritual Strength with Testing and Trials*

you will remove the chance to tempt God by still being there.

> *"Do not associate with a man given to anger; Or go with a hot-tempered man, or you will learn his ways and find a snare for yourself"* (Proverbs 22:24-25).

10. **Surround yourself with supportive Christians.** Surround yourself with Brothers and Sisters in Christ who will strengthen your righteousness and faith. There is strength in numbers, and isolation magnifies deception.

    > *"Two are better than one because they have a good return for their labor. For if either of them falls, the one will lift up his companion. But woe to the one who falls when there is not another to lift him up"* (Ecclesiastes 4:9-10).

11. **Practice spiritual disciplines regularly.** Spiritual disciplines are just that: *discipline for your Spirit*. They are acts of devotion that strengthen faith, increase spiritual growth, and enhance the power of prayer. They show God you are serious about having a relationship with Him; it is experiential Christianity in action. The more time spent in prayer, studying God's Word, and fasting, the less chance Satan has of steering you off the righteous path that leads to God's Grace and Salvation.

    > *"All discipline for the moment seems not to be joyful, but sorrowful; yet to those who have been trained by it, afterwards it yields the peaceful fruit of righteousness"* (Hebrews 12:11).

12. **Keep a prayer journal and daily devotional.** The best way to measure success and victories is to track your progress. Journals serve as written prayers, devotionals for daily study, and keep a record of your successes and failures. Over time, a journal will help you to build a strong defense against Satan's temptations and schemes.

    > *"Thus says the Lord, the God of Israel, 'Write all the words which I have spoken to you in a book'"* (Jeremiah 30:2).

Chapter 07

Advancing Christianity with Faith in Action

"In the same way, let your light shine before others, that they may see your good deeds and glorify your Father in heaven."

~ Matthew 5:16 ~

Chapter 07: *Advancing Christianity with Faith in Action*

7 Goals of Practicing "Experiential Christianity"

The act of having faith, by itself, will not save or empower anyone; it is the objective truth of faith that allows that to happen. For Christians, that objective truth is Jesus Christ, our Lord and Savior. Their faith compels them to study the Bible, build a personal relationship with God, and understand His purpose for all believers. We learn about His redemptive plan, character, and His promises to all who profess faith in Him. Our faith in Christ – and our belief in the truth and promises of His Word – gives us the confidence to act on His purpose in accordance to His Will for us.

When Christians forego acting on God's Word, and neglect applying His purpose to their life, faith becomes an academic exercise devoid of spiritual value. The principles contained in the Bible must be applied to every aspect of Christian life and guide the actions leading to spiritual growth which bring us into a closer relationship with God.

Many Christians have a desire to apply biblical principles to their life; however, they lack an understanding of *how* to do it and *where* to begin. How can a text, written thousands of years ago, help to guide decisions believers will make tomorrow? Are the meanings, morals, and messages still relevant in a modern context? How does one know if a biblical verse, specific to a person or event in the past, can be interpreted and applied in a broader sense to direct contemporary behaviors?

Those are relevant questions to ask, and the answers must be practical if they are to be effective. Thankfully, God knew these questions would arise, and His Scripture reveals answers that are uncomplicated, straightforward, and practical. The first step is *desire*: knowing why you *want* God's Word in your life.

> *The things you have learned and received and*
> *heard and seen in me, practice these things,*
> *and the God of peace will be with you.*
>
> ~ Philippians 4:9 ~

Chapter 07: *Advancing Christianity with Faith in Action*

Goal #1: To WANT God's Word

A biblical life starts with *wanting* God's Word to be *the* guiding force in *every* thought and action. Competing temporal interests can make this challenging for Christians in modern society. When believers decide to want God's Word, they must create a strong foundation to be successful.

A rational person would not build a home in a muddy swamp, using the best materials and expert craftsmen, and expect it to stand. Jesus taught this clearly: *"Therefore everyone who hears these words of Mine and acts on them, may be compared to a wise man who built his house on the rock"* (Matthew 7:24).

In a culture exalting conformity as a virtue, it is not easy to walk with Christ. Young adults – especially those attending universities – want to make friends and avoid social conflict. A believer wanting God's Word must be aware of the consequences of following popular opinion: *"You shall not follow a crowd to do evil; nor shall you testify in a dispute so as to turn aside after many to pervert justice"* (Exodus 23:2).

Older adults pursuing careers face similar challenges in corporate environments. Christians confront the realities of entrenched traditions, and a "groupthink" business culture that shuns deviating from the norm. Once again, a believer wanting God's Word must be aware of the consequences of conforming to this pressure: *"Neglecting the commandment of God, you hold to the tradition of men."* (Mark 7:8).

The greatest challenge posed to building our foundation is not external; it is the result of assigning a higher priority to our human reason than God's Word. We tend not to learn from our past mistakes, and discover our reasoning is often incorrect. His Word *must* be the foundation that supersedes everything else.

> *There is a way that seems right to a man, but its end is the way of death.*
>
> ~ Proverbs 16:25 ~

Chapter 07: *Advancing Christianity with Faith in Action*

Goal #2: To FEED on God's Word

The body needs nourishment to function properly and survive; without food and water, the body weakens and fails under pressure. The same holds true for spiritual life. God's Word is to biblical life what food is to physical life; neither can survive without the other.

Christians must view God's Word the same way they view food – it is not an option; it is an obligation – if they truly expect their strong foundation of biblical life to survive.

It has to dwell richly within the Christian's mind, heart and soul: *"Let the word of Christ dwell in you richly in all wisdom, teaching and admonishing one another in psalms and hymns and spiritual songs, singing with grace in your hearts to the Lord"* (Colossians 3:16). This is the only area of a believers' life in which overconsumption is not penalized and overeating never results in a diet.

Feeding on God's Word requires the use of all five senses, in many instances simultaneously. Unlike food, we take in (and absorb) the nourishment of His Word in a variety of ways.

We use our ears to listen, not only during sermons, but in our discussions with others as well. We use our eyes to read the Bible, and to see opportunities to serve in ways that nourish our faith. Our mouth speaks God's Word in prayer and testifies to him in all we do. Our mind researches His truth in Scripture and reflects on His wisdom every time we decide to speak or act.

The five senses combined allow Christians to memorize God's Word, committing it to the forefront of their mind, and recall it at a moment's notice for any occasion. Scripture is read, understood, spoken, reflected upon, written, and acted upon. It is the source of spiritual nourishment Christians consume daily.

> *Blessed are those who hunger and thirst*
> *for righteousness, for they shall be satisfied.*
>
> ~ Matthew 5:6 ~

Chapter 07: *Advancing Christianity with Faith in Action*

Goal #3: To LIVE by God's Word

To understand God's Word, one must read and understand it. To live by His Word, Christians must memorize it to the best of their ability. An illustration of this is Satan's temptation of Jesus.

During Satan's first temptation, Jesus replied, "*It is written, 'Man shall not live on bread alone*" (Luke 4:4), and it ended. During Satan's second temptation, Jesus replied, "*It is written, 'You shall worship the Lord your God and serve Him only*" (Luke 4:8), and it ended. During Satan's third temptation, Jesus replied, "*It is said, 'You shall not put the Lord your God to the test'*" (Luke 4:12). Satan quit the temptation altogether and left Jesus alone.

Jesus beat all three temptations – and defeated Satan in the process – with Scripture. Jesus had God's Word committed to memory and used it to support His relationship with God the Father. All Christians can imitate Christ, memorize Scripture, and use God's Word anytime it is needed.

Many Christians believe they do not have the capacity or capability to memorize Scripture; common sense and practical experience proves that belief to be false.

How many important phone numbers do you have committed to memory – work, family, and friends – that you can recall when needed? How many computer passwords do you have memorized? How many addresses, names, and websites can you recall without referring to notes? The human brain can memorize and recall anything, but there is a catch: *it must be important enough to remember*.

When Christians give priority to God's Word, memorizing it is easy, fun, and much more beneficial than phone numbers.

The law of his God is in his heart; his steps do not slip.

~ Psalm 37:31 ~

Chapter 07: *Advancing Christianity with Faith in Action*

Goal #4: To GROW in God's Word

When anything stagnates, it tends to become deficient and cease to exist. This applies to physical and spiritual natures. Humans have an intrinsic desire to grow and expand in all areas of their life.

Jesus taught His disciples this lesson with the four examples in the *Parable of the Sower*. In the first example, *"A sower went out to sow his seed. And as he sowed, some fell by the wayside; and it was trampled down, and the birds of the air devoured it"* (Luke 8:5). Treaded ground in the field is as hard as pavement – as difficult to penetrate as a closed mind – and God's Word cannot grow.

In His second example, *"Some fell on rock; and as soon as it sprang up, it withered away because it lacked moisture"* (Luke 8:6), a superficial faith – with nothing more than the shallow roots of an emotional response – withered before it could grow. Unlike faith, emotion changes drastically when tested by external pressures and stress.

In His third example, *"And some fell among thorns, and the thorns sprang up with it and choked it"* (Luke 8:7), concerns of the world – careers, wealth, and leisurely pursuits – took priority and choked out the life in God's Word. Just as fresh water and salt water cannot flow from the same well, God's Word cannot grow in soil fertilized with worldly priorities.

In His fourth example, *"But others fell on good ground, sprang up, and yielded a crop a hundredfold"* (Luke 8:8), the seed of God's Word fell on the fertile soil of a righteous heart, and the results were exponential. The average yield for a crop at that time was tenfold, a fact known to agrarian society. To increase the yield of a crop to a hundredfold is impossible – for Man. When a Christian grows in God's Word, *anything* is possible.

> *Like newborn babies, long for the pure milk of the word,*
> *so that by it you may grow in respect to salvation;*
>
> ~ 1 Peter 2:2 ~

Chapter 07: *Advancing Christianity with Faith in Action*

Goal #5: To MAKE TIME for God's Word

Modern society demands much of our daily allotted time and it seems like there is never enough time available to do the things we plan. Is that true? There are 24 hours in a day, 7 days in a week, and 43,334 minutes in the average month. We can schedule our days and make plans for the week, but we cannot predict what will happen *just one minute from now*. Perhaps time is not the issue. Instead, it is how we occupy time and prioritize our lives. Scripture reveals, *"There is an appointed time for everything. And there is a time for every event under heaven"* (Ecclesiastes 3:1). That includes the study of God's Word.

Many Christians make time to read – biographies of notable theologians, commentaries, and texts about the Bible – but do not spend time reading the Bible itself. No book *ever* written about God's Word will *ever* take the place of reading God's Word itself.

Making time to read the Bible must start at once if one is to build a strong foundation of faith. Some believers are inclined to postpone their time in God's Words until a later date, but the Scriptures warn Christians against having that mindset: *"Yet you do not know what your life will be like tomorrow. You are just a vapor that appears for a little while and then vanishes away"* (James 4:14).

Time management is making the time to carry out priorities; Christians increase the urgency of this by realizing we cannot predict what will happen *just one minute from now*. If we spend 30-minutes each day in God's Word, we make our faith stronger and show God we understand He is the priority. God sees we understand that, *"We must work the works of Him who sent Me as long as it is day; night is coming when no one can work"* (John 9:4). Christians always make time for God's Word.

> *Seven times a day I praise You,*
> *because of Your righteous ordinances.*
>
> ~ Psalm 119:164 ~

Chapter 07: *Advancing Christianity with Faith in Action*

Goal #6: To ACT on God's Word

I will ACT on God's Word.

I will **will** ACT on God's Word.

I will **ACT** on God's Word.

I will ACT **on** God's Word.

I will ACT on **God's** Word.

I will ACT on God's **Word**.

Most Christians understand knowing something to be right – and failing to act in support of it – is equivalent to doing something wrong. It is the "sin of omission," and Scripture takes that seriously.

The Bible provides believers with clear instructions: *"But be doers of the word, and not hearers only, deceiving yourselves"* (James 1:22). To hear the Word of God and do *nothing* is the same as hearing His Word and doing *otherwise*. An act of omission is an act of defiance.

There are several ways Christians can begin to apply God's Word in their daily life, using simple methods and an incremental approach. The first is *visualization*: imagining a situation that affects you, then planning a biblical strategy in response. Scripture teaches us the benefit of planning ahead: *"For which one of you, when he wants to build a tower, does not first sit down and calculate the cost to see if he has enough to complete it?"* (Luke 14:28). Visualize scenarios that affect you the most, then find the Scripture to guide your response.

Another useful method is "personalizing" Scripture for a deeper understanding of the text. Verbally repeating a verse, and placing emphasis on a different word each time, gives varying contexts and helps to commit the verse to memory via repetition. Paraphrasing verses in modern dialects – accurately, of course – also gives additional meaning, and makes Scripture easier to understand. God never intended His Word to be difficult: *"The unfolding of Your words gives light; It gives understanding to the simple"* (Psalm 119:130).

Many Christians find including a biblical verse in prayer helps to remember it and seek God's strength to manifest it at the same time. No matter the method, the point is to act on it.

*Little children, let us not love with word
or with tongue, but in deed and truth.*

~ I John 3:18 ~

Chapter 07: *Advancing Christianity with Faith in Action*

Goal #7: To TRUST God's Word

When people need answers to daily problems beyond their capabilities, they find experts to help them find a solution. Society tends to trust those with specialized training and inside information; we view these experts as uniquely qualified to handle the task. We trust them to guide us down the right path, even though we cannot see the path ourselves. Scripture reveals God's Word serves that purpose, and can be trusted to expertly guide us in daily life: *"Your word is a lamp to my feet and a light to my path"* (Psalm 119:105).

Some Christians trust God with their eternal souls, but do not trust Him with guidance in their daily lives. God's promise of eternal life is available to all who profess faith in Christ, but we do not have to wait until we arrive in Heaven for God to fulfill His promise; eternal life with Him begins now.

> *"Blessed is the man who trusts in the Lord and whose trust is the Lord. For he will be like a tree planted by the water, that extends its roots by a stream and will not fear when the heat comes; But its leaves will be green, and it will not be anxious in a year of drought nor cease to yield fruit"* (Jeremiah 17:7-8).

When believers trust God's Word to guide them in daily life, they learn how to listen to His voice, and trust the wisdom the Holy Spirit reveals to them. Unlike temporal subject matter experts, they do not need to ask for a second opinion to confirm His guidance. Trusting God's Word directs Christians down the right path to their calling as well. When we trust God's Word enough to direct our calling, the Bible tells us we can move forward in confidence: *"Therefore, brethren, be all the more diligent to make certain about His calling and choosing you; for as long as you practice these things, you will never stumble"* (2 Peter 1:10).

> *Trust in the Lord with all your heart, and*
> *lean not on your own understanding.*
>
> ~ Proverbs 3:5 ~

Chapter 07: *Advancing Christianity with Faith in Action*

5 Categories of Timeless Lessons in the Bible

God's Word is a book of wisdom, a collection of timeless truths, written over the course of 1,500 years by 40 divinely inspired authors. Things have changed since the Bible was written – cultures, languages, societal norms, geographic boundaries – with one notable exception: the nature of Man. Our emotions thought processes and limitations have remained remarkably unchanged despite the passage of time. For this reason, the illumination and lessons of God's Word is as relevant today as it was thousands of years in the past.

> *"Acquire wisdom! Acquire understanding! Do not forget nor turn away from the words of my mouth. Do not forsake her, and she will guard you; Love her, and she will watch over you"* (Proverbs 4:5-6).

Hermeneutics, the theological discipline of interpretation of Scripture, seeks to discover the implication of God's Word: the directed truth of the message. This is discussed at length in *Chapter 01: The Power and Promise of God's Written Word*. Once the truth of God's Word has been properly discerned, the next mission is to properly apply this truth to one's life. It is during the process of application many Christians have difficulties.

The Bible does not answer every possible question directly. However, *Scripture interprets Scripture*, and understanding the variety of themes within the text – and the categories of lessons contained within those themes – practical application of God's Word in modern times gets easier to manage. Understanding textual themes offers deeper insight of the authors' intent and reveals broader truths that tend to apply to a variety of life circumstances. One might not find the "perfect" verse for a specific issue, but an applicable lesson always exists.

> *But if any of you lacks wisdom, let him ask of God, who gives to all generously and without reproach, and it will be given to him.*
>
> ~ James 1:5 ~

Chapter 07: *Advancing Christianity with Faith in Action*

Lesson #1: DIRECT COMMANDS

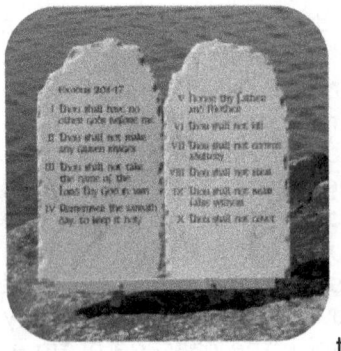

Direct commands are the easiest messages to identify and understand; when God's Word tells Christians to do something, they do it. When He tells them not to do something, they do not do it. The Ten Commandments, given to Moses by God on Mount Sinai, are a familiar example of direct commands. They are non-negotiable – Moses did *not* receive the *Ten Suggestions* – and they are always conditional. With respect to God's commands, conditional does not mean optional. It means if we obey them, blessings follow; if we disobey them, we can expect bad things to happen.

Consider the First Commandment: *"Then God spoke all these words, saying, 'I am the Lord your God, who brought you out of the land of Egypt, out of the house of slavery. You shall have no other gods before Me'"* (Exodus 20:1-3). God's plain language is easy to understand.

Unfortunately, Moses had not come down the mountain with the Ten Commandments, and the Israelites were already defying God by demanding that Aaron create a Golden Calf. God's response to their defiance was just as easy to understand: *"The Lord said to Moses, 'I have seen this people, and behold, they are an obstinate people. Now then let Me alone, that My anger may burn against them and that I may destroy them'"* (Exodus 32:9-10). We must obey God's commands, or else.

Direct commands occur throughout the Bible, in both Testaments. An unmarried couple may want to live together, but *"Marriage is to be held in honor among all, and the marriage bed is to be undefiled; for fornicators and adulterers God will judge"* (Hebrews 13:4). That is a direct command from God's Word. You can choose to ignore it, but Christians already know how God responds to defiance. It does not typically end well.

> *Jesus answered and said to him, "If anyone loves Me, he will keep My word;"*
>
> ~ John 14:23 ~

Chapter 07: *Advancing Christianity with Faith in Action*

Lesson #2: UNIVERSAL TRUTHS

Universal truths apply to everyone, in any situation, all the time. They may be easy to find and clearly said, *"Do not be deceived: 'Bad company corrupts good morals'"* (1 Corinthians 5:33), or they may be contained in a story that does not appear to be related to a specific circumstance. In the latter case, the truth must be discerned, but once discovered it can be applied to a variety of circumstances. An example of this is the *Parable of the Rich Fool*.

"The land of a rich man was very productive. And he began reasoning to himself, saying, 'What shall I do, since I have no place to store my crops?' Then he said, 'This is what I will do: I will tear down my barns and build larger ones, and there I will store all my grain and my goods. And I will say to my soul, "Soul, you have many goods laid up for many years to come; take your ease, eat, drink and be merry."' But God said to him, 'You fool! This very night your soul is required of you; and now who will own what you have prepared?'" (Luke 12:16-20).

You are probably not a rich farmer thinking about building bigger barns, but there is a good chance you have suffered material loss in your life. You may have had money stolen, an electronic device destroyed, or a new vehicle scratched or dented in a parking lot. If so, the universal truth of this Scripture is relevant.

In the original language of the New Testament, the word "required" (ἀπαιτέω / ah-pie-TAY-oh) means "to ask or demand back." This is the type of demand used for a debt or a promissory note. Everything you claim as your own – wealth, possessions, and your life – are on "loan" to you from God. He can demand them back at any time without notice. The universal truth is this: be thankful for everything and attached to nothing but God.

He who walks with wise men will be wise,
But the companion of fools will suffer harm.

~ Proverbs 13:20 ~

Chapter 07: *Advancing Christianity with Faith in Action*

Lesson #3: DIRECT EXAMPLES

Direct examples are biblical lessons we can easily apply to modern life. They can be identified as examples for Christians to follow, "*Be imitators of me, just as I also am of Christ*" (1 Corinthians 11:1), or presented as stories involving actions God wants us to emulate. In the first instance, they are presented as commands; in the second, readers need to grasp the underlying message. Once the reader understands the truth of the message, it has application within a variety of circumstances. An example of this is *The Widow's Mite*.

"And He sat down opposite the treasury and began observing how the people were putting money into the treasury; and many rich people were putting in large sums. A poor widow came and put in two small copper coins, which amount to a cent. Calling His disciples to Him, He said to them, 'Truly I say to you, this poor widow put in more than all the contributors to the treasury; for they all put in out of their surplus, but she, out of her poverty, put in all she owned, all she had to live on.'" (Mark 12:41-44).

In the first century, a "mite" (or *lepton*) was worth $1/128^{th}$ of a denarius, the daily wage. The woman was a widow – she had no husband to support her – and she chose to put all she had into the "collection box" and trust that God would supply all that she needed. Proportionally, she gave infinitely more than wealthy contributors that donated from surplus. The widow trusted God more than she cared about her possessions.

This direct example goes beyond money; it applies to any scarce resource in our possession. When a scarce resource is given freely – money, time, or possessions – it shows God we trust Him to supply (and resupply) our needs, and He rewards our faith. How often have we said, "*we do not have time to help?*"

He who trusts in his riches will fall, but the righteous will flourish like the green leaf.

~ Proverbs 11:28 ~

Chapter 07: *Advancing Christianity with Faith in Action*

Lesson #4: INDIRECT EXAMPLES

Indirect examples are more difficult to identify; they involve people, places, and events that appear to be unrelated to modern circumstances Christians face daily. However, we understand the truth of these lessons, their value is clear. Many of these examples appear in well-known Bible stories taught in Sunday school classes across the world. A good example of this is the story of Joshua and the *Walls of Jericho*. An angel of God told Joshua to seize Jericho, a well-fortified city, and to use unconventional methods in battle.

> "The Lord said to Joshua, "See, I have given Jericho into your hand, with its king and the valiant warriors. You shall march around the city, all the men of war circling the city once. You shall do so for six days. Also seven priests shall carry seven trumpets of rams' horns before the ark; then on the seventh day you shall march around the city seven times, and the priests shall blow the trumpets'" (Joshua 6:2-4).

Imagine the thoughts in Joshua's mind, and the reaction of his top generals when he relayed God's instructions. "*God has commanded us to seize Jericho,*" he tells his generals, "*So get the soldiers prepared for war. You and your troops will be supporting the mission, but we are letting the music guys fight this battle.*"

Joshua did not question God's Word; he had been with Moses in the wilderness and had seen God's miracles himself. They assembled the troops and trumpeters, marched with the Ark of the Covenant around the city for seven days, sounded the trumpets and won the battle.

When God gives believers direction, it can defy common sense and seem illogical. Trust His wisdom over human logic.

> *For My thoughts are not your thoughts, nor are your ways My ways,*" declares the Lord.

~ Isaiah 55:8 ~

Chapter 07: *Advancing Christianity with Faith in Action*

Lesson #5: REASONABLE ASSUMPTIONS

Reasonable assumptions make up most lessons in the Bible. They tend to appear as consistent themes that occur throughout Scripture. The characters, circumstances, locations, and events are different; however, an underlying theme – and a biblical lesson – links them all together. Their generalized nature makes them more difficult to identify, but that same nature makes them easier to apply, in a wider variety of circumstances. An example of this is the story of David and Goliath. David, a young shepherd with unshakable faith in God, has volunteered to fight Goliath, the mightiest of the Philistine warriors – with stones and a slingshot.

> *"Thus David prevailed over the Philistine with a sling and a stone, and he struck the Philistine and killed him; but there was no sword in David's hand. Then David ran and stood over the Philistine and took his sword and drew it out of its sheath and killed him, and cut off his head with it. When the Philistines saw that their champion was dead, they fled"* (1 Samuel 17:50-51).

In modern culture, most Christians do not tend sheep or do battle with giant warriors, so the reasonable assumptions may not be immediately apparent until they read other stories in the Bible. There are several lessons in the theme of this Scripture that we can apply to circumstances in our daily life.

First, the odds against the chances of success do not matter when God is part of the equation. Second, human skill and ability play a secondary role when fulfilling God's Will. Third, peoples' lack of confidence in our ability to succeed have no importance when deciding to act on God's Word. Fourth, age is not a factor when God chooses to make us part of His plan. Finally, an unshakable faith is the only way to make these lessons true.

> *Jesus said to them, "With people this is impossible, but with God all things are possible."*
>
> ~ Matthew 19:26 ~

Chapter 07: *Advancing Christianity with Faith in Action*

7 Learning Styles: Choose the Best for YOU

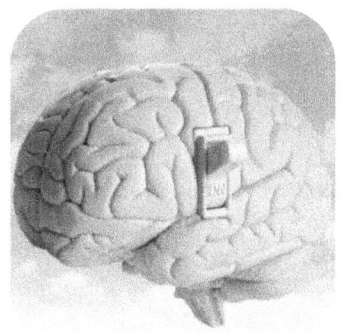

A biblical lifestyle requires Christians to apply biblical principles; the starting point for application is learning. While the methods of application presented in this chapter have universal utility, no one learning style works for every person. If you recognize your style of learning, you can personalize and adapt universal principles in a way that increases your chance for success.

1. **The Visual/Spatial Learner**: A visual learner is most successful when visual aids – such as graphs, pictures or charts – are used during study

2. **The Logical Learner**: The logical learner categorizes and classifies information, and tends to understand patterns and relationships within information

3. **The Kinesthetic Learner**: The kinesthetic learner is most successful when interacting with information in a "hands on," "learn by doing" fashion

4. **The Linguistic Learner**: The linguistic learner is most successful when interacting with information by reading, writing, listening or speaking

5. **The Rhythmic Learner**: The rhythmic learner is most successful when humming, tapping or background music is present while interacting with information

6. **The Interpersonal Learner**: The interpersonal learner is most successful when interacting with others in groups, and sharing in collaborative thought

7. **The Intrapersonal Learner**: The intrapersonal learner is most successful when interacting with information alone, motivated by internal (rather than external) factors

Why is this important? Employing learning methods that are counter to your learning style tend not to work. Asking a rhythmic learner to turn off the radio, or a kinesthetic learner to memorize 30 pages of text by reading alone, is pointless. Adapt your learning style to the task. The method of learning is not important; learning, to apply biblical principles, is what matters.

7 Components of a Successful Biblical Lifestyle

Applying biblical principles to life is the duty and responsibility of every Christian. Without application, the Bible becomes an ancient anthology of historical texts, letters, poems, and psalms. The path of a biblical lifestyle is a challenge for every believer that evolves and progresses over time. The hardest part of the journey is deciding to begin. Have faith and feel secure; you are not alone. God sent His Holy Spirit to guide you and reveal truth you'll need to be successful.

The process of applying biblical truths to modern Christian life has seven basic components. Each component is equally as important as the next and last, and all must be practiced if you are to be successful in your journey. Everything starts with the Bible.

> *"Enter through the narrow gate; for the gate is wide and the way is broad that leads to destruction, and there are many who enter through it. For the gate is small and the way is narrow that leads to life, and there are few who find it"* (Matthew 7:13-14).

1. **Read the Bible daily**: The first step in applying God's Word in our life is to read it, listen to it, and absorb it. Scripture builds the foundation of our relationship with God; it gives us understanding of His Will, His Word, His character, and His expectations for believers in the world. In the process, we learn the history of God's interactions with other faithful believers, the challenges they faced, and the successful resolution to difficult problems. This must be a daily exercise and, like the food we consume to survive, God's Word offers the nourishment needed for a healthy soul and spirit. It strengthens, enlightens, and guides everything else we do that follows.

> *Until I come, give attention to the public reading of Scripture, to exhortation and teaching.*
>
> ~ 1 Timothy 4:13 ~

2. **Study the Bible daily**: Although study incorporates reading and listening, it is different from reading in its approach and goal. We focus time and attention on a specific passage of Scripture, research the deeper meaning, and discern the true sense of what Scripture is trying to reveal to us. It involves notes, the use of sources other than the Bible (dictionaries, lexicons, commentaries, maps, and concordances), and serves to elevate biblical knowledge from a level of familiarity to understanding. In the process, our faith matures and strengthens.

> *For Ezra had set his heart to study the law of the Lord and to practice it, and to teach His statutes and ordinances in Israel.*
>
> ~ Ezra 7:10 ~

3. **Memorize God's instruction**: It is not possible to apply principles that are not known; memorizing verses commits God's Word to our heart. It is held in reserve for times of greatest need when we do not have a Bible on hand. In the same incremental way, we build retirement accounts over time for future use, Christians should lay up God's Word for themselves in their hearts and mind. Jesus did not have Scripture available when he defeated the temptations of Satan in the wilderness.

> *The law of his God is in his heart; His steps do not slip.*
>
> ~ Psalm 37:31 ~

4. **Discover God's meaning**: We must know what God's Word meant to the divinely inspired authors of the Bible before we can figure out what Scripture means to us. What's the literary context (what does the part mean light of the whole? What's the historical context (date, culture, and events)? What's the linguistic context (ancient words with multiple meanings)? What's the theological context (what is God communicating to man)?

> *A fool does not delight in understanding, but only in revealing his own mind.*
>
> ~ Proverbs 18:2 ~

Chapter 07: *Advancing Christianity with Faith in Action*

5. **Meditate on God's Message**: Technology has given Christians more access to God's Word than any other time in history. Unfortunately, the byproduct of advancement is noise and distraction. We are inundated with information, and the study of Scripture requires quiet time alone with God to receive His message in our heart and mind. The spiritual discipline of meditating on God's Word does just that. It empowers us to focus on His message, grasp the meaning, and understand how we can apply His truth in our life according to His Will.

   > *Let the words of my mouth and the meditation of my heart be acceptable in Your sight, O Lord, my rock and my Redeemer.*
   >
   > ~ Psalm 19:14 ~

6. **Correlate principles with issues**: God's Word is the source of principles that guide Christian life. However, life can seem so complex, a starting point for application may be difficult to discern. Begin with issues that impact you personally, research the relevant biblical principles, then visualize how those principles can be applied in practical situations. When researching Scripture, do not neglect the universal truths, direct examples, indirect examples, and reasonable assumption categories for your inspiration.

   > *The beginning of wisdom is: Acquire wisdom; And with all your acquiring, get understanding.*
   >
   > ~ Proverbs 4:7 ~

7. **Apply God's Wisdom**: The key to applying God's Word in life successfully is the "4-P Rule." The application must be *personal* and have meaning in your life. Make it *practical*; is this an issue you deal with regularly? Make it *possible*; is the application realistic? Make it *provable*; can results (positive *and* negative) be observed and improved?

   > *Therefore, prepare your minds for action, keep sober in spirit, fix your hope completely on the grace to be brought to you at the revelation of Jesus Christ.*
   >
   > ~ 1 Peter 1:13 ~

Chapter 07: *Advancing Christianity with Faith in Action*

7 Biblical Strategies to Overcome Adversity

Faith defines the Christian life; it is the force driving our perseverance, passion, and purpose. It guides actions in the temporal world and guarantees eternal life with Christ in Heaven. In a relationship in which God gives fallen and undeserving mankind Salvation, faith is the *only* thing He asks from us in return. Indeed, it is the only thing a finite being *could* offer God: *"For by grace you have been saved through faith; and that not of yourselves, it is the gift of God"* (Ephesians 2:8). Given its position of prominence in Christian life – and the role it serves in our eternal relationship with Christ – it makes sense that God regularly tests our faith.

Yet in many cases, it is during these times of adversity and testing when the faith of Christians is most prone to fail. Could it be possible many believers simply do not understand the nature of their faith, or the role it plays in their relationship with the God who tests it? Scripture reveals testing and trial should come as no surprise: *"The refining pot is for silver and the furnace for gold, but the Lord tests hearts"* (Proverbs 17:3).

If growth and change tend to be uncomfortable (and even painful) in the physical world, imagine how much more that truth applies in the spiritual realm. The Bible is clear: those who aspire to mature in their faith must realize growth results from change, and change is the result of testing. Through difficult testing, God is shaping believers into His image of the masterpiece He wants them to be: *"But now, O Lord, You are our Father, we are the clay, and You our potter; And all of us are the work of Your hand"* (Isaiah 64:8).

If the testing of faith that results in spiritual growth is a divine constant, our reaction becomes the *only* variable in our relationship with God; and it is the *only* thing within our control.

> *Blessed is a man who perseveres under trial; for once he has been approved, he will receive the crown of life which the Lord has promised to those who love Him.*
>
> ~ James 1:12 ~

Chapter 07: *Advancing Christianity with Faith in Action*

#1: Trust the Security of Fundamental Faith

Christians must accept three facts as truth to trust the security of their faith at a fundamental level. First, as fallen humans created in God's image, His purpose for mankind is to conform us to the image of Christ for His Glory. Next, adversity has meaning despite its mystery to us, and God's purpose is always good: *"Therefore, those also who suffer according to the will of God shall entrust their souls to a faithful Creator in doing what is right"* (1 Peter 4:19). Finally, the tests and trials of adversity are secondary to our reaction to them.

The experience of adversity by any name – suffering, trial, testing, etc. – is a painful process that is mysterious by nature: *"Why does God let 'X' happen to 'Y'?"* However, all tests have a purpose. If one could know the reason behind every test, it still would not diminish its impact; any student that is studied for a final exam in school will confirm that as fact. The difference between many Christians and students taking final exams is the students knew they were going to be tested and prepared in advance.

Scripture reveals Christians have been afforded the same advance notice: *"Consider it all joy, my brethren, when you encounter various trials, knowing that the testing of your faith produces endurance"* (James 1:2-3). In the original language of the New Testament, the word "trials" (**πειρασμός** / pie-ras-MAHS) means "probation period," and the word "testing" (**δοκίμιον** / dah-KEE-me-on) means "to test for genuineness." God's Word is telling us to have faith at the fundamental level and prepare for His test. The answers we give – our response to the testing – will be graded after the exam.

Having trust in the security of fundamental faith – God is good, tests have meaning, and responses matter – is a strategy that will withstand any test of adversity you encounter.

> *Therefore we do not lose heart, but though our outer man is decaying, yet our inner man is being renewed day by day.*
>
> ~ 2 Corinthians 4:16 ~

Chapter 07: *Advancing Christianity with Faith in Action*

#2: Discern the Trial's Purpose and Lesson

When adversity and suffering strike, several things happen simultaneously in our mind. We experience a range of initial emotions – we tend to become angry, bewildered, and depressed – all of which impair our judgment. We tend to blame external factors as the source of the problem and remove ourselves as a possible cause. Amid the chaos, it is easy to become overwhelmed, and forget to call them into action.

A Christian's ability to recall Scriptural truths will dictate their capability to discern the trials' purpose and lesson. First, God is always involved: *"For His eyes are upon the ways of a man, and He sees all his steps"* (Job 34:21). Next, God wants us to have wisdom and know the truth: *"Behold, You desire truth in the innermost being, and in the hidden part You will make me know wisdom"* (Psalm 51:6).

Most importantly, God wants us to understand why He is testing us: *"It is good for me that I was afflicted, that I may learn Your statutes"* (Psalm 119:71). The moment the testing begins, Christians have two choices: focus on the problem, or focus on God. Choosing to focus on God shows Him we agree to take part in the lesson, which creates the mindset that allows God to reveal His purpose.

The first step is prayer, with an intentional inward focus: *"Search me, O God, and know my heart; Try me and know my anxious thoughts; And see if there be any hurtful way in me, and lead me in the everlasting way"* (Psalm 139:23-24). The second step is to accept God's revealed guidance, and act on His Will: *"All discipline for the moment seems not to be joyful, but sorrowful; yet to those who have been trained by it, afterwards it yields the peaceful fruit of righteousness"* (Hebrews 12:11). The trials we experience are difficult – discerning the purpose is not easy – but embracing God's Will is joyful under any condition.

*Many plans are in a man's heart, but
the counsel of the Lord will stand.*

~ Proverbs 19:21 ~

Chapter 07: *Advancing Christianity with Faith in Action*

#3: Expect Changing Seasons with Optimism

Our temporal world has seasons, a series of cyclical changes in weather, reoccurring each year with amazing predictability. We cannot prevent them; they appear and affect our life whether we like them or not.

A Christian's life has seasons as well. However, unlike natural seasons in the physical world, spiritual seasons are supernatural, and directed by the sole providence of God. They are not predictable – the "weather" can change at any moment – and they always serve God's intended purpose: *"To everything there is a season, a time for every purpose under heaven"* (Ecclesiastes 3:1). It is not a matter of "if" a season will change for us, but "when," and how we respond to this inevitability matters.

Our society demands we plan everything in our life, as far in advance as possible. When an unexpected change in seasons occurs, plans fall apart, and the balance and timing of life falls apart with it. Scripture reveals while God finds time important, He does not extend that value to human schedules: *"It is not for you to know times or seasons which the Father has put in His own authority"* (Acts 1:7).

In the original language of the New Testament, the word "times" (**χρόνος** / KRAH-nas) means "appointed time," and the word "seasons" (**καιρός** / kai-RAS) means "opportune time." God's makes His distinction perfectly clear: not only does He appoint the time for all seasons, but He also selects the best time for it to occur, according to His Will and purpose.

When God intervenes with a change of season, we may be doing *exactly* the right thing, at *exactly* the wrong time. God's timing and purpose for us are perfect, and a change confirms for Christians that He is actively involved in their spiritual growth and well-being in the physical world.

> *Wait for the Lord; Be strong and let your heart take courage; Yes, wait for the Lord.*
>
> ~ Psalm 27:14 ~

Chapter 07: *Advancing Christianity with Faith in Action*

#4: Face Times of Testing with Courage

We respond to threats in the physical world in one of three ways: fight, flight or freeze. When Christians face times of testing, there is no physical enemy to fight, but the threat directed at their faith is real. How we face the challenge of adversity – with courage, denial, or despair – will depend on the strength of our relationship with God. Scripture reveals the preferred response: *"Be on the alert, stand firm in the faith, act like men, be strong"* (1 Corinthians 16:13). Denial is pointless; the challenge still exists, and it shows God our unwillingness to take part in His plan for our spiritual growth. Despair is worse; it weakens faith and serves as a rejection of God's strength.

When a person professes faith in Christ and turns to the Lord, their spiritual testing begins in earnest. God is shaping His children into the image of Christ, and Satan is trying to destroy their faith with deception and lies.

Scripture reveals that this should come as no surprise to Christians: *"Beloved, do not be surprised at the fiery ordeal among you, which comes upon you for your testing, as though some strange thing were happening to you"* (1 Peter 4:12). In fact, they should expect these adversities with the same level of assuredness that they hold for the law of gravity: *"Indeed, all who desire to live godly in Christ Jesus **will** be persecuted"* (2 Timothy 3:12).

God never leaves His children unprepared or defenseless during times of testing; He wants us to develop courage, wisdom, and a strong foundation of faith in Him. Scripture reveals God gives His strength to those He tests: *"Have I not commanded you? Be strong and courageous! Do not tremble or be dismayed, for the Lord your God is with you wherever you go"* (Joshua 1:9). Leave denial and despair to non-believers in the world; accept God's strength and face times of testing with courage in Him.

*Arise! For this matter is your responsibility, but
we will be with you; be courageous and act.*

~ Ezra 10:4 ~

#5: Gain Wisdom from Times of Testing

God does not subject Christians to adversity for His amusement, nor does He impose testing as punishment. His purpose is to conform the believer into the image of Christ for their spiritual growth, and for His Glory. His testing strengthens our faith and increases our knowledge: *"The fear of the Lord is the beginning of knowledge; Fools despise wisdom and instruction"* (Proverbs 1:7). The ability to learn from our life experience – mistakes, victories, and God's instruction – gives us wisdom, endurance, perseverance, and hope in God's Promises.

> *"Consider it all joy, my brethren, when you encounter various trials, knowing that the testing of your faith produces endurance. And let endurance have its perfect result, so that you may be perfect and complete, lacking in nothing"* (James 1:2-4).

Although testing gives us the chance to learn from our experience, our fallen nature tends to cause us to forget the lessons learned from earlier mistakes. When this happens, the testing may actually be God's *chastening*: *"For those whom the Lord loves He disciplines, and He scourges every son whom He receives"* (Hebrews 12:6). Even so, His purpose is still the same, and His instruction serves to correct us, not punish us. It is God's desire that we have wisdom to avoid making the same mistakes repeatedly.

The primary benefit of learning from times of testing is its cumulative nature with exponential effects; lessons learned in adversity do not add to our capabilities, they multiply them like compound interest: *"After you have suffered for a little while, the God of all grace, who called you to His eternal glory in Christ, will Himself perfect, confirm, strengthen and establish you"* (1 Peter 5:10). Over time, the lessons of God's instruction combine to create whole Christians, greater than the sum of their parts.

> *For a righteous man falls seven times, and rises again, but the wicked stumble in time of calamity.*
>
> ~ Proverbs 24:16 ~

Chapter 07: *Advancing Christianity with Faith in Action*

#6: Do not be Enslaved by a Sinful Past

Christians know when Christ became sin and died on the Cross, the blood of His sacrifice washed away the sins of those who profess faith in Him. When our sins are forgiven – and the slate of our past is wiped clean – we are also given the benefit of a clean conscience. Scripture reveals God's position on this to be clear: *"I, even I, am the one who wipes out your transgressions for My own sake, and I will not remember your sins"* (Isaiah 43:25). Those who do not divest themselves of the guilt of the past tend to have difficulty dealing with adversity.

> *"Do not call to mind the former things or ponder things of the past. Behold, I will do something new, now it will spring forth; Will you not be aware of it?"* (Isaiah 43:18-19).

During a time of testing, a Christian's heart and mind must focus on God; prayerfully discerning His purpose, listening for His guidance, and receiving the lesson of His instruction. A guilty conscience forces one to unnecessarily focus on the past, instead of looking to the future with God. Believers must trust the promises of God that result from their faith: *"If we confess our sins, He is faithful and righteous to forgive us our sins and to cleanse us from all unrighteousness"* (1 John 1:9).

Believers must also accept that a clear conscience is the byproduct of genuine faith in Christ, and the forgiveness of our sins: *"In view of this, I also do my best to maintain always a blameless conscience both before God and before men"* (Acts 24:16). Forgiveness of sin and a cleansing of conscience are not separate events; they happen simultaneously.

Enslavement by the past – after a profession of faith – calls into question one's trust in God. Faith and trust in God are requirements for spiritual growth, the purpose of His testing.

> *Therefore if anyone is in Christ, he is a new creature; the old things passed away; behold, new things have come.*
>
> ~ 2 Corinthians 5:17 ~

Chapter 07: *Advancing Christianity with Faith in Action*

#7: Ask Fellow Christians for Help

Asking for help during times of adversity is not a sign of weakness; it is a sign of strength, faith, and trust in God's Word. In addition to petitioning God personally, Scripture reveals we are required to help each other in times of need: *"Bear one another's burdens, and thereby fulfill the law of Christ"* (Galatians 6:2). God may choose to act directly, but in many instances, He acts through members in the Body of Christ. In this way, the commandment Jesus gave His disciples is fulfilled: *"This is My commandment, that you love one another, just as I have loved you"* (John 15:12).

Unfortunately, some Christians refuse to seek the help of others, even when it is desperately needed. There are times when God will test our faith to humble us, especially following a season of blessing and prosperity. The pride of the one being tested prevents God's ability to help through other believers, and the time of testing is extended as a result. Scripture reveals when pride becomes an obstacle, things do not end well: *"Pride goes before destruction, and a haughty spirit before stumbling"* (Proverbs 16:18). Consider the irony of God testing Christians for humility, and His believers being too proud to discern the test.

The nature of true Christian fellowship demands that we give help to others freely in time of need, and never hesitate to ask for help in our time of need. Believers within the Body of Christ must understand the nature of this two-way obligation: *"Do not merely look out for your own personal interests, but also for the interests of others"* (Philippians 2:4). The sin of pride disrupts individual lives – extended trials, increased suffering, and interference with learning God's lesson – and negatively affects fellowship as well. Christians that God may have chosen to serve and support do not get the chance to take part in that calling. Never be too proud to ask fellow Christians for help.

Now we who are strong ought to bear the weaknesses of those without strength and not just please ourselves.

~ Romans 15:1 ~

Chapter 07: *Advancing Christianity with Faith in Action*

7 Benefits of Applying Biblical Truth to Life

Christians in modern society live in a culture that values high standards in every facet of life. Those who aspire to a "standard of excellence" – and meet that goal with dedication, commitment, and training – are recognized as role models and leaders within their fields. If high standards did not yield benefits, society would not embrace them. If that holds true for the temporal world, how much more important should it be in our eternal relationship with God? In applying biblical truth to modern life, Christians show God they want to live up to His standards and take an active role in His purpose of conforming us to Christ.

In our fallen state, we will never fully achieve that goal – God knows that – but in the absence of high biblical standards, we will miss the chance to achieve the potential of God's purpose for our life. In the words of Italian sculptor Michelangelo, *"The greater danger for most of us lies not in setting our aim too high and falling short; but in setting our aim too low and achieving our mark."* The eternal rewards and temporal benefits are too important for Christians not to try their best.

1. **Enjoying Freedom and Safety**: Christ freed us from the bondage of sin, and the penalty of eternal death, with His sacrifice for us on the Cross. He also freed us from guilt, ignorance, and depravity as part of His redemptive plan. Through our profession of faith, we receive the promises of God and trust His Will, enjoying the safety of eternal life. Conforming to the image of Christ by following God's Word does not restrict our freedom. We may have freedom to drive a vehicle, but if no one honored traffic laws, we would not feel safe enough to enjoy that freedom. God's Laws give the benefits of freedom and safety.

   It was for freedom that Christ set us free;
   therefore keep standing firm and do not
   be subject again to a yoke of slavery.

   ~ Galatians 5:1 ~

Chapter 07: *Advancing Christianity with Faith in Action*

2. **God Answers our Prayers**: The things that separates Christianity from false religions is a God who actively takes part in our life in personal ways. The thing that separates true Christians from lukewarm believers is that God answers our prayers, repeatedly. Scripture reveals God answers the prayers of those who follow His Word, and rejects the prayers of those who do not: *"I hate, I reject your festivals, nor do I delight in your solemn assemblies"* (Amos 5:21). Is there anything better than a prayer answered by God? It is an amazing process: you pray to God, He *hears* you, and He *answers* your prayer in a way that *only* He can. When that happens, we have just had a personal interaction with the infinite Creator of *everything*. It is an amazing experience that strengthens our faith, glorifies God, and gives a powerful testimony for us to share with others.

> *And whatever we ask we receive from Him, because we keep His commandments and do those things that are pleasing in His sight.*
>
> ~ 1 John 3:22 ~

3. **Receive Temporal and Eternal Blessings**: Scripture reveals God wants us to have an intimate relationship with Him, and He gives us the promise of an Eternal Life that starts now. Does a person change when they have an intimate relationship in the world? Everything changes: the way they *feel*, *act,* and *speak*. If that holds true for worldly relationships, how much more would that hold true for a relationship with God? Scripture reveals God's promise of blessing for those in a relationship with Him: *"For the Lord God is a sun and shield; The Lord gives grace and glory; No good thing does He withhold from those who walk uprightly"* (Psalm 84:11). Christians who believe their relationship with God – and His blessings – does not get serious until they get to Heaven are missing an incredible opportunity to enjoy His blessing now.

> *Blessed be the God and Father of our Lord Jesus Christ, who has blessed us with every spiritual blessing in the heavenly places in Christ.*
>
> ~ Ephesians 1:3 ~

Chapter 07: *Advancing Christianity with Faith in Action*

4. **Protection from False Teaching and Apostasy**: One of the greatest threats Christians face in modern society is false teaching. Faithful believers can rely on the power of the Holy Spirit to discern the truth of God's Word, and to protect them from false doctrine: *"Beloved, do not believe every spirit, but test the spirits to see whether they are from God, because many false prophets have gone out into the world"* (1 John 4:1). Millions of people are being deceived by unethical leaders of apostate movements, who pervert the truth of the Gospel for personal gain. A dedicated Christian, committed to applying biblical truth in their daily life, is not likely prey for modern antichrists. In addition, the strength they receive through their faith in Christ prevents them from turning away from God when a "better message" tries to lead them astray.

> *And He said, "See to it that you are not misled; for many will come in My name, saying, 'I am He,' and, 'The time is near.' Do not go after them.*
>
> ~ Luke 21:8 ~

5. **Proving God's Word is Truth**: When a Christian applies biblical truth to every facet of their life, people notice. God sees that as well, and actively works in the believers' life. When God works in the life of a faithful servant of Christ, people around them take interest. When this happens, it is a perfect opportunity to become living proof of the truth of God's Word: *"Come and hear, all who fear God, and I will tell of what He has done for my soul"* (Psalm 66:16). This applies to non-believers and fellow Christians alike. For the former, it is a chance to lead a lost soul to the Lord. For the latter, it is a chance to reinforce the faith of other believers and inject strength into the Body of Christ through fellowship.

> *But when He, the Spirit of truth, comes, He will guide you into all the truth; for He will not speak on His own initiative, but whatever He hears, He will speak; and He will disclose to you what is to come.*
>
> ~ John 16:13 ~

Chapter 07: *Advancing Christianity with Faith in Action*

6. **Engender Confidence and Trust**: One of the chief complaints directed at Christianity is so many of its members appear to be hypocrites; they behave in a manner contrary to the principles of their faith. When Christians live by God's Word – when they practice what they preach – it engenders confidence and trust in people around them. In a society tending to be suspicious of motives, genuine personalities are refreshing: *"Let your light shine before men in such a way that they may see your good works, and glorify your Father who is in heaven"* (Matthew 5:16). Trust is the driving force in any relationship. Non-believers are more likely to be led to the Lord by a Christian they trust, not because of the words they speak, but because of the life they live through their action every day.

> *In all things show yourself to be an example of good deeds, with purity in doctrine, dignified, sound in speech which is beyond reproach, so that the opponent will be put to shame, having nothing bad to say about us.*
>
> ~ Titus 2:7-8 ~

7. **Setting a Standard of Excellence**: Society values standards of excellence and respects the amount of dedication and commitment it takes to achieve them. We require these standards from others – pastors, surgeons, craftsmen, etc. – because the outcome we expect from them is important. The standard of excellence for believers is Christ, and the instruction to achieve this standard is the Bible. God expects nothing less from His believers: *"Do you see a man skilled in his work? He will stand before kings; He will not stand before obscure men"* (Proverbs 22:29). Our standards convey the importance of our faith in Christ, and the priority of God in our life.

> *Finally, brethren, whatever is true, whatever is honorable, whatever is right, whatever is pure, whatever is lovely, whatever is of good repute, if there is any excellence and if anything worthy of praise, dwell on these thing.*
>
> ~ Philippians 4:8 ~

Chapter 07: *Advancing Christianity with Faith in Action*

7 Daily Habits to Reinforce a Biblical Mindset

Habits are regular practices that are done with little thought; they define who we are as individuals and serve as a foundation for our life. Bad habits can be changed, and new habits can be created, with a proper mindset and self-discipline: *"Like a city that is broken into and without walls is a man who has no control over his spirit"* (Proverbs 25:28). Most importantly, habits can help us achieve our goals.

The seven habits listed below help to reinforce a biblical mindset which, in turn, helps to create a foundation for applying biblical principles successfully in modern Christian life.

1. **Wake up early**: If you claim not to be a "morning person" this might make you uncomfortable, but it is no coincidence that our role model, Jesus Christ, woke up early in the morning. Our minds are predisposed to do this, and our clarity and focus peak in the morning. Rising early also reduces the pressure of time constraints, and gives you the chance to plan your time with God: *"I rise before dawn and cry for help; I wait for Your words"* (Psalm 119:147). When the first thought of your day is God, it is easier to keep Him in the forefront of your mind during the rest of the day. If you work at night, the same rules apply; they just happen in the evening. The importance of rising early is not based on the sun or the moon, it is being focused on the word "early."

> *Now in the morning, having risen a long while before daylight, He went out and departed to a solitary place; and there He prayed.*
>
> ~ Mark 1:35 ~

2. **Do not check email or social media**: Business interests and friends can wait; the morning is your time to focus on God and build spiritual strength. Professional issues and personal agendas will only serve to distract your focus and

concentration: *"Set your mind on the things above, not on the things that are on earth"* (Colossians 3:2). Your email and social media can wait until you have brought your faith into focus and made Christ your exclusive priority.

> *And this I say for your own profit, not that I may put a leash on you, but for what is proper, and that you may serve the Lord without distraction.*
>
> ~ 1 Corinthians 7:35 ~

3. **Pray and meditate on God's message**: Prayer is a two-way conversation; we pray, and God listens, God speaks and we listen. Many Christians pray daily, but they are off their knees and on their feet without giving God time to reveal His guidance. When we approach God in prayer, we need to do so in reverence, and with the expectation He will reveal His message to us: *"Let the words of my mouth and the meditation of my heart be acceptable in Your sight, O Lord, my rock and my Redeemer"* (Psalm 19:14). This is also the time to consider the known challenges of the day and asking God to provide biblical responses to those issues.

> *Oh, how I love Your law! It is my meditation all the day. You, through Your commandments, make me wiser than my enemies; for they are ever with me.*
>
> ~ Psalm 119:97-98 ~

4. **Share the Gospel every day**: Personal and professional life will always bring you into contact with new people, regardless of your environment. Take advantage of this opportunity and make it a point to share the Gospel with at least one person every day: *"And let us consider how to stimulate one another to love and good deeds"* (Hebrews 10:24). God's primary mission for all Christians is to make disciples; that can only happen through conversations with other people. Christ's "mission statement" to the disciples, *"Go therefore and make disciples of all the nations,"* propelled the early Church forward, and established Christianity as a global faith. The disciples had to share the

Chapter 07: *Advancing Christianity with Faith in Action*

Gospel of Christ with non-believers, create disciples, and teach them how to replicate their efforts. We must train ourselves to do the same; eventually, sharing God's Word with people you meet will become habitual, comfortable, and rewarding.

> *For if I preach the gospel, I have nothing to boast of, for necessity is laid upon me; yes, woe is me if I do not preach the gospel!*
>
> ~ 1 Corinthians 9:16 ~

5. **Offer praise to others and give God the glory**: Making an intentional effort to offer praise and acknowledgment to someone every day is not for appearing to be a "good Christian." Scripture reveals believers must control their thoughts and words: *"From the same mouth come both blessing and cursing. My brethren, these things ought not to be this way"* (James 3:10). If we must focus on the way we speak to others, it makes sense to focus on praise in the process. Not only does it make you stop for a moment and recognize the contributions of those around you, but it also shows your humility and humanity. Both traits serve to give God glory and shows true genuineness in our faith that creates trust and confidence. People tend to remember thoughts they associate with positive events. If people think about God every time they recall the praise you offered them, you have fulfilled His purpose for you, and God gets the glory for it.

> *Let another man praise you, and not your own mouth; A stranger, and not your own lips.*
>
> ~ Proverbs 27:2 ~

6. **Claim your daily Bible study time**: The importance of achieving a balance between professional life and spiritual growth cannot be overstated. Neglecting your time alone with God's Word will undermine your ability to develop a personal relationship with Christ, stall spiritual growth, and fulfill God's purpose for you. When you spend time each day studying the Bible, you show God where He fits in the order of your priorities: *"For where your treasure is, there your heart will be also"* (Luke 12:34). Claim one hour of the day

as your own to spend time immersed in God's Word; not just reading but studying. This is your non-negotiable time for spiritual growth, and how you prove to God He is in control of your life. Given the demands modern society places on our valuable time, there will always be reasons to use this time for other things; none of them are valid: *"But seek first His kingdom and His righteousness, and all these things will be added to you"* (Matthew 6:33). Consider this an offer from a Holy God that you cannot – and will not – refuse.

> *Now the Berean Jews were of more noble character than those in Thessalonica, for they received the message with great eagerness and examined the Scriptures every day to see if what Paul said was true.*
>
> ~ Acts 17:11 ~

7. **End the day with 30-minutes of quiet time with God**: Adequate sleep is crucial to your physical and spiritual health; nothing disrupts sleep patterns more than a brain that will not relax. Thirty minutes prior to bed, turn off the electronic devices, and allow your mind to focus on God; something it will not do if it stays engaged with the world. Confess your sins, pray for stronger faith, and cleanse your soul in preparation for tomorrow: *"Draw near to God and He will draw near to you. Cleanse your hands, you sinners; and purify your hearts, you double-minded"* (James 4:8). Those who go to sleep peacefully tend to wake up peacefully, and sleep well in the process.

> *I will both lie down in peace, and sleep; For You alone, O Lord, make me dwell in safety.*
>
> ~ Psalm 4:8 ~

On the surface, these habits appear simple and easy to start; they are. However, their value extends well beyond a daily biblical lifestyle. Collectively, they form a strong foundation for building a relationship with Christ and give God a position of exclusivity in your future. Additionally, as your trust in God's providence increases, negative factors – such as stress, anxiety, and uncertainty – will decrease. *We serve an awesome God!*

Glossary of Terms

Ad Hominem Tu Quoque
An informal logical fallacy that intends to discredit the validity of the opponent's logical argument by asserting the opponent's failure to act consistently in accordance with its conclusion(s).

Addiction
The state of being enslaved to a habit or practice or to something that is psychologically or physically habit-forming, as narcotics, to such an extent that its cessation causes severe trauma.

Antinomianism
A derogatory term for the doctrine saying Christians, once saved by Grace through faith, are under no obligation to obey the laws of ethics or morality.

Apologetics
A field of Christian theology that presents historical, reasoned, and evidential bases for Christianity, defending it against objections.

Apostasy
The abandonment or renunciation of a religious or political belief.

Argumentum Ad Hominem
A logical fallacy in which an argument is rebutted by attacking the character, motive, or other attribute of the person making the argument, or persons associated with the argument, rather than attacking the substance of the argument itself.

Argumentum Ad Ignorantiam
A fallacy in informal logic that asserts that a proposition is true because it has not yet been proved false (or vice versa).

Argumentum Ad Populum
A fallacious argument that concludes that a proposition is true because many or most people believe it: "If many believe so, it is so."

Augustine of Hippo
(354 – 430 AD) An early Christian theologian and philosopher whose writings influenced the development of Western Christianity and Western philosophy.

Glossary of Terms

Biblical Aramaic
A Semitic language (Syrian dialect) which was used as a lingua franca in the Near East from the 6th century BC. It gradually replaced Hebrew as the language of the Jews in those areas and was itself supplanted by Arabic in the 7th century AD. (see *Lingua Franca*).

Biblical Fasting
Abstaining from food, drink, or any activity to focus on a period of prayer, meditation, or spiritual growth.

Biblical Greek
The common supra-regional form of Greek spoken and written during Hellenistic and Roman antiquity and the early Byzantine era, or Late Antiquity (also known as *Koine* Greek).

Biblical Hebrew
An archaic form of Hebrew, a Canaanite Semitic language spoken by the Israelites in the area known as Israel, roughly west of the Jordan River and east of the Mediterranean Sea.

Biblical Languages
The languages employed in the original writings of the Bible (primarily Classical Hebrew, Aramaic, and *Koine* Greek).

Biblical Theology
Theology based on the Bible; specifically, theology that seeks to derive its categories of thought and the norms for its interpretation from the study of the Bible in its entirety.

Burden of Proof Fallacy
A logical fallacy asserting the burden of proof lies not with the person making the claim, but with someone else to disprove.

Canon Law
The body of laws and regulations made by ecclesiastical authority (leadership), for the government of a Christian organization or church and its members.

Catechesis
Doctrinal instruction given to a person in preparation for Christian baptism or confirmation, typically using a catechism.

Glossary of Terms

Charles Wesley
(1707 – 1788) An English leader of the Methodist movement, most widely known for writing more than 6,000 hymns.

Christology
The branch of Christian theology relating to the person, nature, and role of Christ.

Commentaries
A Bible commentary is a written, systematic series of explanations and interpretations of Scripture, chapter by chapter and verse by verse.

Concordance
An alphabetical list of the words (especially the important ones) present in a text or texts, usually with citations of the passages concerned.

Critical Thinking
The objective analysis and evaluation of an issue in order to form a judgment.

Denominationalism
Devotion to denominational principles or interests; the emphasizing of denominational differences to the point of being narrowly exclusive.

Diachronic
Relating to, or dealing with phenomena (as of language or culture) as they occur, develop, and evolve over time.

Didache
An early Christian treatise on Christian ethics, rituals, and church organization; written in Greek, dated by most modern scholars to the first century.

Disciple
A follower or student of a teacher, leader, or philosopher.

Dispensationalism
An interpretive system that considers Biblical history as divided deliberately by God into defined periods or ages to each of which God has allotted distinctive administrative principles.

Glossary of Terms

Doctrine
A belief or set of beliefs held and taught by a church, political party, or other organized group.

Eisegesis
The process of interpreting a text or portion of text in such a way that the process introduces one's own presuppositions, agendas, or biases into and onto the text.

Evangelism
The spreading of the Christian gospel by public preaching or personal witness.

Exegesis
The critical explanation or interpretation of a text, especially of scripture.

Fellowship
A friendly association, especially with people who share one's interests.

Fideism
The doctrine that knowledge depends on faith or revelation.

Fratricide
The murder of killing of one's own brother or sister or an individual (as a countryman) having a relationship like that of a brother or sister.

Genre
A category of artistic composition, as in music or literature, characterized by similarities in form, style, or subject matter.

Glorification
The belief in Scripture that deals with the ultimate perfection of Christian believers in their eternal life.

Gnosticism
The thought and practice especially of various cults of late pre-Christian and early Christian centuries distinguished by the conviction that matter is evil and that emancipation comes through knowledge (*gnosis*).

Glossary of Terms

Hermeneutics
The branch of knowledge that deals with interpretation, especially of the Bible or literary texts.

Historical Theology
A branch of theology investigates the socio-historical and cultural mechanisms that give rise to theological ideas, statements, and systems.

Idolatry
The worship of idols; or, extreme admiration, love, or reverence for something or someone.

Impeccable
Incapable of wrongdoing; not liable to sin resulting from a flawless nature.

Imprecatory Prayer
Prayers that call for an evil, curse, or calamity against a person.

Incarnation
To become flesh; the divine nature of God's Son was united but not mixed with human nature in one divine Person, Jesus Christ, who was both fully God and fully Man.

Interpretation
The action of explaining the meaning of something.

John Calvin
A prominent French theologian during the Protestant Reformation (1509 – 1564) and the founder of the theological system known as Calvinism.

Jonathan Edwards
(1703 – 1758) A Puritan theologian, pastor, and devout Calvinist who a key figure in what has come to be called the *First Great Awakening*.

Justification
God's act of removing the guilt and penalty of sin while at the same time declaring a sinner righteous through Christ's atoning sacrifice.

Glossary of Terms

Latin Vulgate
A late fourth-century Latin translation of the Bible that became, during the 16th century, the Catholic Church's officially published Latin version of the Bible.

Lingua Franca
A language that is adopted as a common language between speakers whose native languages are different.

Literary Genre
A category of literary composition; may be determined by literary technique, tone, content, or length.

Litmus Test
A test in which a single factor (as an attitude, event, or fact) is decisive.

Logic
A science that deals with the principles and criteria of validity of inference and demonstration; the science of the formal principles of reasoning.

Logical Fallacy
A pattern of reasoning made invalid by a flaw in its logical structure that can neatly be expressed in a standard logic system, for example propositional logic. An argument that is formally fallacious is always considered wrong.

Mass
The name used by the Roman Catholic Church to describe celebration of the Eucharist and includes the ritual of chants, readings, prayers, and other ceremonies in the celebration.

Martin Luther
(1483 – 1546) A German professor of theology, composer, priest, monk, and a seminal figure in the Protestant Reformation.

Ministry
The work or vocation of a minister of religion; the spiritual work or service of a Christian or a group of Christians, especially evangelism.

Glossary of Terms

Myopia
Nearsightedness; lack of imagination, foresight, or intellectual insight.

Natural Theology
The branch of philosophy and theology which tries to either prove God's existence, define God's attributes, or derive correct doctrine based solely from human reason and/or observations of the natural world.

New Testament
The second major part of the Christian biblical canon that discusses the teachings and person of Jesus, as well as events in first-century Christianity.

Non-Sequitur Fallacy
Literary and rhetorical devices which include the statements, sayings and conclusions that do not follow the fundamental principles of logic and reason.

Old Testament
The first part of the Christian Bible, including thirty-nine books and corresponding approximately to the Hebrew Bible, that contain the chief texts of the law, history, prophecy, and wisdom literature of the ancient people of Israel.

Parable
A short, allegorical story designed to illustrate or teach some truth, religious principle, or moral lesson.

Patristic
Relating to the early Christian theologians.

Peccable
Liable to error; capable of committing sin.

Peer Review
Evaluation of a person's work or performance by a group of people in the same occupation, profession, or industry.

Period Map
A diagrammatic representation of an area of land or sea showing physical features, cities, and boundaries during a specific period in world history.

Glossary of Terms

Polycarp
(69 – 155 AD) The 2nd-century Christian Bishop of Smyrna.

Post Hoc Fallacy
A logical fallacy that's committed when it's concluded that one event causes another simply because the proposed cause occurred before the proposed effect.

Primary Source
An artifact, a document, diary, manuscript, autobiography, a recording, or other source of information that was created at the time under study.

Purgatory
A Roman Catholic process of purification of the soul after death, following the judgment and ordinarily a requirement before entry into Heaven.

Repudiate
Refuse to accept or be associated with; refuse to fulfill or discharge (an agreement, obligation, or debt).

Restorationism
A charismatic Christian movement seeking to restore the beliefs and practices of the early Church.

Rhetoric
The discipline of effective or persuasive speaking or writing, especially the use of figures of speech and other compositional techniques.

Robert Estienne
(1503 – 1559 AD) Also known as Stephanus; a 16th-century printer and classical scholar in Paris, and the first to print the Bible divided into standard numbered verses.

Sanctification
The act or process of acquiring sanctity, of being made or becoming holy.

Secondary Source
Any source about an event, period, or issue in history that was produced after that event, period or issue has passed.

Glossary of Terms

Sectarianism
An excessive attachment to a specific sect, denomination, or party, especially in religion.

Secular
Denoting attitudes, activities, or other things that have no religious or spiritual basis.

Self-Assessment
An assessment or evaluation of oneself or one's actions and attitudes of one's performance at a job or learning task considered in relation to an objective standard.

Soteriology
The study of religious doctrines of Salvation.

Spiritual Discipline
A deliberately self-imposed habit that's biblically based, which nurtures spiritual health and fosters spiritual growth leading to a maturity in the Christian faith.

Spiritual Maturity
The state reached in the life of Christian believers when control, consistency, stability, and wisdom are demonstrated and practiced.

Spiritual Warfare
The Christian concept of taking a stand against preternatural evil forces, based on the belief in demonic entities which influence and intervene in human affairs.

Stephen Langton
(1150 – 1228 AD) An English Cardinal of the Roman Catholic Church and Archbishop of Canterbury who was responsible for dividing the Bible into the standard modern arrangement of chapters.

Synchronic
Concerned with events existing in a limited period and disregarding historical antecedents.

Systematic Theology
A discipline which addresses theological topics one by one and attempts to summarize all the biblical teaching on each specific subject.

Glossary of Terms

Teleology
The explanation of phenomena by the purpose they serve rather than by postulated causes; doctrine of design and purpose in the material world.

Tertullian
(155 – 240 AD) A prolific early Christian author from Carthage in the Roman province of Africa.

Textual Bridge
A passage in a literary work serving as a movement between two other passages significant or greater importance.

Theological Tradition
A behavior, doctrine, or practice of Christians, passed from generation to generation, informing participants within the tradition about their own identity in the church and in the surrounding culture.

Thomas Aquinas
(1225 – 1274) An influential philosopher in the 13th-century Christian Church, theologian, and jurist in the tradition of scholasticism.

Thomism
The theology and philosophy of Thomas Aquinas or of his followers.

Transubstantiation
The Roman Catholic doctrine that the bread and wine, used in the Lord's Supper or Eucharist, become the literal body and blood of Christ at the "consecration" by the ordained priest.

www.ingramcontent.com/pod-product-compliance
Lightning Source LLC
Chambersburg PA
CBHW071337150426
43191CB00007B/761